What to Read When

Dear Dawn,
Read with joy!

Pam Allyn

What to Read When

The Books and Stories to Read with Your Child and All the Best Times to Read Them

Pam Allyn

AVERY ✦ a member of Penguin Group (USA) Inc. ✦ New York

Published by the Penguin Group
Penguin Group (USA) Inc., 375 Hudson Street, New York, New York 10014, USA • Penguin Group (Canada), 90 Eglinton Avenue East, Suite 700, Toronto, Ontario M4P 2Y3, Canada (a division of Pearson Canada Inc.) • Penguin Books Ltd, 80 Strand, London WC2R 0RL, England • Penguin Ireland, 25 St Stephen's Green, Dublin 2, Ireland (a division of Penguin Books Ltd) • Penguin Group (Australia), 250 Camberwell Road, Camberwell, Victoria 3124, Australia (a division of Pearson Australia Group Pty Ltd) • Penguin Books India Pvt Ltd, 11 Community Centre, Panchsheel Park, New Delhi–110 017, India • Penguin Group (NZ), 67 Apollo Drive, Rosedale, North Shore 0632, New Zealand (a division of Pearson New Zealand Ltd) • Penguin Books (South Africa) (Pty) Ltd, 24 Sturdee Avenue, Rosebank, Johannesburg 2196, South Africa

Penguin Books Ltd, Registered Offices: 80 Strand, London WC2R 0RL, England

Library of Congress Cataloging-in-Publication Data

Allyn, Pam.
What to read when : the books and stories to read with your child, and all the best times to read them / Pam Allyn.
p. cm.
ISBN 978-1-58333-334-1
1. Reading (Early childhood) 2. Reading—Parent participation. 3. Children—Books and reading. 4. Oral reading. I. Title.
LB1139.5.R43A48 2009 2008054501
649'.58—dc22

Printed in the United States of America
10 9 8 7 6 5 4 3

Book design by Kate Nichols

For Jim, Katie, and Charlotte

(Always and always, over and over)

Acknowledgments

The best way I can think of to thank the wondrous people who have influenced the writing of this book would be to give them each a ceremonial, metaphorical "book" gift.

To my colleagues at LitLife, brilliant, generous, and wise, I give the book *Because of Winn-Dixie,* because that book is all about community and that is what you are all about. Your love and care for the work of literacy education inspires me every day. To all the teachers and children in the schools within which we work, my gratitude and everlasting admiration. I thank you all for championing the idea of this book and for your insights and steady wisdom that keep LitLife and now LitWorld (thank you, awesome Jenny Koons) moving forward and forward, for as James Baldwin said: "These are all our children."

To the fabulous Rebekah Coleman I give the book *Planting the Trees of Kenya* because you so believe in this dream that words can change worlds and you have done so much to help me in every way and at every turn. Your radiant presence is felt on every page of this book.

To Alyssa McClorey, who arrived like a miracle just when we most needed you, and before you embarked upon your own magical teaching future, and to Flynn Berry, whose graceful and luminous support impacts the writing here, I give you both the book *Words Under Words* by Naomi Nye to nourish your dreams. Jen Estrada, Tara Mastin, and many wonderful interns over the years have helped us collect the books that matter to this community; I give you the poem "Kindness" in gratitude for yours.

To the boys at the Children's Village and their teachers and caregivers, as well as to my humane and thoughtful cocreators of Books for Boys, I give the book *The Dream Keeper,* by Langston Hughes, because he teaches us through his poems that words can provide a refuge and a source of safety and comfort for children who most need it.

From this book, I mark the page with the poem "April Rain Song" for my dear friend of my heart and codirector of Books for Boys, Sue Meigs. Your April birthday brings me much joy because it is a time to celebrate you. I love our years of walks and talks of our hopes for the boys and for our own children.

I mark a page of that book for you, dear Lauren Blum, "The Dream Keeper," for keeping my dreams and yours for all children alive with your faith, love, and inspirational optimism in all people, and for you, dear Jeannie Blaustein, for your wisdom and kindness, for your precious friendship, and for taking tender care of dreams.

To the women who have shared their book knowledge with us, I give you the book *The Librarian of Basra* because your work is beyond important; it is essential. We talked to and worked with fantastic and knowledgeable librarians and educators, booksellers, and book enthusiasts who shared favorite books with us; I am touched by their belief in this work and in their dedication: the magnificent Marva Allen, whose reach has influenced thousands of children to find their own cultural, colorful selves within the pages of stories; wonderful public librarians Amy Fontaine and Rebecca Johnson, who shared such treasures with us; and my dear friend of my heart and soul, Elizabeth Fernandez. How lucky I have been to find a friend who loves words and children and has given so much of herself to our friendship and to our work.

To Lisa DiMona, literary agent beyond compare, I give the book *The Other Way to Listen,* by Byrd Baylor, because you always listen so closely and so carefully to the promise of stories and ideas whispering in the world. I am so grateful.

To the extraordinary team at Avery, especially Megan Newman, brilliant and inspirational publisher, and Lucia Watson, my dear, dear Watson, who makes me smile each time I open her e-mails and whose wise support and fine touch have brought this book to completion, I give you all the picture-book version of "Stopping by Woods on a Snowy Evening," by Robert Frost. It is a poem that takes care with words, as do you. You make all things possible, and your work makes words last. Thank you for your faith in me.

To my wonderful in-laws, Cindy and Lou Allyn, who value reading and provide me my very own reading couch at every visit, I give *The Polar Express,* by Chris Van Allsburg, for all the special times that have created many happy memories for our family, and many cozy reading times together.

To my parents, Anne and Bill Krupman, for all the years of your love, your guidance, your great humor, and our thousands and thousands of life-changing conversations. I give you the memory of my old battered copy of *Blueberries for Sal.* In those pages I keep the first memories of your voices, which carry me on into the world every day and are the beloved voices I cherish always.

To my family of my heart: children, Katie and Charlotte, and husband, Jim, for your presence every, every day, for your wisdom, for your company, for your blessed, blessed spirits and sense of life and purpose and joy. For these reasons, it is hard to choose just the right book to give you. But then I realize: I can give you this one, which contains every and all of the books we once read together. All my love, always.

Pam Allyn
2008

Contents

Introduction: The Sound of Reading Calls Us Home *1*

Part I: The Power of Reading Aloud

1. Why We Must Read to and with Our Children *11*
2. The Four Keys to Helping Your Child Become a Lifelong Reader *18*
3. Supporting Your Child's Reading Life: Frequently Asked Questions *28*
4. Landmark Books *38*

Part II: What to Read Aloud at Every Age

5. How to Read Aloud *51*
6. The Chronological "When": The Reader's Ladder *56*

- ✦ Birth to Age Two: Beginning the Magical Journey *57*
- ✦ Two to Three Years Old: Leaping Toward Understanding *65*
- ✦ Four Years Old: Loving the Story *70*
- ✦ Five Years Old: Balancing Challenge and Comfort *78*
- ✦ Six Years Old: Forging Connections *84*
- ✦ Seven Years Old: Opening Up to the World *90*
- ✦ Eight Years Old: Creating Ideas *95*
- ✦ Nine Years Old: Asking Questions, Shaping Answers *101*
- ✦ Ten Years Old: Exploring New Horizons *108*

Part III: The Emotional "When": Fifty Essential Themes

7. How to Make Best Use of the Fifty Themes *117*

8. The Fifty Themes: All the Best Books for the Moments That Matter Most *120*

Adoption *120*
Appreciating the Natural World *124*
A Bad Day *130*
Bath Time *133*
Becoming Someone Who Loves to Write *135*
Being Yourself *138*
Birthdays/Growing Up *144*
Building the World of Family *149*
Building, Making, and Creating: The World of Mechanical Things *154*
Building Peace, Confronting War, and Talking with Your Child about World Events *156*
Bullying and Hurtful People *159*
Caring for Someone *163*
The Challenges and Joys of Siblings *166*
The Complexity of Sharing *170*
Coping with Illness *172*
Courage *175*
Creating Community *181*
Creating Theater: Making Plays and Scenes Together *185*
Creativity *187*
Cultivating a Sense of Time and Place *191*
Death *194*
Divorce *198*
Falling Asleep *201*
Feeling a Sense of Justice: Changing the World *206*
Feelings about School *210*
Feeling Silly *214*
Heroes *217*
Journeys *222*
Learning New Things *227*
Loneliness *229*
Loving Art *232*
Loving History *236*

Loving Music *241*
Loving Numbers *245*
Loving Science *249*
Loving Sports *252*
Loving Words and Language *256*
Making a Mistake *259*
Making Friends/Friendship *263*
A New Baby *268*
Overcoming Adversity *272*
The Power of Grandparents *274*
Pondering the World *279*
Savoring Food *284*
Spirituality *287*
Separations *289*
Sleepovers *294*
The Value of Your Imagination *295*
Your Body *300*
Your Own Category *303*

Conclusion: Blueberries, Silvery Moons, and a Purple Plastic Purse *305*

Index *307*

What to Read When

Introduction: The Sound of Reading Calls Us Home

My strongest memory from childhood is the sound of my mother's voice reading *Blueberries for Sal.* Little Sal is walking with her pail, and because she is eating so many of the berries, the ones she does manage to save enter her pail with a *kerplink, kerplank, kerplunk*. I loved the way my mother formed those words as she said them. There was something immensely satisfying in her reading of that book to me. It was a combination of the way she spoke and the nature of the story itself: terrifically scary but at the same time tremendously comforting. One rainy day after school, my mother sat next to me on the couch and read that book to me for probably the hundredth time. I can still remember from that particular day the sound of the rain on the windowpane and the sound of her voice forming the words: *kerplink, kerplank, kerplunk*. Sal is happily oblivious to the bear cub nearby and yet we know that mother is also nearby. Nothing will happen to Sal. Nothing will happen to the cub. Something in Robert McCloskey's telling makes you sure.

Years later, it is nighttime, and I am holding one of my daughters, Charlotte, in my arms. She cannot sleep, and so we are sitting together; the chair goes back and forth; her hair smells like milk. We are under the window where the glimmer of a full moon glints down upon us. She reaches her hand up, and it looks to my tired eyes as if she is literally holding the moon inside it. "Good night, moon," she whispers. She is not yet two. "Good night, room," I whisper back. "Good night, old lady," she whispers back to me, and it looks like she winks at me as her hand falls to my shoulder, and she drifts, finally, off to sleep.

The power of reading aloud to draw you and your child near is profound.

As *Goodnight Moon* proves millions of bedtimes over, and as *Blueberries for Sal* proved unmistakably to me, the sound of the human voice can reach across the gulf of age, of all the things that keep us apart, and create a bridge that lasts a lifetime and extends through generations. Through books and stories that are designed to be read aloud, we convey to our children the beauty of language and the joys of rhythm and rhyme; and in the books we choose to read and the way we read them, we also convey the values we hold dear. Every day as you pack a lunch, wave good-bye to a school bus, tie a shoelace, braid a ponytail, the words you want to say to your child hum inside: I love you, be safe, I love you, be free. I love you, I love you, I love you, let the world treat you kindly, come back to me. Here are the values of my life, our family, here is what I hope for you, here is what I dream for you. And yet, for most of us, too many moments slip by and we're lucky to get an "I love you" in edgewise. The good news, wondrously, is that the world is full of literature written by people who know you are longing to make connections and are striving to put a voice to them. This book is your guide to making lasting connections with your child through reading. It is also an essential resource for all the best books to read to your child and all the right times to read them.

Children's literature has long held a cherished place in our culture as a conveyor of values, of belief systems that will give our children courage and help them through a hard day. In Victorian times, children's books were used to convey a strong sense of morals and discipline. Generations later, writers such as Margaret Wise Brown and Maurice Sendak changed the paradigm of children's literature by giving voice to the real lives of children, with their many worries and delights. Through these radically new narratives, the "here and now," as Margaret Wise Brown called them, children were given the opportunity to explore a sometimes confusing universe with a moral compass. How and where will your own child find the human center in an often overwhelming world? Begin the conversation with books that resonate and give you both a point of reference. Whatever the issue at hand—a lost toy, a new sibling, a scary shadow—books and the time spent together reading them can help. There has never been a better time to read aloud to your child. Libraries and bookstores are full of beautiful, astonishing collections that continue to break new ground in their confluence of art and language and depth of feeling. The millions of books available to us also offer an opportunity to redefine childhood in our wired and overprogrammed times, helping us to slow down and reconnect with something timeless and universal. At the same time, the breadth of books with subtle emotion allows us to connect with our children in new and intensely meaningful ways.

And yet, for many of us, there has never been a more confusing time to shop for a book. It's possible to go to a bookstore and stand for what feels like hours in front of rows and rows of books and not know how to choose. They all look beautiful, but who knows what's inside? We know we trust the old favorites, the ones we all remember. But what about the books that speak to the sorrows and the joys of childhood as it is in today's world? These too must be added to our canon. And yet there are thousands. How does a busy parent, grandparent, or caregiver search for the just right book? What is just the right book?

The same way we choose foods to suit our moods—hot soup on a cold winter's night, spicy ribs for a family picnic—we long to choose the "just right" books that will match the moments we find ourselves in with our children. With all those books out there, certainly there must be a book for every moment: a book to mark the moment of leaving, of coming, of newness, of sameness, of change. As adults, we connect with our reading of books in different ways at different times. So what, then, are the books that are right for our children at very particular times in their lives? How can we match the time, place, and circumstances of our lives with just the right book? *What to Read When* will help you find the perfect books for the perfect times. This is the work of parenting no one told you about when you left the hospital or walked through the front door with your newly adopted child. At all life-cycle moments, we adults hunger to capture the moment in words: we read poems to each other at weddings, we tell stories of a beloved friend at a funeral service. It is humanity's greatest gift to be able to see the power of storytelling to pin down experience, to capture it, and render it timeless. *What to Read When* is a guide to the life-cycle moments of childhood—the occasions big and small when you want to bond most with your children—and the books, words, and pictures that will bring both clarity and connection to those moments.

When your child is small, and you turn the pages of *Mr. Rabbit and the Lovely Present*, by Charlotte Zolotow, and the two of you can nearly feel the texture of the fruits he so lovingly chooses for his mother, the rabbit's journey and his gift giving help you to show your child the power of a simple act of generosity. The tender repetition of the language as he adds his fruits to the basket is soothing and familiar. You are reminded that gifts come in all sizes and all forms. This becomes one of the first, precious lessons you can teach your child. Later, when your child is older, six or seven, and you read the chapter book *The Lion, the Witch and the Wardrobe* aloud to this same child you feel one another tense up as Lucy opens the door of the wardrobe and feels the cold rush of air in Narnia for the first time. Here is where Lucy will find the courage she never knew she had and meet beloved friends such as Mr. Tumnus. Here too is where she will face the frailties of human nature when her own brother Edmund betrays her to the icy, cruel White Witch. Here is where Lucy will be brave, even though she is a small girl, and here is where she will learn to forgive her brother and give him another chance. Here is where, as a parent, you will accompany your child through this essential journey of making choices and finding acceptance, standing up for yourself, and knowing when to forgive. Books give you ways to talk to your children about these big ideas. Later, when your child is on the brink of leaving childhood behind, you want to share words with your child that will help her move gracefully into young adulthood. According to the poet Billy Collins, poetry tells the history of the human heart. But I think that all of great literature maps the human heart, and children's literature knows how to do so best of all.

My Life with Words

As a child, books were my transport. Through reading, I discovered worlds of people I had not known before. I read stories about history and places and people that moved me, reduced me to tears, brought me off of my couch and on a journey that never ended. The protagonist in Faith Ringgold's masterpiece *Tar Beach* travels the city of New York by flying: she soars over the city and gets a bird's-eye view of her home. The reading experience for me was much like this: I found myself soaring overhead, even while I could still keep an eye on my reading self: on the couch down below.

Both Jo in *Little Women* and Sal in *Blueberries for Sal* taught me the kind of girl I wanted to be. The heroines of those books were more meaningful to me than most of the girls I saw on television or even met in my 1960s childhood. As a parent of two daughters, now sixteen and fourteen, I read to them as eagerly as I read on the couch all those years ago. It was a delight to return to some of those old books and watch my own daughters cry too when Beth falls ill in *Little Women*, or laugh over Mrs. Piggle-Wiggle's antics, or grip my hand tighter when Milo begins the next adventure in *The Phantom Tollbooth*.

But it has also been my great pleasure to find new books through these readings together, books that had not been written when I was a child. How fantastic that my daughters were present for the birth of a Landmark text, the Harry Potter series, and that they have also been part of a revolution in children's literature as illustrated books by authors like Mo Willems and Brian Selznick break new ground in storytelling through pictures.

I'm often asked in workshops when I stopped reading aloud to my daughters, but the fact is, I haven't stopped. Even now, as teenagers, my daughters revel with me in the nuances of language in a Billy Collins poem that I read aloud to them from the current issue of *The New Yorker*. At the breakfast table, my husband and I read aloud to them from articles on African education, one of the issues currently on our minds as a family. We read to them from books they may still, as fluent readers, have challenges navigating on their own, or books that will benefit from a collective reading through the discussions that ensue. And, simply, because a shared text creates another kind of energy in our family: like going on a long road trip, it is a new venture that bonds us most.

Reading is more than a passion to me: it is a life's work. I am certain that it has the capacity to be exhilarating for every child, and so I have devoted myself to the task of expanding literacy so that one day every child will be able to read to the point of transcendence. There is still so much work for us left to do together, not only for our children, but for all children. I hope to share with you the techniques and the titles I have found to be the most compelling for both children and their teachers and to help you be your child's own best teacher in the purest and most joyous sense of that word.

As executive director of LitLife, an internationally recognized organization dedicated to cultivating the reading and writing lives of children and young adults, I train more than a thousand teachers a year in the teaching of reading and writing. In every classroom, there is one unfailingly successful tool for unlocking the door to literacy for all children, and that is the read-aloud: the book that is read by the teacher to her students: the shared experience. I want every home to have access to this wondrous and miraculous tool. I want you to have all the resources you need to unlock the door for lifelong literacy for your child.

As a literacy educator, I also founded an initiative for foster care children called Books for Boys, and now, LitWorld. Both of these initiatives bring the work of LitLife to all communities of children: from the Children's Village, a residential school for vulnerable children, to a school for HIV/AIDS orphans in Nairobi, Kenya. No matter the gender, the life story, the nature of the community, or the personal story of that child, over and over again I pay humble and grateful witness to the mysterious power of the human voice, the human child, and the text and what they can accomplish together.

Joined together with each other over the pages of a book, adult and child discover new worlds and, with them, a sense of unending possibility. When I read Dr. Seuss to a child who has survived unspeakable horrors in his early life, and he laughs until he cries, or I read *Where the Wild Things Are* to a wounded and hurt teenager who has years of defense built up around him, and he cries, he literally cries, leaning into me and whispering: "No one ever read aloud to me before this moment, and I always wished someone would," then I know that books and the ritual of the read-aloud do truly have the power to change the world.

Reading to your child begins as an exquisitely intimate experience, but it sows the seeds for lifelong literacy. I hope *What to Read When* will be a part of the continuing path toward universal literacy, and it is my honor to share this work with you. I hope you will combine your profound knowledge of your child's needs and desires with the advice I offer within this book to create a joyous, nourishing reading environment at home. You'll find a selection of books here that I've found to be irresistible to children, along with practical advice on how and when certain books are most compelling to read.

The most powerful work you can do for the world begins in your home, with the intimacy of one book. There is no better teacher than you, no better mentor, no better role model. Your connection to literacy will inspire your children to read to their children, and they to theirs. I hope this book will give you the tools, strategies, and the utmost confidence to read, read, read to and with your child. Reading aloud is fun, productive, and life-changing (for you and your child). But sometimes reading with your child also feels hard. I hope this book will help you to embrace the hard parts too, and to be patient both with yourself and with your child and that you will feel the tenderness that growth brings, and your child will feel your tenderness as a teacher. I hope this book will keep you good company on these journeys and help you feel the power of your own life-changing potential, for the work you do matters, so much.

How This Book Works

"Part One: The Power of Reading Aloud" begins with my top-ten list of reasons to read to your kids: values, language, comprehension, story, genre, structure, comfort, critical thought, other worlds and voices, and building a reading life. The list gives parents some of the same practical tools I share with teachers. It also makes the case anew for the power of reading and why, particularly within the context of our information-saturated times, we must read aloud. I will share with you a top-ten list of "Landmark texts." You may not fully agree, but I will offer you my view on why these books are part of an American canon of childhood literature. I hope more will be added as you experience this book and become familiar with new titles.

The book is then divided into two major "whens": the chronological "when" of your child's reading life, and the emotional "when" of your child's reading life.

"Part Two: What to Read Aloud at Every Age" takes you on a journey with your child through every stage of his chronological development. This section describes some general characteristics of books or stories or poems that make them appealing reads for certain times of the day or for certain times in a child's life. This chapter tunes into the exquisite differences of each age group. Six is so different from seven, seven so different from eight. Reading aloud lets you hold those time periods in the cup of your hand, savoring them with your child as she learns to love literature.

"Part Three: The Emotional 'When': Fifty Essential Themes" illuminates the emotional chronology of your child's literary experiences. This is a deeply annotated list that identifies the children's literature best suited for the emotional "whens" in your children's lives. There are favorite book choices on themes ranging from friendships to journeys, new siblings to encounters with bullying, social justice to spirituality, giving all parents an indispensable resource for nurturing thoughtful, creative, and curious readers. The recommendations represent a synthesis of my personal experience with the books as a reader, a parent, and as an educator; the annotations include helpful hints and tips for the best possible read-aloud experience with each book. "How to Read a Picture Book," for example, is part of the curriculum I developed for my organization LitLife and adapted so that parents can use those same powerful teaching techniques at home.

"Conclusion: Blueberries, Silvery Moons, and a Purple Plastic Purse" is a final meditation that I hope will be inspiring, a source of nourishment for you as both a reader and as a parent wanting a lifetime of good reading for your child.

The idea for this book was born from the hundreds of letters, phone calls, and e-mails I have received from parents, teachers, school administrators, caregivers, and grandparents over the course of these past years asking far-ranging questions about how to read to your children, when to read to your children, and of course, what to read. I long to respond to all of you who have written and called, with your words and voices full of love for your children and the hunger to get that reading piece right. This book is my opportunity to do so. I consider it a love letter to all those who love children. I honor you for all the hard work you do in caring for your children and for your desire to do what is right for them. This book is a tribute to you, to all those marvelous questions you have asked me, and to how they inspire me to continue this work. I hope you will enjoy reading *What to Read When* as much as I enjoyed writing it.

Part I

The Power of Reading Aloud

1. Why We Must Read to and with Our Children

There are so, so many reasons to read aloud to your child! The obvious one is that it is really fun and a way to build intimacy with your child. But there are other more subtle reasons why reading to and with your child is as important as giving them nutritious meals each day. Reading aloud will help your child to:

1. Develop Shared Values

The best children's books convey a strong sense of what the author feels about the world and about our responsibility to it, in a way that appears almost invisible. Literature is a moral compass for goodness in the most sweeping sense: it includes looking at human frailties in the face and finding the courage to deal with them. It is much easier to talk with your child about some of these issues in the context of a powerful story, through a character who comes to life on the page. Friendship, kindness, generosity, patience, understanding, and bravery all can be discussed with a smile through the eyes of a frog (*Frog and Toad*) or through the eyes of a badger (*Bedtime for Frances*). Through different lenses we learn, we revel, we grow. My daughter Charlotte recently said to me, "When I read Harry Potter, I know J. K. Rowling believes in what I believe in." That is huge.

2. Fall in Love with Language

Children are fascinated by how things are made, how things fit together. A sentence is the perfect unit to explore together. It is a magical construction that conveys ideas and emotions. Rhythm, grammar, vocabulary, and punctuation all contribute to the architecture of magical language. By reading aloud, you are passing on those rhythms and those nuances of language. When you read aloud from an Eloise Greenfield poem, "Jumprope Rhyme," and your voice skips and trips and lilts over the words, you will too convey to your child a love of language, or maybe you'll be the one to fall in love with it: "Get ready . . . get set . . . jump . . . right . . . in!"

3. Build Comprehension

We can "practice" strategic reading when we read aloud together. Great readers ask questions as they read. Great readers make predictions. Great readers visualize scenes as they read. They use what they already know to construct new understandings. By stopping to think together, by managing hard parts of understanding together, you are modeling the joyful work your child will also always need to do on his own. Reading aloud will help your children learn long after they can read independently. As your child makes her first forays out into the world of reading independence, she still needs to "see" a reader read: what do we all do to comprehend and understand? Great readers pause to think about their reading; they reread parts that felt hard; they make connections with other texts they have read. The read-aloud makes this process visible—your child will use what she learns from watching you when you read aloud to her.

4. Learn the Power of Story

All of humanity loves a story. We tell each other our sorrows, our joys through stories. We tell history through stories. The news itself is simply a composition of people's stories. We reach out across time and space and culture to one another through the telling of story. After the hurricane in New Orleans, or the fall of the World Trade Towers in New York City, or the tsunami in Southeast Asia, people across the world came together to help because they heard the individual stories of others. Every compelling story has a few key elements: characters moving though a plot structured by conflict, a turning point, and a resolution. Through books, our children begin to feel the power of many stories, and also begin to reach for the power of telling their own tales. Their stories matter too.

5. Be Exposed to a Variety of Genres

Genres are containers for thinking. They help us to orient ourselves to the kind of story we are hearing, and its purpose. There are three major genres: nonfiction, fiction, and poetry. Inside each of these genres, of course, are many subgenres. For example, there is informational nonfiction, the kind your child might read to find out more about trucks or butterflies. But there is also persuasive nonfiction, the kind you might read on the editorial pages of your local paper. Fiction transcends facts but is no less true. Short stories, novels, and many picture books tell fantastical stories or stories of people's lives that are built around a strong sense of narrative. The nonfiction writer writes to convey information; the fiction writer writes to help us escape. At the same time, both genres help us to learn more about our world, to peer outside of our own daily lives, whether through escapist fiction or fantastical facts. And to really confuse matters (or clarify them), someone wise once said: "If you want facts, read nonfiction. If you want truth, read fiction." Finally, poetry, the genre most often avoided by adults in their own reading lives. Through this book, I will emphasize the importance of poetry in the lives of your children and hope to help you become confident in reading it to your children for it will provide a way for your children to learn the power of metaphor and to fall in love with language.

6. Learn about Classic Text Structures

Great literature is about both structure and freedom. Every picture book is thirty-two pages long. Every cinquain has five lines in a stanza. Structures are comforting because they are predictable. Within each structure is the author's own voice in all its freedom. When our children start writing for school projects or on their own, they will find that the more they know about classic text structures the more they can fit in their own ideas in ways that their audiences will find truly compelling. So too in reading, knowledge of structures is extremely helpful. By reading aloud, you can sometimes identify structures so your child becomes familiar with them and has a sort of field guide for spotting them.

7. Find Comfort

This is a big one. Never underestimate the power of the read-aloud to bring comfort to your child. The world outside can be hard, especially for a young child trying to navigate his way through social relationships, school, his worries and fears, teachers, and other adults, along with the news of the world swirling around him, most of which he is picking up on in ways you might not even imagine. Books provide ways to talk about all of this. Books say that yes, happy endings are possible. Books say that if the ending is not necessarily resolved, there are people out there practicing courage and also navigating the world just like you. When your child wants to reread certain books over and over, embrace this too. There is something in that book that may be providing a certain kind of critical comfort. My daughter Katie kept *Mrs. Piggle-Wiggle* by her bed for years, and occasionally we would open it up and read excerpts even after she was well on her way as an independent reader. I could always tell that a day had been a little bit hard when *Mrs. Piggle-Wiggle* came back out. She always solved problems in the funniest ways and she was just so dear and comforting to a sensitive young girl navigating new worlds.

Several years ago, I was visiting the Children's Village, a residential school for boys from New York City's foster care system, as a literacy consultant. One morning I went to visit the boys in their homey cottages on campus. There, I was talking with an older boy when he saw the picture books in my bag. He asked me what they were, and when I took them out and began to read them to him, I saw tears fill his eyes. He said, "No one has ever read to me before." From that time, I visited him every week, and before long the other boys in the cottage gathered around too, all snuggling as close as they could. The program that grew out of that moment that summer, Books for Boys, is now a campuswide program bringing readers and books to the boys at Children's Village. When I saw a boy cry for the sheer joy of being read to on that first morning, I realized how vital a read-aloud program would be. Teenage boys, so tough and prickly on the outside, are so tender on the inside. Dr. Seuss and Margaret Wise Brown, Maurice Sendak and Ezra Jack Keats help us to find the tender sweetness inside each of these big boys. And these authors have brought tremendous comfort to the lives of young men who have suffered so much.

Every child, no matter how sheltered, no matter how badly we long to protect her, encounters troubles and confusion. When Charlotte was eight years old, she became preoccupied with what happens to people after they die. She had trouble falling asleep. I gave her a poem, a classic poem about life and death that I had always found very comforting, and she read it with me every night for several weeks. As I watched her eyes close, her exhausted and busy brain finally getting some respite from all its dear and true and honest and important wonderings, I was so grateful to that poem for bringing her some peace of mind. And let's not forget that it's for all of us too! Both my husband Jim and I found that poem to be immensely comforting as well. Share with your child your own fears and that you too are looking for comfort, and that sometimes, when you are lucky, you find it in the pages of a poem or story.

8. Build Critical Thinking Skills

Not all literature is . . . well, great! Or even good. The first time my daughter said to me, at age five, "Mom, I didn't think that book we just read was very good," I was proud. I was proud of her for being able to voice not only what she liked in literature but also what she didn't like. We can encourage our children to form opinions from the youngest age. Read-aloud helps our children practice getting their voices going in response to texts, when in school it will and can be much harder to do so. Beyond expressing whether one likes or dislikes a book, critical reading can go even deeper. We can ask: do you believe this author? We can ask: what do you think this author's point of view may be? By having these conversations with our children, we can counteract the negative forces of racism, sexism, bias, and extremism in our culture that serve only to divide us. And there are plenty of books out there that do not represent girls fairly, or African-Americans, or boys, or Latinos. By speaking up to what might be in the pages of an old book, or even a new one, and having our children do the same, we are raising critical thinkers: just the kind of people our countries need to create peace in the future and a healthier world for everyone.

9. Shape a Lifelong Reading Identity

The opportunity to sit beside your child and point out moments of significance in her own growth is precious. You can say: "I am noticing you really love to read about animals." You can say: "I am so proud of you for reading with me for such a long time. You are really growing as a reader." You can say: "It is just great that you like to hear stories and also poems."It is so crucial that you help to shape a positive identity for your child in the area of reading, especially for a child who may struggle in his independent reading life. School in particular is sometimes constructed in such a way that it is looking at the glass (the child) as half empty, and due to the fact that there are so many children to tend to, teachers may not always take that one extra moment to comment on something very special yet small that may be happening to your child as a reader. This is your opportunity to do that. You can say: "I see how you love the sound of language." "I notice that you are the kind of reader who studies the pictures." Your own "teaching" of the day can be transformative.

10. Visit Many Worlds, Hear Many Voices

This benefit from reading aloud is last but not by any means least. This may be the key reason to read aloud with your child. The world is more global, more connected than ever before. Our children are going to grow up forging relationships with people all over the world. The Internet makes it possible and it is entirely likely that by the time you read this book the face of the Internet will be even more multidimensional than it is as I write these words on my computer. It is so essential from the very beginning that our children recognize that by coming to understand humanity's similarities and differences we can create peace. In some ways, we are all the same, wherever we live and whatever we do. And in other ways, our cultures and our languages and our places of origin shape us and define us and have an impact upon us our whole lives long. Throughout this book, I will share with you stories and poems from across the world in the hopes that we can use the read-aloud as a powerful tool to change the lives of our own children and of all the children of the world. In the book *Sitti's Secrets*, the author Naomi Shihab Nye expresses Sitti's longing for her grandmother who lives so far away, across the world. She pictures her grandmother under her orange tree, and brushing her long hair. They have never spoken the same language, but they know each other through love. In another picture book, the author David Getz describes little Maxine going up in space to the moon in her rocket ship. When she looks down from there, she realizes she cannot see any of the lines you would see on a map of the world, that those lines are the boundaries adults have created, and that all the world is really one. That is what great literature explains: all the world, all of us, are really one.

You Are Your Child's Greatest Role Model

Your child must have people in her life she can look to in order to say: "I want to be like that." If you have always been a struggling reader, or never liked to read as a child, please don't worry. I hope this book will help you as a gentle guide but that it won't negate the real you as a reader, struggles and all. Mentors are real and authentic. Mentors demonstrate struggle as well as success. Mentors show they love something. So if you love the sports pages but hate novels, that's okay and you can share that. But find out what you love about the sports pages. Ask yourself: is it that it's a play-by-play? A great retelling? A collection of pictures? Or is it the way your heart thumps as you read about the end of a great game? Name what works for you and share that with your child. Be positive about *yourself*. Be kind to yourself. Share how reading has meant something to you, how you still work to overcome the struggles, and when something moved you, even if you have to go way back to a book that affected you once, long ago.

Show your reading habits and your own reading rituals, your quirky likes and dislikes. I share with my daughters that I have eclectic taste: I have wept over Jhumpa Lahiri's short stories, lost my heart to *Anna Karenina*, chased imaginary dogs in Albert Payson Terhune's tales of collies, and pored over celebrity snapshots in *People* magazine. I am not a snob at all about my reading, but I am voracious and I want my kids to know that my eclecticism is a part of my life that I value deeply. My husband, Jim, has been on an Abraham Lincoln exploration for two years, reading every biography he can find about him. He recently read about a new translation of *The Odyssey* and bought three different versions so he could compare them. And he loves the sports section in the *New York Times*, reading most often about his favorite Boston Red Sox when the New York papers deign to give them some attention. My father loves the obituaries, and clips them and sends them to me frequently. He is right; they are generally very well written and tell a wonderful story about one life. I would never have thought to include obituaries on my favorite reading list, but thanks to my dad I sure do now.

If you love the backs of cereal boxes or still recall how much you loved the Archie comics, share all that with your child. Ingesting words, like fruit and vegetables, is just plain good for us, no matter where they are coming from. I celebrate this text-messaging generation of young adults, because they are ingesting the written word at rates we never dreamed of at our age. I consider it all reading and urge you to celebrate it all too.

Before you feel overwhelmed by the sheer numbers of books in the world, and the many kinds of ways people read, and what your considerations are as a parent or caregiver, let me reassure you. Raising a reader in your home is actually very, very simple, costs very little, and produces outcomes that are tremendously beneficial not only for your child but for you too. I have four pieces of advice for you to help you along the way. I call them the Four Keys.

2. The Four Keys to Helping Your Child Become a Lifelong Reader

I had a student once whose name was Wayne. He was a deaf thirteen-year-old and had just arrived in my classroom from Guyana. At first, he never said a word and he did not know any sign language. He sat in the back of the classroom and looked angry and frustrated. No matter what I did in those hard first days, he would not connect with me or with anyone else in our room. On our third day together, I brought out a pile of picture books. I sat next to him and began stickering them for our shelves. After a time, I saw his eyes going to the books, his curiosity there even though he wanted still to hide it from me. I continued with my stickering as if I hadn't noticed, to give him a chance. A book popped up. It was called *Jump, Frog, Jump!* by Robert Kalan. And he reached for it. After he looked at it for a few minutes, I asked him: would you like me to read that book to you? And I moved even closer to him, and started to sign and speak the text of the book to him. Now I knew he did not know English, nor did he know sign language (yet), but it didn't matter. He inched even closer and pointed to each picture and I showed him the story through the pictures while he watched my hand intently to decipher each word. It was the first time he smiled at me, when we got to those *Jump, Frog, Jump!* pages. And then he started to get that there was a pattern and that the pages repeated. His face just lit up with that understanding.

As a result of that reading, I realized how much he loved animals. Together, we went through the pages of a pet company's catalog and I explained to him as best as I could that we were going to select something he liked from the catalog to order for our classroom. He and I pored over those pages for many hours. I will never forget how he leaned in close to the book and scoured each picture to "read" whatever he could. At last, he selected what he wanted: African tadpole eggs. We ordered a hundred of them, as recommended by the company. When they were delivered, Wayne cleaned their tank meticulously, which he continued to do every day that spring. He fed them carefully and watched them each day. We got stacks of frog books and tadpole care books and he deciphered the words with me by studying the pictures. Those tadpoles grew to be tiny perfect frogs, swimming delightedly in their pristine waters. Wayne wrote his first line in English that spring. It was a story to tell us of his life in Guyana and it was: "I was the lonely deaf." He made signs and hung them all around the school: "Come to Visit the Frogs in Class 1-B." His literacy was exploding. He took home all kinds of early reading books in his backpack: not only books on frogs now, but books about children and dogs and life in the United States and silly joke books and poetry. He brought them back each day, carefully tending to them as well as he cared for those tadpoles. Now we were able to talk so much more. He told me, in his awkward signs and muffled speech, all about life in Guyana: his grandparents working in their garden, and sweet guavas and pomegranate juices and salt fish and curry chicken. The signs and the speech spilled out of him, in a tumble. He had many stories to tell me that spring. Meanwhile, the frogs were growing. Like Wayne, they grew fast. They thrived in their environment, since it was well suited to their needs, thanks to Wayne. They depended on the routines of his care each day. By the time that spring was coming to its end and summer was peeking around the corner, Wayne was reading voraciously. He sat beside his frogs long after school had ended, a book in one hand, the other on the side of the frog tank. I stayed late in the room doing my cleanup and talking with Wayne about his books and his life.

I will never forget Wayne. I would say he was one of my first, greatest teachers. He taught me the most about what I needed to know about teaching, about learning, about children. Mostly about children: the universal needs of children, no matter where they come from, no matter what their challenges, no matter how they come to us or at what age. Wayne taught me to keep it simple, that there are really just four keys to building the beginnings of a reading life. What Wayne taught me I have categorized for you here in an easy acronym (READ!) so that you can keep these four keys in your heart and let them guide your time with your children. Hopefully with these keys you will open the doors of literacy and a lifelong love of words for and with your child.

R = Ritual

All living beings thrive on rituals. Whether they are as small as what you do each night before you go to bed, or as big as what a community does when there is a milestone, rituals bind us to one another and give us predictability, the kind of predictability that allows us to take risks and try new things. Wayne had never been read to, and so the ritual of the read-aloud was a deep comfort to him, and a boundless joy. It was all so new to him, but once he knew it was every day, he came to trust it, to look forward to it, and to plan for it. So too his after-school reading times with me were predictable and fun: a ritual we both came to look forward to. It was a peaceful ritual, tailored for his unique needs. The read-aloud for the whole class was one thing, but the ritual for him as an individual child was also important.

In your own lives at home, you can create rituals for reading aloud with all your children along with rituals for reading aloud with each individual child. I know it's not easy, especially considering how busy all our lives are. But it's well worth it for the investment you will make. Each child in your family is different. The ritual of reading brings us together in profound ways. The ritual of reading with one of your children gives you the chance to consider the beauty and mystery of this particular child. Each child learns to read at different rates, at different times, and is interested in different things. Carving out a predictable time of day or night to learn about what makes this child so unique is time well spent. Reading together, too, with all ages and diverse interests in your family, is powerful and can be a transformative tool in building family relationships. Reading books to the younger child, an older one snuggles close. Reading books to the older child, the younger one leans in, even if it's over his head for now. Allow this "messiness" in the read-aloud ritual. It is part of the way your family can come together and also a way for all of you to learn more about each another.

Some of the rituals I recommend relate to when to read: not only at night, although the snuggle in bed is just a wondrous thing, but also reading to your child while he sits in the bath, reading to your child in the kitchen while you cook dinner together. He helps you stir and turn the pages and you read, and season, read and season. (I wouldn't say my pot roast always had the right flavorings as a result, but the experience sure was sweet!) Or on Sunday mornings all together, one of you reads from the Sunday newspaper to the family; there is so much in the paper for all of you. The sports section tells stories that are often gripping and universal. Another worthy ritual is to pack a little set of books to bring to the playground. Every time you get ready to go, your child will know where in the backpack to put that little set of books. While she swings on the swing, read Robert Louis Stevenson's *The Swing*. While she plays nearby in the sandbox, read from *Poems for the Very Young* by Michael Rosen, which includes some playground poems. Read the same story before your child starts school each fall. Read *Sheila Rae the Brave* or *Leo the Late Bloomer* or another book you and your child choose together to symbolize that first big day each year. Holidays are of course a great time to consider the read-aloud as part of your ritual. Read *It's the Great Pumpkin, Charlie Brown* at Halloween; *Merry Christmas, Amelia Bedelia* at Christmas; *Latkes and Applesauce* by Fran Manushkin at Hanukkah; *The Gifts of Kwanzaa* by Synthia Saint James during Kwanzaa; *Lighting a Lamp: A Diwali Story* during the Hindu festival of lights.

But many memorable rituals are also created out of ordinary moments, those regular, predictable times we have with our children every day. Reading aloud stamps the seal of the extraordinary on a day rushing by like any other.

E = Environment

Establish an environment that is conducive to reading aloud together. When I was little, I could read anywhere at any time. I would sit on my couch during a family gathering and get some aunt or uncle to read to me through all the noise. That is really not true of all children. Some children need for us to create a very special read-aloud environment where the conditions are just right.

Look around your home environment and ask yourself what might get in the way of a tranquil reading experience. Ask yourself what you could do to set up an environment that reflects a value for literacy. You do not have to have a lot of space and you do not have to have a lot of room. The television is oftentimes competing for children's mental focus and personal space. Have designated times of the day when the television is on and times when it is off. For some people, especially children, it is so difficult to concentrate on literally anything else when the television is on, even if the sound is off. It is interesting to me that we send our children off to read alone, while the television has become the hearth of the family life. If it's there, you will use it. Instead, send the TV off to its own room. Then watching TV becomes something you have to think about doing, rather than just keeping it on because it's there. On a side note, when your children are young, and especially if English is not your child's or your first language, or if you have a child with language development issues, keep on the closed-captioning button so your child can read along with the narrator's voice. It is a free and easy way to integrate print literacy into television time.

I see the future as evolving so that eventually all books and print material will be available online, and so the word "reading" will take on new and different resonance. I think that eventually the way we are going to get books to the most children is by making them available electronically, so I am a big fan of computers and their potential. There are and will be plentiful opportunities to "read" together online. Find ways to investigate the Internet and explore it with your child as an act of literacy; have fun with it together and read aloud from what you find and discover there. Don't worry that your child will not like to read books if he likes to "read" the Internet. Take the approach that we "ingest" words in many forms.

Our children have to put their stamp on the environment too. Let them create the read-aloud environment with you. So what do I mean by "environment"? I mean the physical layout of space where your child (and you) will actually read together; what belongs in the environment, i.e., books, and magazines, writing materials, and more; the sounds and visuals in the environment that may either compel your child toward print or distract your child. When our daughters were little I set up a writing table right in the kitchen for them. This was because in those days I was doing a lot of cooking in the evenings when I got home from work, and so I wanted my kids near me and also wanted to hear what they were saying and thinking. If I set up a writing corner somewhere else, I might not have heard or participated in all I did. While I was cooking the meal, they were chattering and drawing and I could ask them questions about their stories. The same was true about their books. There were baskets of books on that table, and they browsed them, even picture books, while I did what I needed to do. I could add a comment every now and then, or just listen to the pleasurable sound of their voices. From two years old on, they would ask me if they could "read to me" so I could enjoy the story while I worked. I was amazed at how much of their favorite stories they were able to recall from memory and "read" to me.

My biggest tip on putting books into your environment is to place them where kids will actually be able to use them. I know it sounds obvious, but I can't tell you how many times I've been in people's homes and seen beautiful children's books up on very high bookshelves. The incidence for whimsy and just finding something are much lower in that scenario. Your child can't just reach and grab something because it catches his eye. I much prefer to have you ask your child to help you create a workable environment for literacy together. Buy an armful of plastic baskets from the dollar store. Together, organize your books by theme or author into these little baskets, and keep them on the ground or on a low table.

Ask your children where they would most love to read (this will change as they grow) and establish a nook there. Our daughters loved to read together on the couch downstairs when they were little and so I put a little basket for books right near the couch. As they got older, they read more often in their rooms and so together we sketched out how we thought bookshelves would work best for them in their rooms and built them in that spirit. It's natural to be tempted to arrange for quiet separate spaces for your children as they grow more as independent readers, and sometimes this is not the best idea. Your child, who loves to be with you, then begins to associate reading time with alone time, and as much as you think that is the right thing, it will get in the way of your child wanting to read on his own. It's not something he can articulate, but it's something he may viscerally feel. Create spaces that will truly work for your child. If squishing onto an already crowded couch works, if sitting at the hard kitchen table chair works, if reading on his bed works, then affirm and celebrate those (changing) choices and be attentive to how you can help make those choices work best for him. These discussions with your children set the stage for their own lifelong awareness as to what will work for them as readers.

A = Access

All the keys are important, but this one is especially so. People struggle when they are working with material that is beyond their level of understanding or ease. Access is about the right text at the right time. And plenty of them! A study by the National Endowment for the Arts found that homes with ten or more children's books have a profound influence on kids' lives and how well they do in school. Let's give our kids access to books that match them in terms of levels and interests. Consider three levels:

Uphill books are hard but with a strong interest component that compels your kids.

Level books are just right for your kids and feel like a comfortable shoe.

Downhill books appear "easy" but are actually critical for your kids in terms of building their reading abilities. They can read them quickly and the books are generally on topics of interest or comfort for your kids.

Continue reading aloud books at all of these levels to your children even as your children are developing as independent readers and reading harder books on their own. This is really important and will give you some peace of mind if you have to read to multiple children in your family and are worried that your stronger independent reader is still hearing "easier" books. Hearing books read aloud at different levels is helpful and important because it builds your children's fluency levels, stamina levels, and comprehension levels.

Access comes in many different forms: one is the physical presence of books in your home. I have mentioned baskets, simple ones that can be portable in your home or even in the back of your car. Consider plastic ziplock bags too, with each of your children's names on them. These can be restocked and filled before car trips, or rides on the subway, and personalized for each of your children. Even your youngest child will love filling her own ziplock bag before a long (or short) journey away from home.

Nearness to actual books, actual print, will have a tremendous impact upon your child and you too. Don't worry so much about "quality." Comics, graphic novels, joke books, riddles, recipes, and songs count as reading too. Hang your favorite recipe up in the kitchen, and encourage your child to write his own and hang it too. Sing some songs and copy the lyrics together to hang over his bed to practice at night. Find your favorite funny or big or beautiful words and write them down on cards and stick them on the wall near the writing corner (low, so your child can see them). Access to language, to words, is not just about books. It is about the language that is all around us and bringing it closer to home in visual and vibrant ways.

In the mornings before school, Jim reads the news aloud to our girls. I am always fascinated by what he chooses to read to them. He loves history, particularly military history, and so he gravitates toward news stories relating to the military and global politics. He knows a lot about the subject, but he also shows how much he still learns every day by asking genuine questions as he reads aloud. The girls get very excited about these discussions, and I can see how having access to these kinds of texts is making them much stronger as readers. I'd like to encourage you all to do that too, even if you didn't grow up with military history on your mind. Exposing your children to a variety of texts is so essential, even when you yourself don't know a tremendous amount about what you are reading. That's why newspapers are so valuable, either online or on paper.

Along the same lines, my father has always told me that he thinks some of the best writing in the world is in the sports pages of newspapers. To this day, when he reads a great article in the sports section, he will clip it and send it to me. So from the time I was little, I always had a reverence for the sports pages. Red Barber, a legendary journalist, had a sports radio spot while I was in my teens. I used to sit there at the radio and listen to him, marveling at how he turned a phrase. He said things like: "You have to be as fully prepared for the dull game as you are for the great game, or else you won't be prepared for the great one." What a great sentence. He had hundreds of those sayings. He was also just amazing at retelling a game, or doing a play-by-play. Those writers who can use details and strong images to tell a story in sequence are so valuable to our children as mentors. Access to text is not just access to literature. It's access to words: words that have the power to really affect and change your children's lives. Now, on the Internet you and your children can watch together many of the great speeches of the last several decades. Watch clips of Martin Luther King Jr. and Robert Kennedy. Listen to poets reading from their own work, either on the Internet or on sets on tape. All of this is about access: access to the voices of poets and authors and access to the impact words can have.

D = Dialogue

Build bridges for communication through literature, and they will last a lifetime, fostering a positive engagement with your child.

From the earliest moment, reading aloud facilitates a pattern for dialogue with your baby. Facial expression, your tone of voice, and the baby's movement toward you in those tender moments are all the stirrings of the beginnings of dialogue. As your child grows, your back-and-forth, while playful, is also setting the stage for all the future interactions you will have, into your child's teen years and beyond. Is it unjudging? Joyous? Engaged? Inquiring? Later, this dialogue changes, but the question remains: what are the ways you are going to engage with your children's reading lives, even as they develop independence? Our goal is lifelong dialogue with our children: the doors always open, the talk always going back and forth. As my daughter goes off to college, one of the things I will miss most is the sound of her voice as she comes through the door at the end of the school day and then the sounds of the four of us at the table just talking and talking, sharing all the goodness and the hard times of our days. But I know the dialogue will not end. It will look different and sound different, maybe with more texting and e-mailing, phoning and visiting. I trust the dialogue itself, though. It has been there since I said, "Where's Spot?" and she looked at me and burst out into peals of laughter. She was six months old then.

Now that both of our daughters are in their teens, our interactions, our dialogues are sometimes on the run, sometimes in the car, sometimes late at night after we have been waiting up for them, sometimes around the dinner table. The dialogue is about politics, about global issues, about a great poem, about school. The dialogue is textured, layered, complex, and interesting. It has changed a lot since the days of our nonverbal communication or the Spot moments, but in some critical ways it is exactly the same: the back-and-forth remains constant, the active listening on both sides remains constant. In dialogue, the listening is as important as the talking. It is not always easy, and if you have a child or teen who tends to be private and not so overtly communicative, do not fear. Let the silence be companionable. Read aloud from the paper or from an e-mail into the companionable silence. Dialogue is about that thing we create when our children are babies; the nearness of each other.

It is something we forget as parents because we are so eager to fill up the "empty vessels," to pour our lifelong learning into the minds and hearts of our children, out of all our most earnest worries: all the knowledge, all the wisdom we want them to have. And yet the best dialogue is the inquiry: asking our children what they are thinking and what they are wondering about and how they are absorbing information. Some questions to spark inquiry include: "What are your biggest questions about what we are reading?" "How does this book connect to another book we've read?" "What does this story remind you of in your own life?" "How could reading this book change you or your thinking in some way?" These are all questions without right or wrong answers; with your deep interest in your child you will find your child's responses fascinating. And then you don't have to worry about always having the right answers!

Authentic dialogue is a mutual inquiry: you are both exploring ideas together and valuing each other's opinions. This genuinely applies for both your conversations with your two-year-old and for your ten-year-old. I find two-year-olds really funny and interesting. They have lots on their minds. Try as hard as you can to put yourself in the inquiring stance. Don't ask questions about the read-aloud or about the book your child is reading independently as a question-and-answer session. That is a good way to encourage your child to avoid future conversations with you about literature. Instead, ask questions you don't know the answers to, questions that have to do with your child's way of thinking and her perspectives. People, all people, are hungry to share their interests, ideas, and concerns. A two-year-old is no different. "What do you think is going to happen next?" is a better question when you haven't read the book either. Not such a good question if you've read the book a million times, as it seems a bit forced. But "Let's guess what happens next" is more authentic and makes it into a game, with your child knowing that while you have read the book before, you still think it's fun to make predictions. My uncle Shelley was a very quiet man. He did not say a lot, unlike the rest of my family. Yet at our family gatherings, he and I communicated deeply with each other. I would sit by his side and we would hold hands. When he was very sick with cancer at the end of his too short life, we sat quietly by each other's side and I like to think he took as much comfort from my presence as I always did from his. His version of dialogue was simple and pure, not full of rhetoric or unnecessary words. But in his quiet and peaceful manner, he communicated a lot: he listened really well; he made me feel like I could accomplish anything. His smile and his nod of the head told me in volumes how much he appreciated me and how much he believed in me. His beaming gaze at his wife, my aunt Rita, told me how much he loved her and taught me about being a partner for Jim years later. If you are not a big talker, or if your child is not a big talker, don't worry that dialogue has to be a flood of words back and forth. The patterns of dialogue you create with your child should reflect both the authentic you and your authentic child. You can send strong messages to each other without a word having been spoken.

And finally, the tenor of your dialogue will change over time as well. Please do not worry. It is natural. Your five-year-old is open and expansive. The questions pour out of her like a fountain. Your eight-year-old might be a bit more reserved, or even preoccupied by school matters. Literature is a great way to bring out the latent worries and the joys of her life. Your ten-year-old may be beginning to burrow down in a blanket with her own book, or perhaps not. Maybe at school, books have started to represent something that feels hard and uncomfortable. Your unjudging, loving dialogue will say: I am here for you, your biggest champion, always.

3. Supporting Your Child's Reading Life: Frequently Asked Questions

In this book, I focus on the read-aloud: a key factor in helping you to raise lifelong readers. Along the way on your reading journeys, plenty of questions will come to your minds. Some will be about kids and reading in general and others will be about your kids as independent readers. Here, to start us off, are some of the questions I am most commonly asked by parents and teachers. I hope my responses are of good comfort to you, and that this book itself will be a truly helpful companion and guide for you as you do your important work raising your lifelong readers.

Why do boys seem to resist reading more than girls? Is this a myth or reality?

I founded and lead Books for Boys, a nine-year literacy initiative that addresses this question specifically. I have pondered this question deeply and here is what I think: boys do not resist reading more than girls, but they appear to due to the nature of what they are most often offered to read, both by female teachers and by the female members of their families. I can't say conclusively which comes first, this chicken or this egg, but suffice to say, boys read *differently*. Now, it should be said that I'd like us all to be more open-minded on this subject, and equally concerned that we provide our girls *and* our boys with stimulating, equally accessible, equally diverse material. But given that ninety percent of the teaching population is women, we definitely have a perspective skew. Women and girls tend to really like reading narrative text: books with stories. Many boys tend to like nonnarrative texts a lot. They will read to hunt for a bit of information rather than to follow the trail of a story. I can't tell you how many times parents have said to me, after watching a son read a magazine or a video game manual, "But that's not really reading. I want my son to really read."

I think we all must be open to how we define what we value as readers, especially given that in the world of Internet technology, reading itself is changing and evolving. We read faster and we skim more on the Internet, all skills our boys crave to do when there is a big book on some topic or another open in front of them. It may look like they are not really "reading," but this is reading too. I'd like to see our girls do more of that. Boys start to resist when they feel outside of the named experience. Research shows us that boys like outcomes. They like to finish things. As soon as we as parents see our children able to do something, we instantly want them to do it better, faster, longer. If we can accept our boys' reading at their level for longer, reading books they can manage easily and feel success in finishing, chances are they are going to see themselves as readers and want to read more often. Also, offering more of a variety of genres to our children, both in terms of what we read aloud to them and what we celebrate that they are reading on their own, is incredibly helpful. Comics, graphic novels, how-to manuals for video games, the sports pages, this is all reading, but we tend to devalue it all for the sake of narrative fiction with an emotional message. Let's encourage all kinds of reading for both our boys and our girls. I guarantee it will lead to more time spent reading in your home, and that is the key. Once I ran a panel for boys from a diverse range of backgrounds. I asked them what made them choose a book they wanted to read. One of the boys said: "Our teachers always choose the books with medals on the covers, but we really like the ones with dragons on them." I have always remembered, as I go to select books, that what is most important is to read, read, read and to expose our kids to that reading experience. Reach for the dragons, too.

Should I still be reading aloud to my child after he or she is reading independently?

Absolutely! Yes! Yes! (Did I say yes?) There are many powerful reasons why this is so critical. Our children are still developing as readers long after they appear to be reading independently. They are building stamina, comprehension, and fluency skills. The profound impact of reading aloud cannot be underestimated for many reasons. Just as they are beginning to read independently, in general, they are also beginning to foray into the world of independence. Reading aloud to them helps bring them back onto the couch. Reading aloud to them helps bring them back into discussions with you. The ritual of the read-aloud allows you to ask if everything is okay, without asking if everything is okay. It allows you to ask how things are going in school, without asking how things are going at school. It allows you to ask how everything is with his best friend, without asking how everything is with his best friend. The ritual of the read-aloud is at once like a ship that sets out on a journey and the anchor that helps return it to its resting place. So too, your children are going on journeys every single day and the read-aloud serves as an anchor for those journeys. Also, the read-aloud can serve the purpose of providing a model for your children of what is coming next for them as readers; you might choose to read aloud to them a book that is too complex for them as independent readers. For example, your son might be reading fairly simple Henry and Mudge books while you are reading aloud to them a far more complex book such as *Charlie and the Chocolate Factory.* While your child cannot read this book on his own yet, the image of the book in his life, the image of what his independent reading life might be going forward, can prepare him for his future as a reader.

The read-aloud also provides your child with an opportunity to hear vocabulary she would otherwise not hear, because you are reading it. The vocabulary flows into her smoothly as a ship moving downstream.

Finally, there is an almost surprising reason for why the read-aloud is so critical at this juncture. You should read aloud not just *beyond* your child's level, but also *below* your child's level and *at* your child's level. Your child needs to see that the books he is reading independently are not just books that he is "practicing on" until he gets to the "real books" that adults read. Even these very "simple" books are worth reading aloud as well as independently because of their funny, silly stories, or their charming pictures, or their wise use of language. By reading these types of books aloud, as well as the books we consider great literature, we are showing our child that these books help to make us all authentic readers in the world. So too, reading aloud books that are *below* our child's level or *at* our child's level gives us the opportunity to model the kinds of thinking skills that we use when reading unfamiliar texts, such as decoding new words or comprehending the story idea.

Along the same lines, if we read picture books or early chapter books *below* our kids' reading levels, we are modeling a few very important things for our child: the power and purpose of rereading (which I will talk about a little later), and how we use books we know and books that feel easy for us in order to build our stamina, concentration, and fluency. As adults, we often read books and magazines that are really below our reading levels because we have a purpose in our reading. We might be seeking information in a magazine that we would consider "light reading" or we might just simply be tired and really crave a moment with the fast mystery on our bedside table.

Should I give rewards to my child for reading?

When our children were little and came home from school, we would lay out a snack for them. The snack would often be carrot sticks and brownies. They loved the bright orange, crispy crunch of the carrots and the dark, rich sweetness of the brownies. I was very intrigued by watching them, having tried not to put a value on one choice over the other, and found that they were equally interested in both the carrot and the brownie. The same is true for reading. If we help our children to create a reading experience that feels meaningful and sweet, the reading experience becomes its own kind of reward. If we start to use it as something that they have to do in order to watch a video, it becomes clear to them that in some way we are placing more value on the video than on reading. I understand that for some of our children reading does feel stressful, so as parents we look for ways to ameliorate that stress. Since we know that reading is good for our kids, we will do just about anything to get them to do it, including offering rewards. So my suggestion here is to make the reward embedded in the reading experience. If your child needs an incentive to read, create the kind of conditions in which the child will really want to read. For example: put a pot of tea to boil, get out the blanket, create a cozy corner, and sit down beside your child with your own book. Bring a plate of treats (carrots and brownies, for example!) and show your child how you are valuing this experience as much as he is.

All that being said, we do not often celebrate our children in their great efforts to enter the reading experience, so authentic kinds of rewards that feel very connected to what they have been able to achieve can be really fun and significant for your child. We should not reward children for the number of books they have read, but rather for the amount of time they have spent reading. Keep track with your child of the time you both have spent reading; when you both read three hundred minutes (this could be over a period of several weeks), then have a little tea party or a mini-celebration, like a trip to the ice-cream shop.

I know my child can read Harry Potter because he can sound out all the words on the page. So why does he seem unable to finish the book?

Reading is both divinely simple (like riding a bike, once you get the hang of it) and also extraordinarily complicated (like flying a kite, which depends on multiple factors being just right). There are some factors that are nearly invisible on the surface that can really get in your child's way as a reader. Let us look at the four key areas of reading development: *decoding*, *comprehending*, *building stamina*, and *building fluency*. Decoding is the most visible to us as parents, and so we can see it immediately: can they or can't they? Decoding is the word we use to describe the breaking down of sound to read each word. But this is just one of the four areas of strength a child is building, and so it is not surprising to me that sometimes you will see your child decode words on a page and yet still not be able to read the book.

Comprehending the book is often made much more difficult by barriers you may not have even considered. For example, when your child begins to read books with many chapters, he has to figure out the passing of time. Some books jump backward and forward in time and can be extremely confusing. Our children also have to figure out the role of secondary characters. This can be very confusing as well, especially as they make the leap from simpler chapter books with fewer characters to books with many more. (Harry Potter is one such example: even as the books go on in the series, they become full of more and more characters, so even the child who was able to read Book One may struggle in comprehending the subsequent books.)

Stamina is another key ingredient for the growing reader. Just as you know how to run, let's say, and you can do it perfectly, you may only be able to run well for seven minutes. If I asked you to run for two hours, you might think very differently about running. You might even say you couldn't do it at all. Reading is a lot like that. What a child can do perfectly for seven minutes may not be something he can sustain yet for much longer on his own, especially with harder books. The thought of all that hard work may be daunting for him. Your read-alouds are crucial supports because they can help your child explore the world of harder books he craves with you, while still practicing his independent reading skills in books he can manage more easily.

Fluency is another word for reading smoothly. You can help your child learn to read more smoothly (with fewer bumps or awkward pauses) if you demonstrate your own smooth reading by reading aloud with expression from all kinds of books.

How can I encourage my child to read more?

Read with your child: both as the reader and also just as a companion. We tend to encourage our children to do things we may not be doing enough of either! We tell them to go read while we are on our work calls or cooking dinner. Take time for yourself too. Curl up with a good magazine, or a novel you have been longing to read, and make a place beside you on the couch for your child.

Read the same book your child is reading. Buy two copies at the bookstore or reserve two copies at the library. Don't quiz her on what she is reading, but rather savor the moments you enjoy and share them with her. Ask about parts you might be puzzling over. Share your perceptions of a character. Be as authentic as you can be with her. You will be surprised at how much you may like some of the books she is reading. Be very, very open to the books your child really wants to read. Try not to be judgmental. Remember, our parents probably cringed at Judy Blume and some of the authors we read while coming of age, and their parents before that probably cringed at Marjorie Morningstar. Every new generation is going to push the envelope a bit further. Our daughters have loved the genre of young adult girls' lit: *Gossip Girl*, etc. A generation ago, these would have been hard to swallow, but now they have encouraged a generation of girls to read and read and read and to talk at school and on their chats about the books they are reading and sharing. Use your best judgment, and, of course, if you are not comfortable with a selection, share with your child why you might not be. But use it as an opportunity to talk about books.

My child only wants to read magazines, never books. What do you think?

There are so many wonderful magazines to choose from, and if you think about how you read as an adult, chances are you might read more magazines than books. There are skills required for magazine reading that are useful for other genres too, and even applicable for hurdles like test taking. Magazine reading requires us to skip around and to jump from genre to genre, just as standardized tests do. So it is good prep for your kids for the lives they have in school. Beyond that, magazines are rich with persuasive writing, with poetry, short stories, snippets of real life events, and photographs. They are chock-full of the kinds of reading your child will be doing his whole life long. Read these aloud to your child too, in addition to having them available (or browsing them together in the library). In the "Reader's Ladder" section of this book, I will give you some suggestions for magazines to read with your child.

My child wants to reread the same books over and over again. Is this okay? Why is he doing this?

This is more than okay: this is really great. There are good reasons why a child reads and rereads a book, and also good reasons why it is healthy for your child to do so. Children reread because something in a book is extremely compelling to them, whether it is the plot or the characters or the overall sensation. Charlotte reread every book of the Harry Potter series several times over. When I asked her what felt most important about her rereads, she said to me, simply: "I just love the feeling I get when I am in that world with them." The world of Harry Potter: the butterbeer, the train ride to Hogwarts, the buffet table in the big hall, the creaky stairs, and the close, dark air under the Invisibility Cloak. All of this feels more real than imagined and is a world children want to enter and reenter a thousand times over. One of the boys I met at the Children's Village, Genesis, read Harry Potter more than nine times! When I asked him why, he said: "Harry is my best friend." When I was a little girl, I loved *Anne of Green Gables,* and I read that series again and again and again. I just wanted to be with Anne by the Lake of Shining Waters, or sitting with Marilla at the cozy kitchen table on the farm. I could predict the moment when Anne would get into one of her "scrapes" and when Marilla's voice would soften even after Anne had been up to something mischievous. It was as if I knew them as well as I knew myself. Something about the rereading Charlotte and I were doing was beyond comforting. It was the essential aura of the environment, the characters, the plot, the *life* of the book that seemed to matter so much. It was a visceral sense of wanting to be there.

The key thing about rereading books is the unbelievable capacity children have to get inside other worlds. It's a crucial quality to develop in your children, because it is all about cultivating empathy, understanding, and relational experiences not only to humankind, but also to other environments and experiences. In addition, rereading does something else: it helps your child become a faster reader. When a child gets to know a book, and is less weighed down by plot and the introduction of characters, he becomes faster and faster in the sheer skill of words per minute. In a world where speed does matter, and where in college and high school the students who can read quickly are at a distinct advantage, this is a useful skill to hone. Whenever I think about how I became a fast reader myself, I think about *Anne of Green Gables*. First, Lucy Maud Montgomery gave me the gift of the stories I will never forget, the girl named Anne who taught me that girls can speak up and speak out and that having an imagination is the world's most priceless gift. Second, Montgomery gave me another gift: I loved those books so much that I was willing, no, eager, to read them over and over and over. And every time I read them, I got faster and faster and faster, less focused on the sharp plot turn or the emotion of the moment and more just completely inside of the experience.

Finally, rereading does one more key thing for your child. We are all trying to work through our experiences. We are all of us, big and small, trying to make sense of the world in which we live. By rereading, our children are potentially working on something: a difficult character, a resonant plotline, a complex situation the character faces that is resolved in a way that feels powerful to your child. All of this requires reseeing, rethinking, reimagining. It may be on the unconscious level, but nevertheless, rereading does give your child the opportunity to revisit something that may be particularly hard to work out in real life but that is safe to explore and ponder in the pages of a book.

I don't really like to read. How can I encourage a love of reading in my child if I don't like it myself?

Chances are you read more than you think you do. In other words, you may be a reader of newspapers, or comics, or letters, or Web pages. Reenvision yourself as a reader. Talk to your child about the kinds of things you like to read and be proud, not embarrassed. If you have a note that your mother wrote you years ago that you keep folded up in your top drawer and read often, tell your child about that. If you love the sports pages and read them every day, read them aloud to your child. If you really cherish your favorite recipes and you collect them, remembering where you got each one, tell your child about that. Identify yourself as a reader who loves sports, recipes, your mother's words.

You may be a struggling reader. Perhaps for this reason, you have never loved to read. It may be something you have just acknowledged or something you have struggled with your whole life. Here are a few suggestions: first, embrace this opportunity to read with your child. Select picture books that will make you feel comfortable: books with limited print and wonderful pictures that support the text. Tell stories to go with the pictures for your child. He will love the nearness of you and your voice and will not care if you skip some of the words. Second, try to really take on the struggle completely and get some help, no matter what your age. It is never too late to improve upon your own reading. Buy books on tape and follow along with the printed page. Use the Internet to practice your skills. Turn on the close-captioning button of your television and practice reading along when your favorite show is on. Ask a friend you trust a lot to help you practice improving your reading skills by reading together. But, best of all, read with your child. Your child loves you so deeply and so much. He is the least judgmental reading partner you could find. Let him read a page, and then you read a page. As he gets a bit older, tell him about your own struggles and how proud you are of him for being such a reader, that he is helping you too. Life is too short for us not to be authentic with one another, and being authentic with our children is the best place to begin. They will admire and love you and cherish you all the more for it. I promise.

My child seems to be reading below her grade level. When should I worry and what should I do to help her move ahead?

Reading aloud to your child is actually one of the best ways to help your child move forward. Let your child experience the pleasures of reading without the pressure of performance. Give yourselves plenty of time to enjoy books together and to let your child feel the magic and breadth of a reading experience. The second-best way is to make very sure you have provided your child with access to the books that are just right for her to read. If she is always scrambling and reading one or two steps beyond her comfort level, her reading will not improve. The third-best thing to do is to talk directly and frankly to your child's teacher about your concerns and to check in to see what the school is doing to support her. Don't hesitate to be a real advocate for your child. I know this is not easy. Express your concern that your child may not be progressing. If the teacher says to just wait, that it may be developmental, ask for another meeting in four weeks' time to get updates on the progress so that you also are working in partnership with the teacher to look for signs of steps forward. Continue to meet with the teacher to be absolutely sure there is intervention when and if needed.

My child has special needs. Will this book be helpful and can I read aloud in the same ways to my child?

Reading aloud is a great, great support for you and your child. You can introduce your child to books she may not be able to read on her own and help her to feel inside the "reading club" with everyone else because you are exposing her to these texts in your read-aloud time. If your child may never be able to read on his own, the read-aloud is a wonderful comfort and opportunity for you to look at pictures together and for you too to feel that it is a time of day for you both to be close. If your child cannot travel or experience the world in the way others might, picture books and chapter books open up new worlds in the stories and tales told. The couch becomes a magic carpet ride upon which you both can transcend the struggles of the day and find new freedoms, together.

My child only wants to be on the computer. Does this "count" as reading? If not, what should I do?

Let us reimagine what our conception of reading really is. In this era, our children are going to be reading and writing in ways you could not have envisioned even three years ago. Soon, all books may be available online or on handheld devices. In some ways, this is tremendously exciting. The world will open in terms of literacy for lots and lots of people who have not had access to books. It means students will be able to read at their levels whenever they want, wherever they want. In other ways, it forces us to reimagine how we define reading and the role of the read-aloud. Right now, books are still a major vehicle for transmitting information and carrying stories. But we can help our children navigate the shift to the technological age by not judging them for their time online, but rather steering them toward quality use of time on the computer. The Internet leads us to great poems, to stories in the news, to children's literature. We can work with our child side by side at the computer to "read" together the kinds of information she is seeking. Try to be open to what is motivating your child and join him in those journeys. If you create a ritual for the read-aloud every day or every evening, your child will come to relish it and to look forward to it if it is a peaceful time. It is when the computer is off, the television is off, the loud sounds of the day subside, and you are together. This in itself is a compelling reason for your child to shut off the screens and find refuge in the pages of a book with you.

My child prefers me to read to him, even though he can read perfectly well. Thoughts?

This time is so fleeting. I have a drawer in which I keep a little red coat both our daughters wore when they were around two. Sometimes if I open the drawer and catch a glimpse of its little red corners, I will feel a sob in my heart: were they ever that small? We all hunger for each other, for the preciousness of our lives together, for the soft, sweet moments of togetherness on a couch, at the kitchen table on a rainy day. Your child longs for this too. School takes them away from you for many hours, and life itself takes them up and away. Still, the nearness of you and the nearness of your child are the anchor in the windy seas of life. It is no wonder he holds on. We should, too.

4. Landmark Books

There are certain books that have shaped how childhood has been conveyed to us over the years. They resonate with us because they remind us of our own childhoods and because they are, quite simply, great books under any circumstances. However, this country is rich with children who have come from other countries and have different stories that resonate with them and their parents. This book is about honoring all these voices. The story of children's literature in this country reveals much about the changing nature of childhood. It is well worth remarking upon a few important writers who have changed the landscape of children's literature.

I think that we can give it all to our children: a canon of literature that represents some critical turning points in the American experience, as well as an introduction to a new canon of key authors who bring us a multitude of voices and perspectives that will broaden our children's understanding of what it means to live in a global world. In this section I will share with you books I have identified as Landmarks that represent the story of children's literature in the United States to this point, but in no way represent a complete canon. I think these are books that you won't want to miss with your child because they are both great read-alouds and important to us historically.

When the author Sherman Alexie, who grew up on a Native American reservation, accepted the National Book Award in 2007, he thanked Ezra Jack Keats, author of *The Snowy Day*. "It was the first time I looked at a book and saw a brown, black, beige character—a character who resembled me physically and resembled me spiritually, in all his gorgeous loneliness and splendid isolation." These Landmark books all represent some major turning points in American culture, but the truth is that until 1962, when Ezra Jack Keats brought a brown character into the lexicon, this was sadly not the case in the majority of children's literature. However, each of these books I have identified as Landmarks serves some crucial purpose in the American landscape toward furthering both a child's view of the world and also the adult reader's sense of what it means to be a child. Surprisingly, there was very little children's literature before 1939. It may have been because childhood itself was not very highly valued. Children were seen as miniature adults. Child labor laws only came into being in the early 1900s. Up until then, many children in the United States were working long, merciless hours in factories and on farms with little or no protection for their needs or desires. I give some credit to the rise of children's literature in promoting a more nuanced view of the lives of children that has led to better care for and understanding of children. The books that follow are those that I believe have played a major role in redefining the American view of childhood and that also have furthered the field of children's literature in a big way. As always, lists are deeply subjective, and I am sure there may be differences of opinion. I share my selections with you humbly, in the hope you will understand that I am identifying books I see as major change-makers on behalf of the rights of children. These are books I think you will like for that reason and for the fact that they are just great books you'll want to share with your own children. I have listed them in order of their appearance on the American landscape.

Books I Consider Landmarks

Madeline, written and illustrated by Ludwig Bemelmans (The Viking Press: 1939). Fearless Madeline was not afraid of anything, even though drama swirled around her. Miss Clavell was a masterpiece, an understated but anguished parental cry of children's literature: her gown flowing behind her, and her finger pointed upward, she cried, "Something is not right!" It was a drama, an opera, playing out against the backdrop of one small girl's experience.

There was a sense of reassurance in Miss Clavell's immediate reaction that even in the absence of your parents someone else would take care of you. Miss Clavell's alarm demonstrates the realization that something really was not right at all. All of the adults and other children would have to step forward to take care of the children who were on their own, both vulnerable and deeply courageous.

Pat the Bunny by Dorothy Kunhardt (Golden Books: 1940). It was, if not the first touch-and-feel book, then one of the first. Daddy's scratchy face was depicted by rough patterns on the page. The bunny had soft fur you could actually touch. In 1941, World War II was boiling and the year ended with Pearl Harbor. *Pat the Bunny*'s innovation was safe and secure, unlike the rest of the world, which seemed out of control. The tactile nature of the book also reassured through physicality: we are near to you, beloved child.

Make Way for Ducklings by Robert McCloskey (The Viking Press: 1941). The war exploded all conventions about women. While the men were at war, women took over their jobs in the factories and kept the country running. The mother duck in McCloskey's tale is brave and bold and she steps out into the world, even with the responsibility of all those children! And what a family she had. The image of them proudly crossing the street with the policeman's kind help is iconic in American children's literature, with mother at the helm.

Curious George by Margret and Hans A. Rey (Houghton Mifflin Company: 1941). Margret and Hans A. Rey fled France on bicycles right before the arrival of the Nazis in 1940. The *Curious George* manuscript was in their bag with them. (Read your child *The Journey That Saved Curious George* by Louise Borden to find out more about the Reys' personal story.) As Jews, they knew they were in mortal danger if they did not leave. Hans built them each a bicycle and that was how they escaped. Quirky, unpredictable, and ever optimistic, *Curious George* is the story of the Reys themselves: unlikely escape artists, bringing smiles to a grim and scary world.

The Runaway Bunny by Margaret Wise Brown, illustrated by Clement Hurd (Harper: 1942). Margaret Wise Brown was revolutionary in her understanding of the lives of children in that she understood the wrenching intensity of childhood. She captured those small moments of separation in a child's experience that feel so excruciatingly complex to him, and through her stories she wrapped some comfort around those times. The mother bunny says: Where you go I will find you. No matter what the little bunny says he will do or where he will go, the mother will be there. Margaret Wise Brown's books are a constant reassurance to the child that there is order in the world and that adults will provide it. And that the child lives in a very different universe, one fueled by the imagination and by the details of ordinary life: the confluence of both.

Goodnight Moon by Margaret Wise Brown, illustrated by Clement Hurd (Harper: 1947). Margaret Wise Brown's bunny sits in his bed, with his ordinary things around him. He hears the voice of the narrator (mother? father? caretaker?) reciting the list of all the familiar objects: goodnight room, goodnight moon. The room is contained and controlled by order. Sleep, the nighttime, is somewhat like death: hard to bear, hard to cross over to. The rhyme is somewhat off: "Goodnight old lady whispering hush," which symbolizes the strangeness of nighttime itself. Although order is there, the child senses the unease of coming separations. Margaret Wise Brown understood the severity of that separation, the intensity and longing of the young child for streaming daylight and the familiar. *Goodnight Moon* has become a Landmark because it addresses the breadth of longing and loneliness just under the surface for all of us, but especially for the child facing the night.

Charlotte's Web by E. B. White, illustrated by Garth Williams (Harper: 1952). *Charlotte's Web* is unlike any story that came before, and there has not been another like it since, although many writers since then have tried to imitate it. None have come close. E. B. White was once asked why he wrote for children. He said he did not write for children; they were just smart enough to know what he was talking about. What adult has not felt a catch in her own voice when reading aloud to a child the scene where Fern is outraged that her father has considered the possibility of killing Wilbur, and then again when Charlotte weaves the word "friend" into her web? It's impossible not to.

This great book has a great story at its heart. Its narrative, like all E. B. White wrote, is clear, simple, and strong. It is not unrelated that E. B. White was also half-responsible for one of the most wonderful grammar books of all time, *The Elements of Style*, which he cowrote with William Strunk. In it, the authors make the case for simple declarative sentences, without unnecessary complexity. It is ironic that schools teach students to be more and more complex in their sentence construction, and grade accordingly. Teachers will often urge students to drop the word "said" and replace it with another more "interesting" verb. But if we are to heed E. B. White, simple is best. *Charlotte's Web* is an example of a perfect story served by perfect grammar. There is nothing fancy or overly complicated in his writing, but it packs a power that is nothing short of miraculous.

I will caution you, however, that the biggest mistake most parents make in reading *Charlotte's Web* with their children is that they read it when their children are too young. The book addresses the intense issue of death and especially the death of a beloved friend too soon for young children. Do not be deceived by the funny and sweet-talking pigs and silly barnyard animals.

This is as serious a book as there is. My recommendation is that you wait until your child is seven to read it aloud, but use your judgment based on the sensitivity of your child.

The story of *Charlotte's Web* was all about ordinary times, the life of a farm, of a barnyard. And yet, E. B. White turned that on its head. A spider that can write? A pig that can talk? A little girl who stands up to the men in charge? That is what the book was about: under the guise of ordinary things, the extraordinary was possible. The words were exquisitely paired with the brilliant Garth Williams's pen-and-ink drawings, so rendered as to bring life and humanity to the faces of Wilbur and his friends. A special note: Charlotte was never pictured; a deeply wise choice by Williams,who left her beauty to our imaginations.

Freedom Train: The Story of Harriet Tubman by Dorothy Sterling, illustrated by Ernest Crichlow (Doubleday: 1954). Just as the civil rights movement began to gather steam, Dorothy Sterling published *Freedom Train,* a chapter-book biography about Harriet Tubman and the Underground Railroad. The book became the first in a series that focused on black history. In her recollections of how these books came to be, Sterling wrote: "I was excited, but also bewildered and angry. Why had I never heard of Harriet Tubman or Sojourner Truth, Frederick Douglass or William Lloyd Garrison? Here was a wealth of inspiration, dozens of inspiring stories to tell to young readers." Sterling's *Freedom Train* opened the door to new images of heroes, to stories that had not been told in ample and rich detail to children, and to an opportunity for a new generation of children and young adults, boys and girls, to find their voices through social change.

The Cat in the Hat by Dr. Seuss (Random House: 1957). In the spring of 1954, *Life* published an article about illiteracy and children. The article argued that perhaps children were not reading because they were bored by the books used to teach them how to read.

Theodore Geisel's publisher read this article and sent him a list of 250 words and asked him to write a book with those "teaching" words in it. Geisel used 220 of those words to write *The Cat in the Hat*, a tour de force: making not only meaning from those 220 words, but also brilliant wordplay. Later, his publisher bet him (fifty dollars!) that he could not write a book using fifty words or less, and this was how Dr. Seuss came to write *Green Eggs and Ham*. The same publisher knew something big was happening in children's books and he created Random House's Beginning Readers' Collection, the first division at a publishing house ever made specifically for children just learning to read.

Dr. Seuss proved that learning to read could be fun. His deceptively simple text was a frame for complex ideas (as in *The Butter Battle Book*), and also the subtle themes of uniqueness (*Horton Hears a Who!*) and control versus chaos (*The Cat in the Hat*). His capacity to order language that was accessible enough for the developing reader but still conveyed meaning was simply revolutionary. Before this, children in school were learning to read on primers that spoke down to their innate intelligence and open curiosity. Dr. Seuss exploded all that with 220 carefully chosen words that allowed children to practice new language skills in the context of meaning, interest, and humor.

To give you a sense of Dr. Seuss's own history, a little known fact about him is that he won an Academy Award for Best Documentary Film in 1948 for *Design for Death*, about the perils of war and the ways to mold a society to avoid future wars. All his books allude to this struggle for peace. *The Butter Battle Book* is the most overtly political book of them all (the creatures fight over how bread should be buttered), but all of his books bespeak the tenderness of peace and the chaos of conflict. And in 220 words or less!

Horton Hears a Who! by Dr. Seuss (Random House: 1954). This book was published at the start of the civil rights movement, at the moment of decision in *Brown v. Board of Education*. Dr. Seuss's refrain in the book that "a person's a person no matter how small" seemed like a novel idea at the time and contributed to the growing sense that all voices do count, and do matter, and that children must be treated equally in all circumstances.

At Children's Village, where the boys come from deeply deprived circumstances and from vulnerable family conditions, the great artist Keith Haring came to visit many times during his lifetime. Recently, I had the honor of meeting his parents at an event there. I shared with them how much the older boys love Dr. Seuss, that he seems to resonate with the older emergent reader perhaps because his humor never condescended to children. Keith Haring's mother stared at me in surprise and delight and started to recite *Green Eggs and Ham*. She then said that she had read all those books to Keith as a child and she remembered every word. She shared with me that when Keith grew up he bought the entire series and carried it with him wherever he lived. I found it profoundly moving that the boys at Children's Village, so deprived of the dignity of childhood, understood exactly what a very famous artist knew even through his adulthood: that underneath the deceptive simplicity of his texts lay an uncanny understanding of the world.

The Snowy Day, written and illustrated by Ezra Jack Keats (The Viking Press: 1962). Ezra Jack Keats was profoundly affected by a picture of a little boy he saw in *Life* magazine. Keats said he often hung pictures in his studio that inspired him, and this one, he said, held special appeal. He loved looking at this picture and loved the image of this boy, and soon he started drawing him and creating stories about him. In his lifetime, Keats wrote several stories about the boy he named Peter. Perhaps his most famous was his first, *The Snowy Day*, published in 1962.

Keats says, "Then began an experience that turned my life around—working on a book with a black kid as hero. None of the manuscripts I'd been illustrating featured any black kids—except for token blacks in the background. My book would have him there simply because he should have been there all along. Years before I had cut from a magazine a strip of photos of a little black boy. I often put them on my studio walls before I'd begun to illustrate children's books. I just loved looking at him. This was the child who would be the hero of my book."

Earlier, I quote the young adult writer Sherman Alexie as saying that seeing a child of color in Keats's book *The Snowy Day* changed his life. I know this to be true for many children, children I have taught and worked with over the years in a variety of schools. In 1962, the book must have been all the more powerful, as there were no other books then reflecting the experience of black children.

In American culture, we were looking *up*: space satellites and men in them were orbiting our planet. All things seemed possible. On November 14, 1960, little Ruby Bridges, age six, walked with federal marshals into her newly desegregated school. Later she would say it was prayer that sustained her, that she was not afraid as she walked although people stood nearby jeering and shouting at her as she went on her way. The story of a little boy, Peter, living in his urban environment seemed extraordinary too in its own way. Like the satellite orbiting the Earth, or Ruby Bridges taking a deep breath and walking through a sea of taunting adults, Peter's presence as hero in a book for children also seemed like something of a miracle: a shining star in the night sky.

Where the Wild Things Are, written and illustrated by Maurice Sendak (Harper & Row: 1963). Sendak's great book played on the notion of children's fantasies of fear and bravery with his uniquely drawn fanged monsters, who were kind of cute and kind of scary at the same time. He was on the opposite end of the spectrum from Margaret Wise Brown's tender details. He burst out into the child's imagination, reminding us that inside the day-to-day lives we create for and with our children are our children's own fantasies and complex imaginative terrains. As a child himself, Sendak was often ill and spent much of his time looking out of windows. He later talked about this influence, often recalling a childhood confined to a couch and a view of the world as an observer. Sendak wrote: "There was a little girl across the street named Rosie, and I must have forty sketch pads filled with Rosie pictures and Rosie stories. She was incredible. She had to fight the other kids on the block for attention, and she had to be inventive. I remember one time, when she came up with the explosive line: did you hear who died? Rosie started telling the kids that she had heard a noise upstairs—a noise like someone falling, furniture breaking, and gasping, choking sounds. She went to investigate, and her grandmother was on the floor. . . . While Rosie was talking, her grandmother came up the street, carrying groceries from the market. The kids waited until she had gone into the house before turning to Rosie with the request: 'Tell us how your grandma died again.'"

Sendak's monsters are strange looking but also strangely lovely. It is likely that children can see that first, as they are much less likely to judge a book by appearances, and much more likely to see the humanity and gentleness in even the most odd-looking monster. Best of all was Max, who went off to see the monsters and play with them, but when he returned home his "supper was still hot." As mad and crazy as the world can be, home is still a sanctuary and will always be there.

Bread and Jam for Frances by Russell Hoban, illustrated by Lillian Hoban (Harper & Row: 1964). Russell Hoban was a true guardian of the value of the child's perspective. His books were a guide for parents looking for ways to honor the child's unique spirit and not tamp it down, while still maintaining their parental authority. It was a way to look at parenting that was inspired perhaps in part by Dr. Spock and his legendary parenting books, which encouraged both attention to the child's unique interests and perspectives, and also a gentle and firm sense of structure and parameters.

At the end of *Bread and Jam for Frances*, Frances sits in her pleased way at her lunch table with her little salt shaker so lovingly prepared by Mother. You get the clear sense that Frances lost none of her dignity or her independent spirit, but in the end, Mother got her way too.

Where the Sidewalk Ends, written and illustrated by Shel Silverstein (Harper & Row: 1974). Shel Silverstein got right to the core of what children were really thinking about (gross stuff!) with a wicked wit that children got right away, of course. The brilliant, brilliant editor Ursula Nordstrom was the one who convinced Silverstein to start writing for children. His poems were surprising and powerful because they spoke to the ordinary times of childhood, while offering an element of magic, sarcasm, and tenderness, a combination every seven-year-old could understand. Up until this time, most poetry for children was done in a repetitive rhyme scheme or somewhat pedantic style. Silverstein, on the other hand, was in on the clubhouse. He was writing from a child's point of view, yet with an edge to warn children of the perils of too much fun. (One of his poems was about a boy who watched television so much he turned into one.)

Chock-full of tiny gems, hilarious in their perfection, and full of grimly kooky but sympathetic characters, Shel Silverstein's work was truly modern, in the best sense of the word, taking all the stuff of everyday life and the silliness of it and putting a shape to it. His stark black-and-white covers became iconic and beloved. Silverstein himself was never sentimental, even though he experienced the devastating loss of both a wife and a child during his all-too-short lifetime. His tenderness for children and his understanding of the humor and pathos of childhood were all perfectly captured in his pithy poems.

The Harry Potter series by J. K. Rowling (Scholastic). I am deeply grateful to J. K. Rowling not only for writing the magnificent collection that is Harry Potter but also for doing so as our daughters and the boys I know at the Children's Village were growing up. I feel immensely lucky that they all got to participate in the birth of a Landmark. On midnight the night of the publishing of her seventh book, bookstores around the country had parties to celebrate the publication of this, the last book in the series. On that night, our local bookstore's doors were open, cake was served, and the people of our community spilled together out onto the street, laughing and waiting for the magic minute when we'd get the last book in our hands. As I looked around that night, I saw many parents with their eyes shining with tears, just as mine were. We were all feeling the awesome power of a book bringing us together. The brilliance of Harry Potter, in addition to many other things, was that it was the story of a young boy who had already experienced a huge amount of loss in his life, but by going to a most magical place, Hogwarts, he was able to recapture magic, and therefore childhood. The upside-down common sense of that, that you have to grow up in order to recover childhood, was sheer genius. In addition, as in all the very great children's books, this author recognizes the innate wisdom of children, their sense of justice, and themes that are not easy to grapple with. Rowling has said that the books comprise "a prolonged argument for tolerance, a prolonged plea for an end to bigotry."

These books were a balm for a post-9/11 world. For children who lost parents to 9/11 or watched their teachers break down in sobs and knew that something terrible had happened, the birth of Harry Potter may have been a way to deal with the pain of that loss. The understanding that a small boy could stand up to the darkest demons and fight back and work for good was no small thing. That there is good and there is evil in the world is an unavoidable fact. That childhood could be the door through which a society becomes free from evil is a powerful idea. Hogwarts represents not only a place where children can take on the responsibilities of adulthood, but also a place where the magic and mysteries of childhood are also found, and used to create more good in the world.

Rowling's balanced treatment of even the worst villain, and her understanding of the complexity of what it means to be a hero (Harry is certainly not perfect) is deeply respectful of children. In the final book in the series, we come away with a new understanding of one of the worst villains in the series. Beyond all that, Rowling creates a *world*, a new world with new names and new species and new ideas. For children who love entering a new place, whose minds are seized by the details and exquisitely rendered scenes of a new world, Harry Potter was nothing short of a miracle.

What are the next Landmarks, the new Landmarks? I think that many of the books listed in the following chapters have the makings of a Landmark in them. You and your spouse, or your life partner, or friends, or anyone else involved in the raising of your child, can discuss what we read in these contemporary times and ponder together which books speak the most to our era. Please e-mail me at whattoreadwhen.com if you have more suggestions for Landmark books.

Part II

What to Read Aloud at Every Age

5. How to Read Aloud

Sometimes as parents and grandparents we feel a lot of pressure because it is assumed we just instantly know how to do everything. Even if in our "prior" lives we were just really good at fixing things or riding the subway or presenting a legal brief and had no experience at all with children, we are suddenly expected to know how to feed another living soul, strap that baby efficiently into a car seat, and the thousands of other things we as caregivers are expected to do. Reading aloud is one of those things. When I had my babies there was no manual on this subject at all and I will never forget that even as a teacher with some experience in how to do such things, I needed to practice at home with my own squirmy infants to learn how to do so many things. All the research shows us that reading aloud is the single most important thing you can do to ensure a lifetime of reading enjoyment and good habits in your kids, and yet it is not easy to find advice as to how to do this successfully.

In this section, you will find a guide to reading with your children at every age. But before diving into the age groups, I'd like to begin with a brief guide on how to read aloud. You will of course find your own way, especially with your child as a guide for your style, but herewith I share some basic fundamentals to help you along.

I hope this step-by-step guide will help you feel comfortable and inspired to read aloud every day to your children, providing them with the "brain food" they need to grow and to flourish.

How to Read Aloud

Warm Up

I have always loved the feel of books, the smell of them, the shape of them, the look of them, the wrinkly, plastic casing on the covers of library books, the newness of books peeking out from a bookshop window. I have loved all these things about books since I was very young, probably because I knew my mother and father felt the same way. I remember very well my mother cradling the stack of books in her arms on our way home from the library and the look of immense satisfaction on her face. And I remember my father reading to me from a very old copy of one of his favorite picture books, turning the pages ever so slowly.

Your physical appreciation for books is one way of modeling to your children the engagement you feel with books themselves.

- ✦ Marvel at the beauty of the physical book, noting the illustration, photography, or other distinguishing characteristics.
- ✦ Read aloud the title and the author's name. Do you know any other books by that same author?
- ✦ Check out the copyright page. When was the book published? Is it old or new? What do you know about the time it was published?
- ✦ Based on the look and feel of the book, what can you predict about its mood?
- ✦ Read the author's note if there is one. For example, Jean Craighead George writes a beautiful note in *Look to the North: A Wolf Pup's Diary*, which gives depth to the reading of the book.
- ✦ Read the dedication. Wonder aloud who that person might be. What does the dedication tell you about the life of the author?

Pause and Talk

A book can always be read through without a pause-and-talk moment—but used with care, these moments can enrich your child's understanding of a book as well as your shared reading experience. The more you read aloud with your child, the easier it will be to figure out when and where a good pause-and-talk might come in handy.

- ✦ Take your time opening to page one and linger a moment as you enter the world of the book.

- Turn the pages slowly, with anticipation.
- Make predictions together about what is going to happen next.
- If you need to stop for bedtime or are otherwise interrupted, talk about plans for continuing the reading at a later time. Make a plan. Let your child know you will be coming back to the book and that you are looking forward to it.
- Use a bookmark or a Post-it note as a way to mark your page, even in a picture book, to build a sense of ritual around the continuation.
- Use Post-it notes to mark favorite words or pages or pictures in the book so later, when you reread the book, you will remember that moment of discovery. Date the Post-it and jot a note to remind you both of what made you stop and marvel.

Reflect and Connect

Linger over the ending and connect with the book and each other.

- What does this ending make you think about?
- Does the book remind you of anything that's happened in your own life?
- How could this book change you?
- Reflect quietly as you close the book. Let the story sink in before you go back to the routines of your lives.
- Make plans. Would you like to read another book by this author? Would you like to see another book by this illustrator? What book should we read next? Talk about genre. For example: "Tonight we read a nonfiction book by Anne Rockwell about cars and trucks. Tomorrow, let's read a fiction book about cars and trucks."
- Rate the book. Is this book one of your favorites? Would you recommend this book to a friend? A brother or sister?

Let's look together at one book, and explore the possibilities of what you might talk about as you read with your child. Sometimes you will not want or need to say much except to read the text itself. And sometimes the book is so moving that to stay still with the picture on one page and look at it together is enough. The silence is reverence for the moment. But other times, the book gives us the opportunity to engage in really interesting conversations with our children. Take a journey with me through this one book to explore the possibilities.

Ways to Read *Andy and the Lion*

written and illustrated by James Daugherty

Warm-up This is an old book. Let's look at the copyright date, which is always inside the front pages. We see that it was written in 1938. That was a very hard time for this country, when people were not able to find jobs and so they needed stories that would lift their spirits.

We can see from the author's page that James Daugherty wrote other books too. He wrote about Daniel Boone and Abraham Lincoln, and he even wrote a book called *Of Courage Undaunted*. He's interested in people who have strength and do unusual and brave things.

The jacket flap says: "Of course James read *Androcles and the Lion* when he was young." So we know this story is based on that story, which was a myth. If you like this book, when we go back to the library maybe we can find that myth to see how it is the same or different from this story.

Let's take a look at the cover. Who are the characters going to be in this story? Yes, a boy and a lion. Can you tell by the front picture what you think might happen in this story? Yes, it looks like they might be friends, and the dog too. But it is unusual for a boy and a lion to be friends, don't you think? I have a feeling that the story will tell us more about that. Let's read and see.

Are you comfortable? Make yourself really comfortable and I will too.

Pause and Talk "It was a bright day with just enough wind to float a flag. Andy started down to the library . . ."

Part One: Andy has been reading about lions and listening to stories his grandpa tells about lions. He dreams about hunting lions and then he wakes up and gets ready for school.

- Can you make a prediction here based on what you saw on the cover and what you have read so far about what might happen in Part Two?

- What kind of character does Andy seem to be? How do you know this already? What are the clues that tell you this about him?

Part Two: Andy meets the lion. The lion chases him, but then the lion shows Andy there is a thorn stuck in his paw. He is in pain. Andy removes the thorn for the lion.

- What do you think about Andy's decision to help the lion? What is his attitude toward the lion? Have you ever been in a situation where you first judged someone the way Andy judged the lion, but then realized the person needed you?
- Andy put his own fear aside to take care of the lion. That is a very special quality. What do you think?

Reflect and Connect

Part Three: Andy goes to the circus and sees a terrible lion that scares the people. But then Andy realizes it is "his lion" and begs the townspeople not to hurt the lion. In the end, there is a great parade with Andy and the lion and Andy is given a medal for his bravery.

- When do you think Andy is the most brave? What do you think about the character of the lion? Have you ever read another book that reminds you of this one? For me, it is *Blueberries for Sal*. I remember feeling that Sal was brave too, in her way. She was not afraid of the bear, because she trusted in the goodness of animals. Not all animals are safe, like they are in books. We certainly want to be careful around lions and bears! But I love stories where animals that seem scary are really kind inside, especially when someone else can see their kindness and bring it out of them.
- Let's take a moment to linger with the last page, on the picture of Andy walking back to the library with his book, with the lion following along. I love these illustrations and am wondering if you do too?
- What did you think of this book? Will you share your thoughts with me?

6. The Chronological "When": The Reader's Ladder

This book is divided into two major sections and both address what I call the "when" of your children's reading lives. In this section I will take you on a chronological reading journey, age by age. As this book focuses on reading to your children, I have leveled each section according to what books I think are appropriate to be read *to* your children at these ages, not by what they can read on their own. As independent readers, your children may be reading the same books *later* as well. Generally speaking, you can introduce books at a higher level a full year or two ahead of the same books your child can be reading independently. And not to confuse matters, but sometimes you will want to read books at the same level or even at an easier level for your child *to* him for various reasons I have shared with you: to affirm his good and wise choices for his reading, to share his independent reading life with him, and to bring more family members into the circle of the reading experience.

Much like we may mark the wall with our child's inches as he grows and grows, the books that accumulate on your bookshelves represent the stages of development and the precious memories you are building together as a family. The Reader's Ladder honors these inch-by-inch growth marks as your child celebrates each birthday.

Author and illustrator Maurice Sendak once said: "Children have a sensuous approach to books. I remember one letter I received from a little boy who loved *Where the Wild Things Are*. Actually, I think the letter was written by the boy's mother, and he sent me a picture he had drawn. So I wrote him back and sent him a picture. Eventually, I received another letter, this time from his mother: 'Jimmy liked your postcard so much he ate it.' That letter confirmed everything I suspected."

Sendak was being funny in his wry way, but he was right that children do have a sensual relationship with books, and at the youngest ages I will specifically recommend books that feel good and even taste good when necessary. Trying to chew the corners of a book when you are a baby is a natural thing, which is why I love board books and soft bath books, which so understand the desire of the baby to literally ingest words!

People have often asked me over the years which of the ages I have taught I most prefer. And I always think about it and then say: "The one I am with now!" I have worked closely with every age level, and each age has its beauty, its poignance, its miracles. In the following section, I have tried to capture the specialness of each age from birth to ten as we go on this reading journey together. You can find a listing of all these books at whattoreadwhen.com.

Birth to Age Two: Beginning the Magical Journey

You marvel at the face of your baby, at her hands, her toes, her smile, her luminous new skin. Your life is full with the work of her care, and the joy of her presence. It is a richly intense time for you as a new parent: you are moved to easy tears, you cannot believe the love inside you, a love you never even knew you could feel. At the same time, you are exhausted in a way you have never been before. It's sheer, passionate vigilance, really. You are listening for her cry when she is sleeping, and watching over her while she is awake. You never feel truly rested ever again.

This early time is critical both for reading aloud to your baby and also for exposing her to the world of books. Both for building your own relationship with your baby and also for welcoming her into a very long relationship of her own with books, now is the time to encircle your baby with the love of language.

Hold your baby in the crook of your arm, and get really comfortable on the couch or in a soft chair. The books you select for this reading time are books that you should love to read aloud, so your baby can hear the sound of your voice relishing the story and the language. These books should be rich with rhythm so your read-aloud voice becomes familiar and beloved by your child. The books I recommend here are books whose authors have paid special attention to the lilt and sound of language itself. Lose yourself in the beauty of that language. Reread the story several times over when you are learning how to read these titles aloud to your baby. She will recall the repetition, and it will increase your own read-aloud skills too.

Books that are well written for this age group provide you with a natural scaffolding for learning how to read aloud well to your baby. The language provides you with the elements by which your voice will rise and fall with predictable intonation and patterns. These are extremely soothing for your baby. She already knows your voice, but the more formal structure of the read-aloud adds one more dimension for her to know you by and to internalize the sounds of your voice.

Show your baby you love books through your body language and the tone of your voice as you begin the read-aloud: demonstrate excitement and interest of your own as you settle in. Show your baby how you love books by lingering first on the front cover. Most good readers do this before beginning to read, and it is not too early to demonstrate some of these behaviors to your child. Then open the book and turn the pages slowly, sharing with your baby through your anticipatory comments and tone that you enjoy this experience too. Point out the pictures you like, and point occasionally as you read to direct your baby's eyes to the page. Do not worry if your baby does not look directly at the page. And don't overpoint; then the read-aloud loses the flavor and tone of intimacy and becomes more of a "lesson." But it is great to naturally point out what you see and admire about the illustrations as you go. The key here is to be as natural and authentic as you can, which is why it is so important to select literature that really will resonate with you too.

Black-and-White Books for Newborns

Scientific research has shown us that babies develop their sense of color rather slowly, not immediately. They are particularly aware of defined destinctions between black and white tones. There are some great books that are published in black-and-white to appeal to the visual acuity of the small baby.

Baby Animals Black & White by Phyllis Limbacher Tildes (Charlesbridge Publishing: 1998)
Black & White by Tana Hoban (HarperCollins Publishers: 2007)
Black on White by Tana Hoban (Greenwillow Books: 1993)
Look, Look! by Peter Linenthal (Dutton Children's Books: 1998)
White on Black by Tana Hoban (Greenwillow Books: 1993)

Rhythmic Cozy Books to Build Rituals

Right from the beginning, establish rituals that will last you for many precious years to come. Reading aloud to your baby before bedtime is ideal. But don't wait until your baby is crying with exhaustion to start the reading process. Anticipate your baby's approximate bedtime, and plan your read-aloud for ample time before then; it will segue into the final bottle or breast-feed of the evening. You do not need to read for very long. In these early months, five to seven minutes is plenty. You can increase the time you read to your baby by approximately two minutes per month in the first year. If you see she really enjoys the intimacy of it, and listening to your voice, then of course increase by greater amounts of time.

Try to end a read-aloud before your child begins to squirm. You may well wonder how you will know that's coming. Look for body cues that would indicate it is time for transition: a bit of shifting in your arms or rubbing her eyes. You will grow accustomed to this if you practice looking for the clues. Most of all, savor these gentle moments for you and your baby. If she falls asleep as you read, read on for a few more pages, noting her weight in your arms, the smell of her sweet skin, the shape of her eyes, the feel of her warm, round body in the crook of your arm. This is as much for you as it is for her. You too deserve these moments of tender sweetness.

Don't save the ritual of the read-aloud just for bedtime, though. Since tiredness will interfere with the positive reading process, it is also essential to create other regular opportunities to read aloud to our children. Keep a basket of books in the kitchen for reading aloud right before a meal begins. If your child wakes early, create a ritual where you bring your baby into your bed in the morning and read and snuggle there. Then you get a few extra moments of relaxation too, and what a nice way to begin the day.

Hold him and show him the pictures. It is helpful to introduce these books to your baby very early, by reading them aloud while he sits or leans comfortably against you or lies in your lap. Make sure it is easy for his eyes to follow the picture and that he is not straining to see. Then there is some familiarity with the books as your baby turns four months old and is ready for a tiny bit more independence with them.

Chicka Chicka Boom Boom by Bill Martin Jr. and John Archambault, illustrated by Lois Ehlert (Aladdin: 2000)

Fiona Loves the Night by Patricia MacLachlan and Emily MacLachlan Charest, illustrated by Amanda Shepherd (HarperCollins Children's Books: 2007)

Goodnight Moon by Margaret Wise Brown (Harper: 1947)

Koala Lou by Mem Fox and Pamela Lofts (Voyager Books: 2004)

The Mommy Book or *The Daddy Book* by Todd Parr (Little, Brown and Company: 2002)
More, More, More Said the Baby by Vera B. Williams (Greenwillow Books: 1990)
The Napping House by Audrey Wood and Don Wood (Red Wagon Books: 2000)
Papa, Please Get the Moon for Me by Eric Carle (Simon & Schuster Children's Publishing: 1991)
Pat the Puppy by Edith Kunhardt Davies (Golden Books: 2001)
The Wheels on the Bus by Paul O. Zelinsky (Dutton Children's Books: 1990)

While sitting in her high chair, your baby is attentive to all the new things you put in front of her. Lay out some board books on her high chair table and watch as her eyes go to one or another. When her eyes rest on one, immediately choose that one and put it in front of her, complimenting her with your tone of voice, saying, "What a great choice! Do you want to read this one?" This is not a futile or silly exercise. Your baby is already communicating with you intensively through her eye contact. If you practice noticing her cues, you will reinforce the idea that people choose books and this is something she will do for the rest of her life. There are many wonderful board books with strong visual images.

Baby Face Books

Babies love books with baby faces in them, just as they begin to love looking in the mirror, thinking they see another friendly baby. It is really great to show them these board books with faces on them. These readings build their sense of themselves and their empathy too. They smile at the faces of other babies naturally and it is a good quality to nurture. The great author Walter Dean Myers notes in his introduction of one of his beautiful poetry books: "Children throughout the world recognize other children. . . . The nationality or race of the child never matters." I love the idea that we are introducing our children to children, all over the world, through literature, from such a young age.

Baby! Baby! by Vicky Ceelen (Random House Books for Young Readers: 2008)
Baby Faces by Margaret Miller (Little Simon: 1998)

Bright Baby Touch and Feel series by Roger Priddy (Priddy Books)
Mrs. Mustard's Baby Faces by Jane Wattenberg (Chronicle Books: 2007)

Board Books

Board books are marvelous inventions for your baby as she becomes able to sit on the baby blanket or in her high chair. They are sturdy and washable and survive spilled bottles, chewed corners, and other hazards of baby life. You delight as she can begin to sit by herself. Her sturdy little body is compact and adorable. But she tires easily. And so do you. Board books will keep her occupied and entertained for many short periods of time.

Boats by Byron Barton (HarperFestival: 1998)
Bright Baby series by Roger Priddy (Priddy Books)
Charley Harper's ABC's by Charley Harper (AMMO Books: 2008)
Dog by Matthew Van Fleet, photographs by Brian Stanton (Simon & Schuster: 2007)
Heads, Shoulders, Knees and Toes by Annie Kubler (Child's Play International: 2002)
The Little Fire Engine by Lois Lenski (Random House Books for Young Readers: 2000)
My First Body Board Book (Dorling Kindersley Publishing: 2004)
My First Farm Board Book (Dorling Kindersley Publishing: 2004)
My First Word Book by Jane Yorke (Dorling Kindersley Publishing: 2002)
Planes by Byron Barton (HarperFestival: 1998)
Trains by Byron Barton (HarperFestival: 1998)
Trucks by Byron Barton (HarperFestival: 1998)
What-a-Baby series board books by Cheryl Willis Hudson, illustrated by George Ford (Cartwheel Books: 1997)

Tactile Books for Newborns

Babies also love strong visual images, with vibrant colors, as well as books with texture and three-dimensionality. There are hundreds of these available to you. They are not necessarily "great" literature per se, but they serve a hugely important function of giving you the opportunity to share the reading experience with your baby in the midst of all your other experiences, in the kitchen, in the car. Many of these books focus on concepts: body parts, names of animals, household objects, members of the family. For this reason also, board books are integral to the early literacy experiences you will share with your child. When you see your baby's eyes go to one area on the page of a text, reinforce that "reading" by saying, "Do you see the cow? Do you see the baby's face? Do you see the red dog?" Even board books have levels of difficulty. The more print on the page, the smaller the picture images will be, which is why the difficulty level will increase, regardless of the type of print on the page or the story itself.

As you turn the pages with your baby, tell the book through the pictures you see. For example, if your baby loves the *Baby Faces* book by Margaret Miller, you can go through it and say, "Now the baby looks sad. Now the baby looks like she is happy. Maybe she is going to bed?" Your baby can hear how books and your read-aloud voice go together and that books convey ideas.

You can begin introducing concepts through the read-aloud very early. Babies and toddlers love books with clear, lively pictures and opportunities for talk. Practice a back-and-forth, like the game of peekaboo. Books offer an opportunity to practice back-and-forth communication. Ask your baby questions. Even if he doesn't understand what you are saying yet, your inquiring voice and your engagement will set the stage for book talks for years to come.

Baby Cakes by Karma Wilson, illustrated by Sam Williams (Little Simon: 2006)
Baby Touch and Feel series by DK Publishing (Dorling Kindersley Publishing)
Concept series by Bernette Ford, illustrated by Britta Teckentrup (Boxer Books)
Dear Zoo: A Lift the Flap Book by Red Campbell (Little Simon: 1982)
Hooray for Fish! by Lucy Cousins (Candlewick Press: 2005)
Inside Freight Train by Donald Crews (HarperFestival: 2001)
My First Opposites Board Book (Dorling Kindersley Publishing: 2007)
Baby Einstein: My First Book of Numbers, concept by Julie Aigner-Clarke, illustrated by Nadeem Zaidi (Hyperion Books for Children: 2007)
Peekaboo Baby by Margaret Miller (Little Simon: 2001)
Peekaboo Kisses by Barney Saltzberg (Red Wagon Books: 2002)
Peek a Who? by Nina Laden (Chronicle Books: 2006)

Touch and Feel Animal Colors by DK Publishing (Dorling Kindersley Publishing: 2000)
Where Is Baby's Belly Button? by Karen Katz (Little Simon: 2000)
Whose Knees Are These? by Jabari Asim, illustrated by LeUyen Pham (LB Kids: 2006)
Whose Toes Are Those? by Jabari Asim, illustrated by LeUyen Pham (LB Kids: 2006)
Zoo Animals by DK Publishing (Dorling Kindersley Publishing: 1997)

Popular Books in Board Book Format

Some of the most popular books are available in a board book format. You can read the larger book-size format before bed as you sit in the baby's quiet room, and then have the same book available in board book format in your kitchen or car. Your baby will learn to recognize the look of the cover, or seminal character, and this will reinforce her knowledge of books and a sense of familiarity and comfort with them. Some books do not translate well to board book format because there is just too much print on each page, and it is overwhelming for your baby. Here are a few that make the transition nicely.

Clifford the Big Red Dog by Norman Birdwell (Cartwheel Books: 2005)
Goodnight Moon by Margaret Wise Brown, illustrated by Clement Hurd (HarperFestival: 1991)
The Runaway Bunny by Margaret Wise Brown, illustrated by Clement Hurd (HarperCollins Publishers: 2005)

Songs

Music and song are a great tool for developing literacy at this age. The music itself structures the language learning and carries your child along on the rhythm of sound. The beat and the rhyme of song all give your baby an opportunity to hear the patterns of language, the length of words, and the syllabic beat of linguistic structure, plus, it's just plain fun to sing out loud. One thing I always loved about singing to my babies was that they never criticized my (horrible) singing voice. They really did a lot for my self-esteem.

"Baby Beluga" by Raffi
"You'll Sing a Song and I'll Sing a Song" by Ella Jenkins

Concept Books

As your baby develops, his understanding of the world is growing, day by day. A sense of concepts is deepening. As your child progresses from one to two, he is absorbing more and more of the construct of the world. Concept books abound and are teaching tools that represent joyous togetherness as your child explores the power of language. Here are some of my favorites:

Baby Einstein's My First Book of Shapes by Julie Aigner-Clark, illustrated by Nadeem Zaidi (Disney Press: 2007)
Charlie and Lola's Opposites by Lauren Child (Candlewick Press: 2007)
Diego Discovers Colors, Animals, Shapes and More by Kara McMahon, illustrated by Warner McGee (Simon & Schuster: 2008)
Eric Carle's Opposites by Eric Carle (Grosset & Dunlap: 2007)
First Words (Usborne Look and Say) by Felicity Brooks, illustrated by Jo Litchfield (Usborne Publishing, board book edition: 2005)
Flip-a Shape: Go! by SAMi (Blue Apple Books: 2007)
The Foot Book: Dr. Seuss's Wacky Book of Opposites by Dr. Seuss (Random House Books for Young Readers: 1996)
Opposites (Learning with Animals) by Melanie Watt (Kids Can Press: 2005)
A Starfish: A Shapes Book by Bernette Ford (Boxer Books: 2008)

Books for the Bath

These books tend to be silly and fun, as they should be for someone reading in the bathtub. There are hundreds of options. I have selected the ones that make babies laugh the most and are friendly companions to the bathtub experience. There is another reason to have these available to your baby in the bath. You are sending a very strong message that books belong everywhere, not just in a shelf in the baby's nursery. Lifelong readers read everywhere. You notice that people who love to read and do it well read everywhere, everywhere. Sponge books convey that message, for sure, and here are two great ones:

Bath Buddies: Little Turtle by Jo Moon (Campbell Books: 2007)
Soft Shapes series by Ikids (Innovative Kids: 1999)

Two to Three Years Old: Leaping Toward Understanding

These years are full of such joyous, surprising leaps of language and understandings that every day will be a new surprise and pleasure for both you and your child. He is active in the world, climbing, learning, wondering, growing by the minute. His language is tripping over itself as he revels in his newfound masteries and also bumps into trouble spots: words he does not know or cannot say easily. He makes errors with language that are endlessly fascinating to you and often hilarious. I well remember my daughter saying to me at the age of three: "Mom, my lips are dry. I need some chopsticks!" So too I remember us laughing at my baby brother Teddy pointing at the sky and crying out: "Look at the hocktincopter, everyone!" The stumbles are endearing and enchanting; we can't get enough of them. They represent our toddler's entry into the world of language, a wider world he will soon belong to in full force when he enters school.

Interest Development Books

Reading should be as active as possible at these ages. Your child may be the kind of toddler who is running around from morning until night. We want to incorporate reading into his life too, even though the playground may hold infinite appeal. Here is where interest development is so important. Be on the lookout this early for your child's passions and interests. They are there, and can be nurtured through your connections with your child through literature. They can mirror the activities your child loves and be companions for you as you travel on these journeys together. Put baskets of books in your child's room and in your play area. Ask your toddler to help you make "interest" book baskets, so when you go to the library you can fill them with the life passions your child is feeling to his very bones right now.

Cars and Trucks and Things That Go by Richard Scarry (Golden Books: 1998)
Dig Dig Digging by Margaret Mayo, illustrated by Alex Ayliffe (Orchard Books: 2008)
Dinosaurs, Dinosaurs by Byron Barton (HarperTrophy: 1993)
Planes by Anne Rockwell (Puffin: 1993)

Happy Endings

Don't underestimate the value of books that are mass-marketed, such as the Disney books or the Berenstain Bears books. They don't look as elegant or beautiful as some of the other books I recommend to you throughout this book. But they serve a powerful purpose in your child's reading life. First, it is inevitable that your child will, in this day and age, be exposed to these stories as movies or on television or the Internet. These books have been translated into many languages, so no matter where you live it is likely your child will find them. It is great to bridge the things he is now exposed to in popular culture to his reading experiences. Beyond that, the brilliance of these books in my view is that they have tapped into what we all so urgently want and need: a happy ending. Our two- and three-year-olds are just beginning to step out into the world. They are experiencing feelings of significant worry and longing when you or your partner go to work in the morning. They experience frustration when they can't swing as high as they would like at the playground, or when their ice cream falls out of its cone. A reassurance about happy endings, then, is more essential than ever before in her life, and perhaps more than it ever will be again. A wonderful literacy educator wrote me once that when I shared the assurance that reading mass-marketed books such as Disney's was not just okay but even important, she felt a huge sense of relief. She said that when she brought her daughter home from Guatemala through an international adoption, her daughter craved only the *Little Princess* and other similar stories. She said it wasn't until she heard me speak on the topic that she realized that more than anything, her little daughter craved the reassurance that the world would right itself, and at the end all would be well. We all have that craving. Walt Disney and the Berenstains were and are ingenious and intuitive in that fundamental understanding of childhood: it is by no means always a sunny journey. The child is peeking out into the world and seeing what's there. He wants to know that happy endings are possible, and the predictability of these texts offers that comfort. I love these books and I think you will too.

The Berenstain Bears series by Jan Berenstain and Stan Berenstain (Random House Books for Young Readers)

Disney's Storybook Collection, Disney

Princess Stories retold by Kate Tym, illustrated by Sophy Williams (Chrysalis Children's Books: 2005)

The Ordinary Is Extraordinary

Even when the life of the character seems somewhat exotic, the most marvelous children's book writers capture the ordinariness of everyday routines. A young child finds the combination of the novel with the deeply ordinary and simple to be evocative and deeply soothing. These two books by Lois Lenski are old classics, soothing in their simplicity.

Cowboy Small by Lois Lenski (Random House Books for Young Readers: 2006)
The Little Fire Engine by Lois Lenski (Random House Books for Young Readers: 2000)

Early Print Awareness

The writer Eudora Welty remembers being riveted by the swirl of alphabet letters in her books from her childhood. "My love for the alphabet, which endures, grew out of reciting it but, before that, out of seeing the letters on the page. In my own storybooks, before I could read them for myself, I fell in love with various winding, enchanted looking initials drawn by Walter Crane at the heads of fairy tales. In 'Once upon a time,' an *O* had a rabbit running it as a treadmill, his feet upon flowers. When the day came, years later, for me to see the Book of Kells, all the wizardry of letter, initial, and word swept over me a thousand times over, and the illumination, the gold, seemed a part of the word's beauty and holiness that had been there from the start." Your young child is becoming aware of the look and concept of print. The alphabet is the key to the door of lifelong reading and writing, and your child is riveted by it. He sees, rightly, that it is a code signaling entry to lots of different understandings: directions (the stop sign), identity (names on the nursery school door), pleasure (literature), information (books on animals). He is not quite sure yet how it all fits together, but he knows he wants to be part of all it has to offer. The books I list for you here have predictable print in predictable places at predictable times. Notice print with your child: "Look, there's the word 'dog,'" or simply point to the words as you read books in this category. Your child will begin to see the one-to-one correspondence between written words and your voice telling the story or naming the labels on the pages. Notice also the alphabet itself: the swirls Eudora Welty loved are the brilliant composition of the code we all abide by, not only for our daily living but also for entry into worlds of magic and knowledge. These books introduce your child to the miracles of print and the beginnings of how to break down that code:

Dr. Seuss's ABC: An Amazing Alphabet Book by Dr. Seuss (Random House Books for Young Readers: 1996)
Jambo Means Hello: Swahili Alphabet Book by Muriel L. Feelings, illustrated by Tom Feelings (Penguin Young Readers Group: 1992)
Maisie series by Lucy Cousins (Candlewick Press)
My Car by Byron Barton (HarperCollins Children's Books: 2003)
National Geographic Little Kids Magazine
Spot series by Eric Hill (Penguin)
1001 Things to Spot on a Farm by Gillian Doherty, illustrated by Teri Gower (EDC Publishing: 1999)

Songs

It is wonderful and important for your child to hear the music in language and singing is the best way to convey the essential rhythms of language through the lilting beauty of song. There are some songs that are gentle and are perfect to either lull your child to sleep or wake him to start the day just right, plus they build your child's emerging literacies:

Baby Beluga (Raffi Songs to Read) by Raffi
Children's Songs: A Collection of Childhood Favorites by Susie Tallman
"Quiet Time" by Raffi
The Singable Songs Collection by Raffi
Songs to Grow on for Mother and Child by Woodie Guthrie
Smithsonian Folkways Children's Music Collection
Woody's 20 Grow Big Songs by Woody Guthrie

Books at this age teach and teach and teach, with your guidance. Here are some wonderful books to build knowledge in your child and that are just plain fun to read together.

Counting Books

At three, our children are absorbing concepts every minute, every day. Counting is something that feels great and satisfying and is so concrete and easy to learn through an awareness of print.

One Little Bunny! (Amazing Baby) by A. Wood, illustrated by Mike Jolley and Emma Dodd (Silver Dolphin Books: 2008)

Ten Black Dots by Donald Crews (HarperTrophy, revised edition: 1995)

Label Books

Words are pouring over them, through them, into them. Books that label things are essential reading at this time and they will be very responsive to them.

The Everything Book by Denise Fleming (Henry Holt and Company: 2000)

Richard Scarry books

Pop-up Books

Pop-up books, too, provide their own kind of pleasure, as well as an opportunity for learning and exploration, along with exposure to the sensory joys of reading.

Dear Zoo: A Pop-up Book by Rod Campbell (Little Simon: 2005)

Munch! Munch! Who's There? by Karen Jones (Barron's Educational Series, board book edition: 2005)

Tactile Books

Books with texture and interaction are great for your child just now. They engage him completely and help him to become an active part of the reading experience.

Dog by Matthew Van Fleet, photography by Brian Stanton (Simon & Schuster: 2007)

Tails by Matthew Van Fleet (Red Wagon Books: 2003)

Potty-training Books

Let us not ignore the books that instruct in all the key ways. (And I should mention I do not love the more graphic books on this subject. Let there be some measure of privacy and a great measure of dignity, even at a very young age.) There are some really awful books on toilet training out there, but my two favorite sets are:

Once Upon a Potty (for boys and girls) by Alona Frankel (Firefly Books: 2007)

The Princess (Prince) and the Potty by Wendy Cheyette Lewison (Aladdin: 2005)

You may find your child at age three becoming more squirmy during a read-aloud, not wanting to sit still, preferring to run and play. Don't fight this impulse. Instead, find shorter books, or even bookmark picture books so you don't feel the compulsion to finish everything every evening. Read while your child plays. Read while your child is in the bath and you are supervising. Find other ways and places to read. The traditional image of a parent reading to a child nestled up in the bedclothes is sometimes a bit stifling for you and your child. Be creative with your more active ones and read in silly ways, in silly places, at silly times.

Four Years Old: Loving the Story

The four-year-old is full of vim and vigor and a new sense of himself in the world. He is feeling like a big kid now. Off to nursery school, he wears his backpack proudly and gazes at it before and after school with delight. He is an imaginative force. At home, he plays for hours with his blocks, a pretend kitchen set, and dress-up clothes. He talks to himself, creating worlds of stories based on what he sees around him. My friend once called me saying that her son picked up the toy phone at the age of four and she heard him pretending to order in from the local pizza place. She said he had her inflections down perfectly, in addition to the order. She said to me: "Pam, I've been outed! My kid is showing the world how we eat dinner most nights!"

Four-year-olds are integrating the "real" world with their imaginative play in numerous ways. In these years, my husband and I could barely use our couch, as it was so often being used for our daughters' worlds of play. "Don't sit there," Katie, age four, shouts to me one day as I am about to settle in to read the paper. "That's a ship, and we are the fairy princesses set out to save the people on the sea!"

For four-year-olds, much of life is about building and creating. In Susan Kempton's book *The Literate Kindergarten* (2007), she writes: "When I say play, I am not talking just about recreation and fun. In a broader sense, play encompasses all sorts of sensory-based environments where children can explore and interact, both with others and with a variety of materials. In these environments, children are most themselves. Play is their natural language and thus the best way to see their learning process." I would like to stress to you: play is fun, but it is also brought on by a deep human desire for connectedness and imagination that creates strong communities and provides sustenance to growing minds. It is a critical step in the process toward acquiring literacy. Stuart Brown, president of the National Institute for Play, recently said that play is part of "the developmental sequencing of becoming a human primate. If you look at what produces learning and memory and well-being, play is as fundamental as any other aspect of life, including sleep and dreams." Imagination is key to the development of the literacy process. It is an extension of and support for the emerging sense of the reading experience, helping children to understand aspects of stories. In literature, the story elements are characters, setting, plot (problem/solution), and movement through time. The structure of story usually includes the beginning, which sets the stage, two or three major plot events, and a conclusion.

This could be complicated terrain, were it not for the fact that human beings are hardwired for story. We love to tell stories and we love to hear stories. Throughout all of history, humankind has worked hard to tell its values and convey its history through stories. Creation stories from different cultures tell the story of the birth of the people, and how they came to be a community. As your child grows, in school he will read chapter books, textbooks, articles, and essays. All of this reading requires a strong sense of understanding of the story elements, as well as story structure. Supporting your child's play helps him develop the muscles to tell a good story, understand story elements, and become aware of the structures that support story.

I encourage you to provide routines and spaces that demonstrate your appreciation and support for play. When you are selecting day care, be sure there are comfortable play environments and peaceful, regular opportunities for play. Rather than rushing around to a thousand activities you have to pay for, set up a play corner in your apartment or house (dress-up clothes, some kitchen pots and containers, Post-it notes, and washable markers) and ensure for your child time to putter in that space every day. I guarantee that you will see future benefits to this mode of parenting, especially in the area of literacy development.

Compelling Stories

The books we should be reading aloud to our children at the age of four reflect a sense of story and the sheer joy of a good one. It is really great for your child to listen to books with powerful story elements.

Alfredito Flies Home by Jorge Argueta, illustrations by Luis Garay, translated by Elisa Asmado (Groundwood Books: 2008)
Arthur series by Marc Brown (Little, Brown and Company)
Caps for Sale by Esphyr Slobodkina (HarperCollins Publishers: 1987)
Corduroy by Don Freeman (The Viking Press: 1968)
Frances books by Russell Hoban (HarperTrophy)
Grandmother's Pigeon by Louise Erdrich, illustrated by Jim LaMarche (Hyperion Books for Children: 1996)
Harry the Dirty Dog by Gene Zion, illustrated by Margaret Bloy Graham (HarperFestival: 2006)
Little Bear books by Elsa Holmelund Minarik, illustrated by Maurice Sendak (HarperTrophy)
Make Way for Ducklings by Robert McCloskey (The Viking Press: 1941)
Strega Nona by Tomie dePaola (Editorial Everest: 1999)

Folktales and Fairy Tales

This genre of literature has a powerful sense of story and story structure. But some of these texts can be scary for our young four-year-old. I have selected several here that are both well told and also deeply respectful of the fears a four-year-old might have. There are a few I have left off simply because I have a personal aversion to them, and think they are really not appropriate for young children ("Hansel and Gretel" is one example). People have strong feelings about these fairy tales, because so many of us grew up reading them. But the world of children's literature has exploded in the last twenty years and what is available to your children now in terms of story is ever so much richer and more appropriate for children of this age than some of the traditional fairy tales. These selections are gently told, but very tuned in to the essence of the original tale. They are not so gentle that they miss the point of these significant tales. They also have the added bonus of remarkable artwork, which I think is extremely important at this age, both to stimulate your child's senses and also to draw him to print in the most compelling ways. Here are my favorites:

Between Earth & Sky: Legends of Native American Sacred Places by Joseph Bruchac, illustrated by Thomas Locker (Voyager Books: 1999)
Little Red Riding Hood retold and illustrated by Jerry Pinkney (Little, Brown and Company: 2007)

Lon Po Po: A Red-Riding Hood Story from China by Ed Young (Penguin: 1996)
The Mitten: A Ukrainian Folktale by Jan Brett (Putnam Juvenile: 1989)
The Persian Cinderella by Shirley Climo, illustrations by Robert Florczak (HarperCollins Publishers: 2001)
The Rough-face Girl by Rafe Martin, illustrated by David Shannon (Penguin Young Readers Group: 1998)
The Three Snow Bears by Jan Brett (Putnam Juvenile: 2007)
Yeh-Shen: A Cinderella Story from China by Ai-Ling Louie, illustrated by Ed Young (Penguin Young Readers Group: 1996)

Recipe Books

Your four-year-old loves to be with you, no matter where you are. Bring reading with you everywhere you go, then. The kitchen is a perfect place for the exploration of books about food. Read even these great recipe books aloud to your child with expression, as you stir and wait for the finished prize together.

Green Eggs and Ham Cookbook: Recipes by Dr. Seuss and Georgeanne Brennan (Random House Books for Young Readers: 2006)
Growing Vegetable Soup by Lois Ehlert (Harcourt Children's Books: 1990)
Pretend Soup and Other Real Recipes: A Cookbook for Preschoolers & Up by Mollie Katzen and Ann Henderson (Tricycle Press: 1994)

Reading Readiness

Not all four-year-olds are ready to read on their own, but let me share with you that I think they are often more ready than we think. It worries me that we often deny our children the opportunity to move forward as readers because we are afraid to "push" too hard. While I honor the care that raises that concern, I also want you to feel free to embrace (not push) the fact that some of your children are going to be enthralled by the written word from the moment they begin to get the idea that there is a code to crack. Don't hold them back. You wouldn't hold them back if they felt an affinity for soccer or the piano. Reading is a human desire and a human capacity, and it's every bit a propensity for some of our kids as kicking a ball around. See it more as part of play and delight and it will seem less jarring to imagine pushing your child as a reader. If you notice your child has a real interest in words on the page and you want to do more for your child, there are some simple books that help your child practice early reading by you reading them aloud as a way to model this early reading.

There are companies that write series of books with "controlled" texts that help our youngest emerging readers step up to new levels comfortably. They are small books, packaged as sets, sometimes by theme, sometimes by genres. On the company Web sites, you will find a list of young readers' books. Companies making these series include:

Bob Books series by Bobby Lynn Maslen, illustrated by John R. Maslen (Scholastic)
Kids Want to Know series (Scholastic)
The Wright Group

Exploration Books

At age four, your child is deeply inquisitive about everything. She asks you questions about the smallest bug crawling on the ground and about the largest dimensions of our world, about the moon in the sky, and the most philosophical ideas. Sometimes her questions are wrenchingly poignant. You look at her and realize just how young she is, how recently she has come to this Earth. Everything is new to her. She believes in miracles and can see them in places we have forgotten to notice. Literature is a wonderful way to respond to her smallest and her biggest questions. And you will learn from her, too. Read these books to explore together:

Actual Size by Steve Jenkins (Houghton Mifflin Company: 2004)
Castle by David Macaulay (Houghton Mifflin Company: 1982)
Chameleons Are Cool by Martin Jenkins, illustrated by Sue Shields (Candlewick Press: *2001)*
DK Eyewitness series by DK Publishing (Dorling Kindersley Publishing)
Dogs by Gail Gibbons (Holiday House.: 1997)
I Wonder Why Camels Have Humps and Other Questions About Animals by Anita Ganeri (Kingfisher: 1997)

I Wonder Why Stars Twinkle and Other Questions About Space by Carol Stott (Kingfisher: 1994)
I Wonder Why the Sea Is Salty and Other Questions About the Oceans by Anita Ganeri (Kingfisher: 2003)

The Rhythms of Language

Your four-year-old is listening for the sound of music in language. Bouncing on your knee, she will love to hear "The Wheels on the Bus" or "Someone's in the Kitchen with Dinah." Songs and poems and chants are humming in her head. She loves the way words go together and the families of words. There are many books that support this learning and this growth. Read them aloud, clap along with their rhythms. All of this is good for your child. There are also several fine books which have sets of poems and songs as the text for picture books. The ones I have featured here are those that have both great, catchy lyrics and beautiful illustrations. They are also a gentle way to introduce your child to Landmarks in children's poetry and songs.

Arroz con Leche: Popular Songs and Rhymes from Latin America by Lulu Delacre (Scholastic: 1992)
Honey, I Love and Other Love Poems by Eloise Greenfield, illustrated by Leo and Diane Dillon (HarperCollins Publishers: 1978)
Favorite Nursery Rhymes from Mother Goose by Scott Gustafson (Greenwich Workshop Press: 2007)
Read-Aloud Rhymes for the Very Young edited by Jack Prelutsky (Knopf Books for Young Readers: 1986)
Stopping by Woods on a Snowy Evening by Robert Frost, illustrated by Susan Jeffers (Penguin Young Readers Group: 2001)
The Wheels on the Bus by Raffi (Crown Books for Young Readers: 1990)
The Wheels on the Bus: A Book with Movable Parts by Paul O. Zelinsky (Penguin Young Readers Group: 1990)

Favorite Song Collections for Four-Year-Olds

Amazing Adventures of Kid Astro by Ralph's World
Catch That Train by Dan Zanes
Growing Up with Ella Jenkins by Ella Jenkins
One Light One Sun by Raffi

Rocket Ship Beach by Dan Zanes
Songs Children Love to Sing by Ella Jenkins
A Year with Frog and Toad original sound track
Yellow Bus by Justin Roberts

Funny Books

Your four-year-old can be the silliest person on Earth. He finds lots of things funny, and he is pretty hilarious himself. Let him see the absolutely magnificent humor to be found in literature, so he knows it is a place where he can go to laugh out loud. Dr. Seuss was brilliant in so many ways, but especially in his razor-sharp understanding of a child's exquisite sense of humor. When asked how he came to his ideas, he said, "Once I was drawing and suddenly I found myself drawing an elephant in a tree. And I said: what in the world is that elephant doing in the tree? And that's how I came to write this book." You could just imagine Dr. Seuss cracking himself up too. This is not just child's play. After a long day of working and caring for your children, you could use a laugh too. Read these together:

Big Dog . . . Little Dog by P. D. Eastman (Random House Books for Young Readers: 2006)
Horton Hears a Who! by Dr. Seuss (Random House: 1954)
I Spy Ultimate Challenger! A Book of Picture Riddles (Scholastic: 2005)
A Light in the Attic by Shel Silverstein (HarperCollins Publishers: 1981)
Please, Baby, Please by Spike Lee and Tonya Lewis Lee, illustrated by Kadir Nelson (Simon & Schuster Children's Publishing: 2007)

Books about Creating

Four-year-olds love to create. They are mud-castle-makers, the kings and queens of cookie dough preparation. Give them a pile of crayons and markers and stickers, and lo and behold, the end result is an enchanted representation of whimsy and verve. Making and creating are part of being a literary person. Recently, I was in South Africa in a township without running water, electricity, or paved roads. I watched for a long time as a group of children played with a ripped cardboard box. They turned it around and made it a little house, and then they climbed on it and it became a ship. It was their own creation for their games and their stories. I am constantly amazed by how children take the simplest tools and use them to create. Early creative endeavors help to develop brains toward critical thinking and the creation of more complex ideas. Later on, when reading harder books, they will make and create ideas about the books they read. Their brains are growing at a rapid rate at this age, and the work they are doing to develop ideas may best manifest itself through play and art. Their creativity in play is also sowing the seeds for complex thinking about reading. Here are some books for you to read aloud to this age group that are inspired by the theme of making and creating.

Do Pirates Take Baths? by Kathy Tucker, illustrated by Nadine Bernard Westcott (Albert Whitman & Company: 2007)
Emma's Rug by Allen Say (Houghton Mifflin Company: 2003)
Fannie in the Kitchen: The Whole Story from Soup to Nuts of How Fannie Farmer Invented Recipes with Precise Measurements by Deborah Hopkinson, illustrations by Nancy Carpenter (Simon & Schuster Children's Publishing: 2001)
Salad People and More Real Recipes: A New Cookbook for Preschoolers & Up by Mollie Katzen (Ten Speed Press: 2005)

The Here and Now

In the 1960s the legendary author Margaret Wise Brown made a discovery. She found that children really understand the preciousness of the "here and now" of their experiences and that they wanted to read about them. But they also liked a bit of magic. Through picture books, we can offer our children both the magic of the imagination and the concrete universe of childhood as described by the "here and now." Margaret Wise Brown's discovery informed the next generation of children's literature. It is because of her that we have all the board books I described in the earlier pages, including concept books and books that describe the daily life of the very young child. Now, some of our greatest authors manage to imbue even that here and now with a touch of the magical, which is their genius. They convey to the growing child that his experience is worth reflection, compassion, and celebration. In *Toy Boat*, the child loses his boat, briefly, but in the end they are reunited. Even in the most intense separations, there is the possibility of the sweetness of the happy ending and the understanding and appreciation of treasures that matter and the importance of coming home again.

Balloon on the Moon by Dan McCann, illustrated by Nathan Hale (Walker Books for Young Readers: 2008)
Corduroy by Don Freeman (Penguin Young Readers Group: 2008)
Paddington Here and Now by Michael Bond (HarperCollins Publishers: 2008)
Toy Boat by Randall DeSeve, illustrated by Loren Long (Philomel Books: 2007)
Where the Wild Things Are by Maurice Sendak (HarperCollins Publishers: 1967)

Five Years Old: Balancing Challenge and Comfort

I still remember the first day when Katie came home from kindergarten and she stood on the front porch taking her backpack off and trying to show me all the papers and instructions from school. I went to her and knelt down to wrap her up in my arms, as she stood there trying to be such a big girl. The first thing I remember so vividly is how she smelled different. The air of the outside world was upon her. She smelled like chalk and sweet gum from a friend on the bus, and peanut butter. It could have broken my heart right then and there. It's that we want to say: take care of her, world! Take care of her, will you, world? She is now a senior in high school. And I still feel that way. On the day she got her driver's license, she stood on the front porch rummaging in her bag to make sure she had everything she needed for her maiden voyage, and my heart broke again.

All through the years, they grow, but inside of them is that five-year-old, that same tenderhearted, tiny girl with her head inside her backpack, with the scent upon her of the outside world.

Your five-year-old is capable of making intense connections everywhere. The blue color inside the fish tank reminds her of the baby blanket on her bed; the sound of laughter on the playground makes her think of her little brother. She is a traveler in a new world with longings for the old one. These books balance her cravings for independence and her continued need for the familiar. Also look for books on the transition to school in Chapter 8: "The Fifty Themes."

Kindergarten Books

Corduroy Goes to School by Don Freeman (Viking Juvenile: 2002)
Kindergarten Rocks! by Katie Davis (Harcourt Children's Books: 2008)
Miss Bindergarten Gets Ready for Kindergarten by Joseph Slate, illustrated by Ashley Wolff (Penguin Young Readers Group: 2001)
My Kindergarten by Rosemary Wells (Hyperion Books for Children: 2007)
Welcome to Kindergarten by Anne Rockwell (Walker & Company: 2004)
The Wheels on the School Bus by Mary-Alice Moore, illustrated by Laura Huliska-Beith (HarperCollins Publishers: 2006)
Wow! School! by Robert Newbecker (Disney Press: 2007)

Play and reflection are part of literacy development. "Only connect," said the writer E. M. Forster. This is the work of the five-year-old. The child abides by the power of imagination. She is building worlds out of things, and things out of worlds. These are the processes by which we will foster literacy: play, imagination, and collaboration.

The imaginative life of a child is one in which any idea can fit into different containers: a couch becomes a magic ship, a pair of sneakers becomes the hooves on a horse. This is an optimal time to expose your child to a range of genres: fiction, nonfiction, and poetry. She sees all the possibilities. Her embrace of the sun's warmth becomes a poem. Her joy in skipping to lunch becomes a song. Her exploration of "why" questions draw her to all-about concept books in the nonfiction section of the library.

Books about Making Things

Your five-year-old likes to see how things get set up, how things are made. He likes to take something apart and put it back together. He is now learning that books are made by authors, and so there are some wonderful books about how books get made that he will enjoy as well. Here are some of my favorites:

How a Book Is Made by Aliki (HarperCollins Children's Books: 1988)
Transformed: How Everyday Things Are Made by Bill Slavin (Kids Can Press: 2007)
What Do Authors Do? by Eileen Christelow (Houghton Mifflin Company: 1997)

Books about Language and Words

Your five-year-old is aware of language and the beauty of words themselves, aware of the look and sound of words and alphabet letters. For your five-year-old, print represents a key to a world of older friends, of big brothers, of mother and father. She sees written language in all its glory, and she wants to be part of it too. Her mind is humming with the newness of words all day long. One time, I asked a group of five-year-olds what was the most important thing about reading and writing they had learned in that year. And one of the students, Allison, said: "I remember I used to think a *w* was a *d* because it sounded like that: double-u." There are many wonderful books for this age group that celebrate the marvels of language and the alphabet. These are alphabet books that are attentive to a child's love for language, as well as books that celebrate the eccentricities of language.

A Is for Africa by Ifeoma Onyefulu (Penguin Young Readers Group: 1997)
The Alphabet Book by P. D. Eastman (Random House Books for Young Readers: 1974)
C Is for China (World Alphabets) by Sungwan So (Frances Lincoln Children's Books: 2004)
The Construction Alphabet Book by Jerry Pallotta, illustrated by Rob Bolster (Charlesbridge Publishing: 2006)
Jambo Means Hello: Swahili Alphabet Book by Muriel L. Feelings, illustrated by Tom Feelings (Penguin Young Reader's Group: 1992)
M Is for Majestic, A National Parks Alphabet by David Domeniconi, illustrated by Pam Carroll (Sleeping Bear Press: 2007)

Poetry and songs enhance that sense of the joyousness of language. Don't be afraid to read poetry to your child. Even if every line is not always easy to understand, your child will appreciate the beats and moods of each poem and it all helps in building literacy. Here are some great ones:

A Child's Garden of Verses by Robert Louis Stevenson, illustrated by Tasha Tudor (Simon & Schuster: 1999)
Jambo and Other Call and Response Songs and Chants by Ella Jenkins
Sing a Song of Popcorn by Beatrice Schenk De Regniers (Scholastic: 1988)

Talking Like the Rain by X. J. Kennedy, illustrated by Jane Dyer (Little, Brown and Company: 1992)

Question Books

There is no one better at asking a question than a five-year-old. These books will help satisfy their desire to know the ins and outs of just about everything.

I Wonder Why I Blink and Other Questions About My Body by Brigid Avison (Kingfisher: 2003)
What Makes Popcorn Pop and Other Questions About the World Around Us edited by Jack Myers (Boyds Mills Press: 1994)

Funny Books

Your five-year-old is the funniest he's ever been, but not the funniest he ever will be. He is starting not only to understand how funny the world is; he can make jokes too. The development of a sense of humor is completely underrated in child development books. I watched in fascination over many years as my daughters grew in their capacity to understand humor, to be subtle in their own humor, and to tell a really funny story. The capacity for humor is well worth cultivating. It is a brain activity and strengthens the brain. All children have an innate sense of humor and you will play a significant role in helping to develop it at home.

Children's literature is a great tool for cultivating a healthy sense of humor. There are so many giggly books to practice on. A continuum of humor might include moments like when a baby smiles at the face of a baby on the page; a toddler giggles at the silly picture of the dog on the lift-the-flap book; a preschooler laughs at the antics of Spot getting lost; a five-year-old begins to see more subtle humor on the page like an amusing picture or a really funny moment in a plot. In addition, he begins to see language as a way to construct humor himself. You can foster the development of your child along this continuum by providing reading opportunities that are just plain silly! Plus, it's really good and healthy for your kids to laugh a lot (and for you too!). These following books are particularly silly. Get your funny bones ready.

The Cow Who Clucked by Denise Fleming (Henry Holt Books for Young Readers: 2006)
The Dumb Bunnies by Dav Pilkey (Scholastic: 2007)

The Everything Kids' Knock Knock Book: Jokes Guaranteed to Leave Your Friends in Stitches by Aileen Weintraub (Adams Media Corporation: 2004)

500 Hilarious Jokes for Kids by Jeff Rovin (Penguin Putnam: 1990)

George and Martha: The Complete Story of Two Best Friends by James Marshall (Houghton Mifflin Company: 1997)

Let's Go Swimming with Mr. Sillypants by Mary K. Brown (Random House Books for Young Readers: 1992)

Martha Speaks by Susan Meddaugh (Houghton Mifflin Company: 1995)

Miss Nelson Is Missing! by Harry G. Allard and James Marshall (Houghton Mifflin Company: 1998)

Mrs. Piggle-Wiggle by Betty MacDonald, illustrated by Hilary Knight (HarperCollins Publishers: 1985)

Oink by Tom Lyons (Hats Off Books: 2005)

The Stupids Step Out by Harry G. Allard, illustrated by James Marshall (Houghton Mifflin Company: 1997)

365 Penguins by Jean-Luc Fromental (Harry N. Abrams: 2006)

1000 Knock Knock Jokes for Kids by Michael Kilgarriff (Random House: 1986)

Research Books

I spoke with a five-year-old at a school about what he most enjoyed reading. He said, "I have a chameleon at home, so I like to do research on what he likes to eat and drink and so I read books about that." How wise! And what our five-year-olds want to research may be exactly that: the support for the important details of their lives. What better way to introduce our kids to the value of exploration and research than to seize their interests and passions early on and introduce them to books that will help them puzzle out the answers to their most fervent wonderings. Here are some great ones to inspire wonderings:

Amazing Snakes! by Sarah L. Thomson, photographs by Wildlife Conservation Society (HarperCollins Children's Books: 2006)

Astronaut Handbook by Meghan McCarthy (Random House Books for Young Readers: 2008)

Big Building Site (Dorling Kindersley Publishing: 2006)

Kites: Magic Wishes That Fly Up to the Sky by Hitz Demi (Dragonfly Books: 2000)
Sporting Events: From Baseball to Skateboarding by Gabriel Kaufman (Bearport Publishing Company: 2005)
Why Do Dogs Have Wet Noses? by Stanley Coren (Kids Can Press: 2006)

Magazines

This is a wonderful time to introduce your child to magazines by reading aloud from them to your child. By doing so, you are modeling that you value this sort of reading as meaningful too. Most adults read about ninety percent nonfiction, especially in the form of magazines and newspapers. It is a great form for learning more, and so we want to cultivate this habit very early on in our children's lives. There are many great magazines that you can either buy, or look at online, or subscribe to for your children. Read them aloud, before bed, and at all your ritual times just like you would a picture book, so they can feel their power in your lives.

General Interest Magazines

Click; www.cricketmag.com
Dig; www.digonsite.com
National Geographic Kids; www.nationalgeographic.com/ngkids/index.html
Owl; www.owlkids.com

Arts & Literature Magazines

Highlights High Five; www.highlights.com
Ladybug; www.cricketmag.com
Stone Soup; www.stonesoup.com

Sports Magazines

Sports Illustrated for Kids; www.sikids.com

Culture Magazines

Appleseeds; www.cobblestonepub.com

Six Years Old: Forging Connections

"Spectacularful ideas are always sproinging up in my brain."
From *Clementine* by Sara Pennypacker

Many of my favorite characters from children's literature seem to be about six years old. The Frances books by Russell Hoban, the Little Bear books by Else Minarik, and *Sheila Rae the Brave* and *Chrysanthemum* by Kevin Henkes are all books about animals personified to seem completely like all the six-year-olds I have ever known. Frances, Sheila Rae, and Little Bear are all feisty, brave, worried, shy, curious, cuddly, and spirited. They are totally and utterly themselves, but they need a hand. They will break your heart on some level, for they are trying to be big kids in the world, with their lunch boxes in hand, or their backpacks weighing heavily on their shoulders, but they are still so tiny and vulnerable and fragile. Their skin is still soft and luminous, so you can recall what they felt like as newborns. But their teeth are falling out, and they are growing up, all of which is intense, miraculous, strange, and sometimes even a bit scary. One of the most viscerally physical experiences of childhood, losing teeth is nothing to simply pass by. It is a very big deal for your child, and literature helps to celebrate these milestones, as well as to provide a bit of magic to lighten the journey.

Tooth Milestone Books

This time is transcendent: your child is in a constant state of awakening to the bright life of consciousness. Most of what happens over the course of this year will make up the first conscious memories they will keep for the rest of their lives. How wise of these fine writers to place their characters in that context: wide-awake, lively minds, deep in the process of creating memory banks and building a sense of themselves. These are books that capture a deep essence of this time for both you and your child as the characters themselves seem to be that very same age. They are sophisticated enough to relate the strong emotion of this age, but still playful enough to convey the spirited life of a six-year-old. With you, the six-year-old can begin to explore the world and open up to all the other stories that are there for him. Books represent a way to speak to those turning points. These books are about unique experiences, perspectives that offer a gentle introduction to the multitude of voices in the world.

Junie B. Jones series by Barbara Park, illustrated by Denise Brunkus (Random House Books for Young Readers)

Frog and Toad series by Arnold Lobel (HarperCollins Publishers)

Little Bill series by Bill Cosby, illustrated by Varnette P. Honeywood (Scholastic)

Miss Rumphius by Barbara Cooney (Puffin: 1982)

Poppleton *series* by Cynthia Rylant, illustrated by Mark Teague (The Blue Sky Press)

Arthur series by Marc Brown (Random House Books for Young Readers)

Books about School and Home

Six-year-olds are hovering between home and school. They have one foot still in early childhood, one foot in later childhood. Thumbs creep near their mouths during the school day, and even pop in on occasion. And yet, they wear a pair of new sneakers to school and practice their balance on the wall of the playground. They are becoming big kids. They go to sleep dreaming of school and they go to school dreaming of home. They may have siblings, and if so, they are spending lots of time after school and in the evening among them. It is odd to go to school and leave all that behind. They are in school for six hours, or even more if they are in an after-school program, and that is a long, long time in the life of a six-year-old. Yet our six-year-olds are learning to negotiate issues of fairness and trying new things, whether they be food or friends. By reading aloud to your child, you can form a bridge with the text for your child between his two worlds.

Brand-new Pencils, Brand-new Books by Diane deGroat (HarperCollins Children's Books: 2005)

Charlie and Lola: But Excuse Me That Is My Book by Lauren Child (Penguin Young Readers Group: 2006)

I Will Never Not Ever Eat a Tomato by Lauren Child (Candlewick Press: 2000)

It's Not Fair! by Amy Krouse Rosenthal, illustrated by Tom Lichtenheld (HarperCollins Publishers: 2008)

The Recess Queen by Alexis O'Neill, illustrations by Laura Huliska-Beith (Scholastic: 2002)

Comfort Books

Your six-year-old might seem big, but he longs for the warmth of your arms. Like Frances and Little Bear, he unpacks his own lunch at school and puts everything away; he can zip up his jacket on his own and spend hours making worlds of pretend outside. With all of the changes happening in his life, familiar books can offer a much-appreciated sense of security. The world of his home, no matter where or what that world is, is quite big enough for him. These books are cozy and lovely. There is no doubt there is love in the world.

Are You My Mother? by P. D. Eastman (Random House Books for Young Readers: 1960)
Hug by Jez Alborough (Candlewick Press: 2002)
Koala Lou by Mem Fox, illustrated by Pamela Lofts (Harcourt Children's Books: 1994)
The Runaway Bunny by Margaret Wise Brown, illustrated by Clement Hurd (HarperCollins Publishers: 2005)
We Had a Picnic This Sunday Past by Jacqueline Woodson, illustrated by Diane Greenseid (Disney Press: 2007)

Books That Cultivate Imagination

Six-year-olds love to dig into dress-up boxes and try on personas: first a princess, then a witch. They are wizards and cowboys, queens, superheroes, and presidents. There are some great picture books that really reflect the vivid imagination that colors the experience of the six-year-old. Six-year-olds build forts and make things out of paper and boxes and bedsheets. They put all of the objects they can find to use, cultivating their imaginations all the while. Their books should reflect their imaginary ventures, so they can recognize themselves in the pages. Here are some I recommend:

Clouds by Anne Rockwell, illustrated by Frané Lessac (HarperCollins Publishers: 2008)
Dreamland by Roni Schotter, illustrated by Kevin Hawkes (Orchard Books: 1996)
Fancy Nancy by Jane O'Connor, illustrated by Robin Preiss Glasser (HarperCollins Publishers: 2005)

Meet the X-Men by Clare Hibbert (Dorling Kindersley Publishing: 2006)
The Raft by Jim LaMarche (HarperCollins Publishers: 2002)
Roxaboxen by Alice McLerran, illustrated by Barbara Cooney (HarperCollins Publishers: 2004)
Snowflake Bentley by Jacqueline Briggs Martin (Houghton Mifflin Company: 1998)
Tuesday by David Wiesner (Sandpiper: 1997)
Weslandia by Paul Fleischman, illustrated by Kevin Henkes (Candlewick Press: 2002)

Stories about Scrapes

Six-year-olds like stories about scrapes where the character is *almost* going to have a big problem, but then it all works out. Probably because they often feel the same, like they are nearly going to make a mistake and then don't (or sometimes do), these books have enormous appeal. From a parent's point of view, these books are a great opportunity to build empathy in your child: help him to understand a character's point of view and to learn how to relate to the little bumps in the road he too experiences.

Alfie Gets in First by Shirley Hughes (Lothrop, Lee & Shepard Books: 1981)
Good Boy, Fergus! by David Shannon (Scholastic: 2006)
Library Lion by Michelle Knudsen, illustrated by Kevin Hawkes (Candlewick Press: 2006)
The Mixed-Up Rooster by Pamela Duncan Edwards, illustrated by Megan Lloyd (Katherine Tegen Books: 2006)
Scaredy Squirrel by Melanie Watt (Kids Can Press: 2006)

Poetry Books

Six-year-olds love onomatopoeia, rhyme, and the funny sound of the language. Here are some terrific books which hold the mysteries and bountiful joys of language:

Beast Feast by Douglas Florian (Voyager Books: 1998)
Dear World by Takayo Noda (Penguin Young Readers Group: 2003)

Favorite Poems Old and New edited by Helen Ferris Tibbets, illustrated by Lenard Weisgard (Random House Books for Young Readers: 1957)
Honey, I Love by Eloise Greenfield, illustrated by Jan Spivey Gilchrist (HarperCollins Publishers: 2003)
Insectlopedia by Douglas Florian (Harcourt Children's Books: 2002)
A Pizza the Size of the Sun by Jack Prelutsky, illustrated by James Stevenson (HarperCollins Publishers: 1996)
Sports: Rhymes about Running, Jumping, Throwing, and More by Jack Prelutsky, illustrated by Chris Raschka (Random House Books for Young Readers: 2007)
Where the Sidewalk Ends by Shel Silverstein (HarperCollins Publishers: 2004)

Skill Books

Recently, I was talking to Jack, who is six. As he was telling me all about his day at school, he was snapping his front finger and thumb together: *snap, snap, snap*. I asked, "Did you just learn how to do that?" He nodded and grinned, so pleased I had noticed (even though he had been snapping madly right in front of me!). This is the essence of the six-year-old: telling stories while practicing skills. There are some wonderful books to help our six-year-olds learn something new. Here are some to read and enjoy together:

Easy-to-Do Magic Tricks for Children by Karl Fulves, illustrated by Joseph K. Schmidt (Dover Publications: 1993)
Kids' Magic Card Tricks by Terry Eagle (Barron's Educational Series: 2003)
Kites for Everyone: How to Make and Fly Them by Margaret Greger, illustrated by Del Greger (Dover Publications: 2006)
Window Art by the editors of Klutz (Scholastic: March 2007)

Telling Stories

Story is key for the six-year-old. Everything is a story. They are out of breath as they tell their own. They love when magic and reality intersect in stories, and things happen that are surprising and a bit quirky. Here are some storybooks I love that are a bit longer for the growing reader and have a very strong sense of story:

Brother Rabbit: A Cambodian Tale by Minfong Ho, illustrated by Jennifer Hewitson (HarperCollins Publishers: 2007)
The Mouse and the Motorcycle by Beverly Cleary, illustrated by Louis Darling (HarperCollins Publishers: 1999)
My Father's Dragon by Ruth Stiles Gannett (Random House Books for Young Readers: 1987)

Series Books

You can read to your six-year-old from series books, which they may already be reading on their own or will read sometime in the next year or two. The secret of the collections is that you will not be able to put them down. It is also good to demonstrate the kind of reading readers do when they read series: figuring out the "trick" of the books, how some things stay the same book to book, and how the characters are predictable. Stop and talk about these things as you read.

Clementine series by Sara Pennypacker, illustrations by Marla Frazee (Hyperion Books for Children)
Frog and Toad series by Arnold Lobel (HarperCollins Publishers)
Henry and Mudge series by Cynthia Rylant, illustrated by Suçie Stevenson (Simon & Schuster Children's Publishing)
Ivy and Bean series by Annie Barrows (Chronicle Books)
Little Bill series by Bill Cosby, illustrated by Varnette P. Honeywood (Scholastic)
Little Bear series by Else Minarik, illustrated by Maurice Sendak (HarperCollins Publishers)
Magic Treehouse series by Mary Pope Osborne (Random House Books for Young Readers)
Mr. Putter and Tabby series by Cynthia Rylant (Harcourt Children's Books)
Nate the Great series by Mary Weinman Sharmat (Random House Books for Young Readers)

Entering Magical Worlds

The journeys of six-year-olds always combine magic and reality. They have newfound skills and powers, with the sheen of babyhood still upon them. Your six-year-old is ready for longer read-alouds and chapter book read-alouds with magic in them. The stories complement the sense of the real journeys of their lives, which are just beginning. Six-year-olds are very conscious of the magic of the world, whether it is in the night sky or right in front of them, or in the life of their imaginations. There are some books that reflect this unique capacity to imagine many worlds.

Comets, Stars, the Moon, and Mars: Space Poems and Paintings by Douglas Florian (Harcourt Children's Books: 2007)
Dinosaur Dream by Dennis Nolan (Simon & Schuster Children's Publishing: 1994)
The Dragons of Blueland by Ruth Stiles Gannett, illustrated by Ruth Chrisman Gannett (Random House Books for Young Readers: 1987)
Stuart Little by E. B. White, illustrated by Garth Williams (HarperTrophy: 1974)
Tupelo Rides the Rails by Melissa Sweet (Houghton Mifflin Company: 2008)

Seven Years Old: Opening Up to the World

The seven-year-old, with his toothless smile, is a physical marvel. He stumbles while running across the playground, because his legs probably grew while he slept last night. He looks slightly different every day, because he is growing teeth and losing them at a rapid rate. Suddenly, he is able to think outside the concrete experience of his in-the-moment life, and plan ahead, envisioning what is not yet there. He also worries about things more than ever before because he can imagine a variety of possibilities. What will happen if you are not there to meet him when he gets off the school bus? What if his playdate goes badly? What if he doesn't get in line in time at his after-school care program? There are many wonderful picture books that help us converse with our children about their worries. A few include:

Froggy Goes to the Doctor by Jonathan London, illustrated by Frank Remkiewicz (Penguin Young Readers Group: 2004)
Froggy Learns to Swim by Jonathan London, illustrated by Frank Remkiewicz (Penguin Young Readers Group: 1996)
There's a Nightmare in My Closet by Mercer Mayer (Penguin: 1992)

Savoring the Moments

Seven-year-olds worry, but they also revel in the rich moments that are special to their age. An ice-cream cone with a grandparent or a subway ride with you are grand adventures. Seven-year-olds are true companions, old enough to understand when you have had a hard day, and young enough to need that day to fall away so she can crawl right back into your arms, preparing for the new and better day ahead. These books help you to savor the moments together:

In Daddy's Arms I Am Tall: African-Americans Celebrating Fathers by Javaka Steptoe (Lee & Low Books: 2001)
Tell Me a Story, Mama by Angela Johnson, illustrated by David Soman (Scholastic: 1989)
The Two of Them by Aliki (HarperCollins Publishers: 1997)

Love of Story

Our seven-year-olds are captivated by a love of story: they are learning that a narrative anchors them, gives them a way to put their daily challenges into perspective, and transports them to magical lands. It is really essential to continue to build that strong sense of story with them. Don't give up on picture books, even if your child seems to be reading a lot independently already. Picture books accomplish so much in small spaces, through the use of strong story elements: character, plot, and the arc of a story. All of these elements are crucial for your child's development: having a well-developed sense of what composes a strong narrative will help your child in all aspects of his life: it will help him learn how to tell his own story, the story of who he is in the world, and it will build his capacity to empathize and understand other people's stories.

Charlotte's Web by E. B. White (HarperCollins Publishers: 1952)
The Gift of the Sun: A Tale from South Africa by Dianne Stewart, illustrated by Jude Daly (Frances Lincoln, Ltd.: 2007)
Mama Panya's Pancakes: A Village Tale from Kenya by Mary Chamberlin (Barefoot Books: 2006)
Martina the Beautiful Cockroach: A Cuban Folktale by Carmen Agra Deedy, illustrated by Michael Austin (Peachtree Publishers: 2007)
Swimmy by Leo Leonni (Random House Books for Young Readers: 1973)

Whistle for Willie by Ezra Jack Keats (Penguin Young Readers Group: 1977)

Books with Magical Elements

Big Anthony: His Story by Tomie dePaola (Penguin Young Readers Books: 2001)
The Borrowers by Mary Norton, illustrated by Diana Stanley (Harcourt Children's Books: 2003).
Catwings by Usurla K. LeGuin (Scholastic: 2003)
Doctor DeSoto by William Steig (Farrar, Straus and Giroux: 1990)
Shrek! by William Steig (Sunburst: 1993)
The Van Gogh Café by Cynthia Rylant (Harcourt Paperbacks: 2006)

Books on Science

A Drop of Water: A Book of Science and Wonder by Walter Wick (Scholastic: 1997)
Water Dance by Thomas Locker (Harcourt Children's Books: 2002)
Wolfsnail: A Backyard Predator by Sarah Campbell (Boyds Mills Press: 2008)

Poetry

Poetry can be an essential and beautiful part of the seven-year-old's reading diet.

Poetry is hidden everywhere in the life of a seven-year-old: inside the petal of a flower, inside the story of Sundays at Grandma's house. There are many wonderful books of poetry that will speak powerfully to kids at this age, as well as providing moments of silliness and fun that can ease a long day or start a new day off just right.

If You're Not Here, Please Raise Your Hand: Poems about School by Kalli Dakos, illustrated by G. Brian Karas (Simon & Schuster: 1985)
New Kid on the Block by Jack Prelutsky, illustrated by James Stevenson (HarperCollins Publishers: 1984)
Plum by Tony Mitton, illustrated by Mary GrandPre (Scholastic: 2003)

Poetry Speaks to Children (with CD), edited by Elise Paschen and Billy Collins (Source Books, Inc.: 2005)

A Poke in the I by Paul Janecko, illustrated by Chris Raschka (Candlewick Press: 2005)

Popcorn: Poems by James Stevenson (Greenwillow Books: 1998)

The Robots Are Coming, and Other Problems by Andy Rash (Scholastic: 2000)

Soul Looks Back in Wonder edited by Tom Feelings and Maya Angelou, illustrated by Tom Feelings (Penguin Young Readers Group: 1999)

Under the Sunday Tree by Eloise Greenfield, illustrated by Amos Ferguson (HarperCollins Children's Publishing: 1991)

Rereading Our Favorites

While we all rush by, busy and moving quickly, the seven-year old will still tug at your hand to bend down and take another look. They want to keep that beloved book by their beds because the act of rereading feels important, soothing, and instructive. And how right they are. In reality, they are building their reading muscles, becoming more fluent readers, and increasing their stamina and comprehension by revisiting familiar texts or reading texts on their own that for years you have been reading aloud to them.

Seven-year-olds want to feel the closeness of family, of their friends, of cherished texts and authors. And yet they are stepping out, dipping their toes in the waters of deeper learning and deeper relationships, growing up. Here are some chapter books to introduce to them at this time that they will remember forever.

Ballet Shoes by Noel Streatfeild, illustrated by Diane Goode (Random House Books for Young Readers: 1999)

Freckle Juice by Judy Blume, illustrated by Sonia Lisker (Simon & Schuster Children's Publishing: 1971)

The Most Beautiful Place in the World by Ann Cameron, illustrated by Thomas B. Allen (Random House Books for Young Readers: 1993)

A Mouse Called Wolf by Dick King-Smith, illustrated by Jon Goodell (Random House Books for Young Readers: 1999)

Silly but Important Series

Seven-year-olds can be very goofy and don't always want to be serious at any time, especially not before bed. There are some books many of our seven-year-olds are ready to read on their own at this time but also really enjoy reading with you. They are building stamina in every way in every aspect of their lives: from how fast they run to how long they can read. Model how you appreciate these series books for the purpose they serve the growing reader by reading them aloud.

Bailey School Kids series
Geronimo Stilton series
Weird School series by Dan Gutman

Magazines

Seven-year-olds love feeling like a part of the important day-to-day rituals of grown-ups. They watch you read the paper at the table and they want one to read too. They watch their teacher read a magazine at her break and they want to do that too. Here are some great ones:

Science Magazines

Ask; www.cricketmag.com
Kids Discover; www.kidsdiscover.com
National Geographic Explorer;
www.magma.nationalgeographic.com/ngexplorer/index.html
National Geographic Kids;
www.nationalgeographic.com/ngkids/index.html
Owl; www.owlkids.com
Ranger Rick; www.nwf.org/rangerrick

Arts & Literature Magazines

Highlights; www.highlights.com
Spider; www.cricketmag.com
Stone Soup; www.stonesoup.com
WordDance; www.worddance.com/magazine

Sports Magazines

Sports Illustrated for Kids; www.sikids.com

Culture Magazines

Appleseeds; www.cobblestonepub.com
Skipping Stones; www.SkippingStones.org

Bilingual Books

It's a wonderful time to celebrate the multiplicity of languages in literature through the fun of the read-aloud.

Hairs/Pelitos by Sandra Cisneros (Dragonfly Books: 1997)
I'm Just Like My Mom/Me parezco tanto a mi mamá by Jorge Ramos, illustrated by Akemi Gutierrez (Rayo: 2008)

Eight Years Old: Creating Ideas

> *"I was eight. I knew the green damp, dark smells that bloomed on the hill. I could track the places where black ash grew. Eight must be old enough."*
>
> —From *The Basket Moon* by Mary Lyn Ray

Integrating Outside Knowledge

The outside world is having a greater and greater impact on eight-year-olds. They fall asleep at night, still thinking about all the new things they have learned, while holding on to their favorite stuffed animal. The following four books represent the integration of outside knowledge. One, a picture book about a unique place and time; another, a book of poems that brings language to the fore. Still another, a short chapter book about a life of poverty and transcendence; and the last, a nonfiction book about facts to provoke much discussion. The books themselves are not related, but the eight-year-old is absorbing and integrating a myriad of information throughout the day and each of these books reflects the joy of that.

The Basket Moon by Mary Lyn Ray, illustrated by Barbara Cooney (Little, Brown and Company: 1999)
Gathering the Sun: An Alphabet in Spanish and English by Alma Flor Ada, illustrated by Simon Silva (Rayo: 2001)

Just Juice by Karen Hesse, illustrated by Robert Andrew Parker (Scholastic: 1999)

What's So Bad about Gasoline? Fossil Fuels and What They Do by Anne Rockwell, illustrated by Paul Meisel (HarperCollins Publishers: 2009)

Nonfiction Matters

There are many mental demands on a child of eight. The school environment has kicked it up a notch, and your child is expected to perform at a much higher level academically, somewhat suddenly. There is pressure in this, but also there is much excitement, as they are able to absorb a great deal of content and integrate it into their understandings of the way the world works. Expose them to plenty of nonfiction at this age. It's also a great genre to read with them and to them, even as they are reading more fiction on their own.

A Cool Drink of Water by Barbara Kerley (National Geographic Society: 2006)

In Their Own Words series by George Sullivan (Scholastic)

A Little Peace by Barbara Kerley (National Geographic Society: 2007)

National Geographic Dinosaurs by Paul M. Barrett and J. L. Sanz, illustrated by Raoul Martin (National Geographic Society: 1996)

National Geographic Encyclopedia of Animals by Staff of National Geographic and George McKay (National Geographic Society: 1996)

Paths to Peace: People Who Changed the World by Jane Breskin Zalben (Penguin Young Readers Group: 2006)

Books about Natural History: For Fun Expeditions

A trip to the rare stones and gem room in your natural history museum or out on the trail of exploration together could be paired with a shared read of books about geology. Tuck these books into your backpack and you are on your way to a great day.

How to Dig a Hole to the Other Side of the World by Faith McNulty (HarperCollins Publishers: 1992)

Looking at Rocks (My First Field Guide) by Jennifer Dussling, illustrated by Tim Haggerty (Grosset & Dunlap: 2001)
Rocks and Minerals (Eye Wonder) by DK Publishing (Dorling Kindersley Publishing: 2004)

Cooking Books

Another kind of science is the science of cooking. This is a great age to inspire a delight in the kitchen, with good books as your guide. Read these with a budding cook.

Cooking with Children: 15 Lessons for Children, Age 7 and Up, Who Really Want to Learn to Cook by Marion Cunningham (Knopf: 1995)
DK Children's Cookbook: Quick and Tasty Recipes for Young Chefs by DK Publishing (Dorling Kindersley Publishing: 2004)

Books about Friendship

Your eight-year-old is thinking a lot about friendship: it feels dynamic, lively, complex, and often hard too. As you'll see in the "Making Friends/Friendship" section of the *"What to Read When"* list, there are many books out there that address the complexities of friendship. Particularly for this age, there are some really good chapter book read-alouds that speak to this dimension in powerful ways and will help you talk about some of the bumps in the road, as well as the joys.

Because of Winn-Dixie by Kate DiCamillo (Candlewick Press: 2001)
Frindle by Andrew Clements, illustrated by Brian Selznick (Aladdin: 1998)
The Hundred Dresses by Eleanor Estes, illustrated by Louis Slobodkin (Harcourt Paperbacks: 2004)
Poppy by Avi (HarperCollins Publishers: 1999)
The Stories Julian Tells by Ann Cameron, illustrated by Ann Strugnell (Random House Books for Young Readers: 1989)

Rituals

While eight-year-olds ponder all the intricacies of friendships, home is all the more important to them as a refuge and sanctuary. They are curious about the rituals of others, and about building their own. They like the fact that you make pancakes every Sunday or that on Friday nights you all eat together. They understand the value of food for bringing the family together, and often get a visceral feeling of joy when the family does gather around the table. Even if your family is small, maybe just you and your child, he craves family rituals. You don't need to be fancy or have lots of money to make rituals—even the simplest ones are precious to your child. Literature can name some of these and help you talk with your child about the essential rituals you want to build into your own family life. Your child can help create them. Here are some books that savor the pleasures of ritual:

Dim Sum for Everyone by Grace Lin (Dragonfly Books: 2003)
Dumpling Soup by Jama Kim Rattigan (Little, Brown and Company: 1998)
Mei Mei Loves the Morning by Margaret Holloway Tsubakiyama, illustrated by Cornelius Van Wright and Ying-Hwa Hu (Albert Whitman & Company: 1999)
Thunder Cake by Patricia Polacco (Putnam Juvenile: 1997)

Series

Eight-year-olds love both the predictability of life and new adventures. As such, series books are ideal for their reading lives this year, and there are hundreds of them. These are swift reads when you read them aloud, but they scaffold your child's independent reading life: you can send him off with a fun stack of the continuations after you read the first one together. Don't think reading aloud books like *Captain Underpants* or *Goosebumps* is a waste of time because they are not "serious." They are important. When read independently, they help your child build stamina and confidence as a reader. But by reading them together, aloud, you are reinforcing that you value all the different kinds of reading for their age and developmental level. You can talk about the characters and help prepare your child for the next steps in independent reading. Favorite series to read aloud to your child include:

A–Z Mysteries series by Ron Roy, illustrated by John Steven Gurney (Random House)
Beast Quest series by Adam Blade, illustrated by Ezra Tucker (Scholastic)
Bunnicula series by Deborah Howe and James Howe, illustrated by Alan Daniel (Aladdin)
Cam Jansen series by David A. Adler, illustrated by Susanna Natti (Puffin)
Captain Underpants series by Dav Pilkey (The Blue Sky Press)

David Macaulay Books

I would like to make a special mention of the books of David Macaulay. His collection is perfect for browsing together. He shows such a deep regard for the sophistication of a child's inquiries and passions. Eight-year-olds are endlessly curious and so interested in how things are built, how they are made, and how they work.

Castle (Houghton Mifflin Company: 1982)
Pyramid (Houghton Mifflin Company: 1982)
The Way We Work: Getting to Know the Amazing Human Body (Houghton Mifflin Company: 2008)

Poetry

At eight, our children are keenly tuned in to the sounds of language. They are silly and serious, joyous and pensive. Poetry collections your eight-year-old will love include:

Baseball, Snakes, and Summer Squash by Donald Graves, illustrated by Paul Birling (Boyds Mills Press: 1996)
Brown Angels: An Album of Pictures and Verse by Walter Dean Myers (Sagebrush Education Resources: 1996)
Creatures of Earth, Sea, and Sky by Georgia Heard, illustrated by Jennifer Owings Dewey (Boyds Mills Press: 1997)
The Dream Keeper and Other Poems by Langston Hughes (Knopf Books for Young Readers: 1996)
Maples in the Mist: Poems for Children from the Tang Dynasty by Min-

fong Ho, illustrated by Jean Tseng and Mou-Sien Tseng (Lothrop, Lee and Shepard Books: 1996)

Moon, Have You Met My Mother? by Karla Kuskin, illustrated by Sergio Ruzzier (Laura Geringer: 2003)

Poetry for Young People: Langston Hughes edited by David Roessel, illustrated by Benny Andrews (Sterling Publishing: 2006)

Poetry for Young People: Robert Frost edited by Gary D. Schmidt, illustrated by Henri Sorensen (Sterling Publishing: 1994)

Where the Sidewalk Ends by Shel Silverstein (HarperCollins Publishers: 2004)

Reflective and Funny

Your eight-year-old sees conventions as the tools of their new worlds. The comma, the quotation mark, the ellipses, and the semicolon all seem to hold some kind of power, and your third grader wants to know exactly what that power is and how they can use it to shape ideas. They are reading chapter books, series books, and nonfiction, and you want to help them to become aware of grammar in ways that will enrich their lives, not scare them. The best way of all is that when you come to a sentence you love, just stop and admire it. Ask your child what he thinks about it—if it's long or short, punchy or tender.

Perhaps it is that they are, right now, entering the age of reason: they are in an existential time. My daughter, in third grade, came home one day to tell me a strange and wonderful moment she had had on the playground. She said: "I was just standing there while everyone was running around me, and suddenly it was the first time I could picture myself outside myself."

Another time, I was watching an eight-year-old drawing a road around a castle in a picture and then sitting there just staring at it. When I asked what he was thinking about, he said, "That is the first time I have drawn something that disappears from my view." They are more aware than ever of the passing of time and their own place in the world. Books that are reflective and funny and somehow convey something serious all at the same time are simply the best. These are all chapter books that I think really capture the spirit of this age, and they are great, great read-alouds. Of these four selections, one is classic (*Mary Poppins*) and the rest are recent, but they all convey whimsy and provoke discussion all at the same time. All the main characters are feisty and strong, just like we hope our own children are and will be.

Diary of a Wimpy Kid series by Jeff Kinney (Amulet Books: 2008)
The Goose Girl by Shannon Hale (Bloomsbury Publishing: 2005)
Mary Poppins by P. L. Travers, illustrated by Mary Shepard (Harcourt Children's Books: 2006)
Peter and the Starcatchers by Dave Barry and Ridley Pearson (Disney Editions: 2004)

Nine Years Old: Asking Questions, Shaping Answers

Your nine-year-old is busy. She is busy with her imaginations, lively experiences, curiosity, investigations, friendships, home relationships. The mind of a nine-year-old is wide awake, humming, singing with possibility.

Fiction with a Touch of Magic

Your nine-year-olds may have a pretend game with a group of friends that goes on and on, where parts are added and discarded over weeks at a time. They constantly generate outlets for their creativity: writing songs, performing plays, doing art projects. This is an age that is ideal for realistic fiction with a touch of magic. These books are extraordinary for independent reading, but also are fantastic for a shared read with you.

Chasing Vermeer by Blue Balliett, illustrated by Brett Helquist (Scholastic Paperbacks: 2005)
Dragon Rider by Cornelia Funke (Scholastic: 2004)
Ella Enchanted by Gail Carson Levine (HarperTrophy: 1998)
The Invention of Hugo Cabret by Brian Selznick (Scholastic: 2007)
The Lightning Thief by Rick Riordan (Miramax: 2006)
The Miraculous Journey of Edward Tulane by Kate DiCamillo, illustrated by Bagram Ibatoulline (Candlewick Press: 2007)
The Penderwicks: A Summer Tale of Four Sisters, Two Rabbits, and a Very Interesting Boy by Jeanne Birdsall (Yearling: 2007)
Redwall series by Brian Jacques (Puffin)
The Tale of Despereaux by Kate DiCamillo, illustrated by Timothy Basil Ering (Scholastic: 2004)

Tuck Everlasting by Natalie Babbitt (Square Fish: 2007)
Warriors series by Erin Hunter (HarperTrophy)
A Wrinkle in Time by Madeleine L'Engle (Square Fish: 2007)

Old Stories, New Readings

This is also a good time to revisit old stories in new ways. They are quite capable of thinking interpretively and thinking across multiple books about big ideas. Get passionate together about literary ideas that are at their levels of understanding. For example, there are really interesting renditions of the Cinderella story told from different cultural perspectives. They may long to revisit a story such as Cinderella but are now at the age when doing so might seem too babyish to them. However, they will find it fascinating to look at the Chinese Cinderella or the Caribbean Cinderella and talk about similarities and differences in the context of the cultures through these wonderful books:

Cendrillon: A Caribbean Cinderella, by Robert D. San Souci, illustrated by Brian Pinkney (Aladdin: 2002)
The Egyptian Cinderella by Shirley Climo, illustrated by Ruth Heller (HarperTrophy: 2002)
The Irish Cinderlad (Trophy Picture Books) by Shirley Climo, illustrated by Loretta Krupinski (HarperTrophy: 2000)
Mufaro's Beautiful Daughters by John Steptoe (HarperTrophy: 1993)

Anansi Stories

As with Cinderella, there are many versions of the Anansi (or Ananse) story. This too may be familiar to them from when they were little, or a story they have been read in school, but now, as an older child, they can ponder with you the differences through the lens of culture. And the stories are still plenty of fun.

Ananse and the Lizard: A West African Tale (hardcover) by Pat Cummings (Henry Holt and Company: 2002)
Ananse's Feast: An Ashanti Tale by Tololwa M. Mollel, illustrated by Andrew Glass (Clarion Books: 2002)
Anansi and the Magic Stick by Eric A. Kimmel and Janet Stevens (Holiday House: 2002)
Anansi the Spider: A Tale from the Ashanti by Gerald McDermott (Henry Holt and Company: 1987)

The Illustrated Anansi: Four Caribbean Folk Tales (hardcover) by Phillip Sherlock, illustrated by Petrina Wright (Macmillan Caribbean: 1995)
The Pot of Wisdom: Ananse Stories by Adwoa Badoe, illustrated by Wague Diakite (Groundwood Books: 2008)
Trickster Tales (World Storytelling) by Josepha Sherman (August House: 1997)

Creation Stories

In a similar vein, if this is something you would like to explore with your child, there are many versions of the creation story told from all different perspectives. Your nine-year-old is sophisticated and innocent all at once, and so it is a good time to think about these simple stories, which are not so simple at all, as you read together from these books:

Four Corners of the Sky: Creation Stories and Cosmologies from Around the World (hardcover) by Steve Zeitlin, illustrated by Chris Raschka (Henry Holt and Company: 2000)
In the Beginning: Creation Stories from Around the World by Virginia Hamilton, illustrated by Barry Moser (Harcourt Paperbacks: 1991)
The Woman Who Fell from the Sky: The Iroquois Story of Creation (hardcover) by John Bierhorst, illustrated by Robert Andrew Parker (HarperCollins Publishers: 1993)

Early Talent

Nine-year-olds are your greatest allies in any good idea waiting to be hatched, any class project waiting to be done, any fun adventure waiting to be launched. They are coming into their own. You can begin to see the stirrings of true talent: the child whose singing voice suddenly stops his class in its tracks, the child who can zing through ten books in two weeks, the child who draws a face with a startling understanding of human emotion. Suddenly, what looks like play is also the early witness to the kinds of passions and interests the child will have as an adult. Browse the books in Part Two, especially in the "Loving . . ." section, because they too may tap into and inspire your child's talents. Here are some that are perfect for your nine-year-old.

Dancing in the Wings by Debbie Allen, illustrated by Kadir Nelson (Puffin: 2003)
Diego by Jonah Winter, illustrated by Jeannette Winter (Dragonfly Books: 2004)
Frida by Jonah Winter, illustrated by Ana Juan (Arthur A. Levine Books: 2002)
Janice VanCleave's A+ Science Fair Projects by Janice VanCleave (Jossey-Bass: 2003)
Take It to the Hoop, Magic Johnson by Quincy Troupe, illustrated by Shane Evans (Jump at the Sun: 2000)
Woody Guthrie: Poet of the People by Bonnie Christensen (Knopf Books for Young Readers: 2001)
101 Things That Go (How to Draw) by Dan Green (Top That! Kids: 2004)

Plays

As your child is entering into a world of his own through literature and through school, it's a wonderful time, especially on a Sunday or during a holiday, to read aloud from plays and other performance pieces together. It's a way to keep the lightness and fun of the read-aloud going, even as your child is able to read so much more alone. Giggles, drama, and seriousness, all part of the life of a nine-year-old. Enjoy these:

Cinderella Outgrows the Glass Slipper and Other Zany Fractured Fairy Tale Plays by Joan M. Wolf (Scholastic Professional Books: 2002)
Free to Be . . . You and Me by Marlo Thomas (Running Press: 2002)
How to Eat Like a Child: And Other Lessons in Not Being a Grown-up by Delia Ephron (Harper Perennial: 2001)
Joyful Noise: Poems for Two Voices by Paul Fleischman, illustrated by Eric Beddows (HarperTrophy: 2004)
12 Fabulously Funny Fairy Tale Plays by Justin McCory Martin (Instructor Books: 2002)

Poetry

You can read aloud from poetry to your child or take turns reading these poems aloud together, dramatically. Poems are great to read right before bed, when your child is tired from too much homework:

A Child's Calendar by John Updike, illustrated by Trina Schart Hyman (Holiday House: 1999)
A Family of Poems edited by Caroline Kennedy, illustrated by Jon J. Muth (Hyperion Books for Children: 2005)
Kids Pick the Funniest Poems by Bruce Lansky, illustrated by Stephen Carpenter (Meadow Brook Press: 1991)
Meet Danitra Brown by Nikki Grimes, illustrated by Floyd Cooper (HarperCollins Publishers: 1997)
My Black Me: A Beginning Book of Black Poetry edited by Arnold Adoff (Penguin Young Readers Group: 1995)

Social Justice

Nine-year-olds are compelled by the idea of justice and injustice. Picture books offer a safe way to explore these very intense ideas.

An Angel for Solomon Singer by Cynthia Rylant, illustrated by Peter Catalanotto (Scholastic: 1996)
Chicken Sunday by Patricia Polacco (Putnam Juvenile: 2008)
The Day Gogo Went to Vote by Eleanor Batezat Sisulu, illustrated by Sharon Wilson (Little, Brown and Company: 1999)
Planting the Trees of Kenya: The Story of Wangari Maathai by Claire A. Nivola (Farrar, Straus and Giroux: 2008)
Wangari's Trees of Peace: A True Story from Africa by Jeanette Winter (Harcourt Children's Books: 2008)
Because of Winn-Dixie by Kate DiCamillo (Candlewick Press: 2001)

Books for Building Complex Thinkers

Nine-year-olds are builders, constructors, fort makers, play makers, plan makers, and goal setters. They are part of our worlds, yet they also like to be just who they are, deeply themselves, quirky, intriguing, eccentric. Let us create, then, reading times together, times that are rich with ritual. These books encourage complex thinking if you read them aloud and reserve time for discussion throughout.

Alex Rider series by Anthony Horowitz (Puffin)
The Chronicles of Narnia by C. S. Lewis (HarperCollins Children's Books: 1950)

D'Aulaires' Book of Greek Myths by Ingri and Edgar D'Aulaire (Delacorte Books for Young Readers: 1992)
From the Mixed-up Files of Mrs. Basil E. Frankweiler by E. L. Konigsburg (Aladdin: 2007)
Harry Potter series by J. K. Rowling (Arthur A. Levine Books)
Mrs. Frisby and the Rats of NIMH by Robert C. O'Brien, illustrated by Zena Bernstein (Simon & Schuster Children's Publishing: 1986)
The Phantom Tollbooth by Norton Juster, illustrated by Jules Feiffer (Random House: 1961)
Trumpet of the Swan by E. B. White (HarperTrophy: 2000)
The Young Merlin Trilogy by Jane Yolen (Magic Carpet Books: 2004)

When one of my daughters was nine and the other seven, we took a long journey to Prince Edward Island. They both loved the book *Anne of Green Gables*. I had read it to them that winter and we came up with the idea to visit the island author Lucy Maud Montgomery had made so famous in her Anne series. To get to this island, you must travel a long way from our hometown in New York. We took a boat and then made the long drive to the remote island. While on the road, we decided to listen to the book again on tape in order to get ready for the world of Anne. As we drove over the many-miles-long extension bridge, we were coming to the end of this marvelous and magical story. I turned to say something to my husband just as we got to a very moving place in the book. He was the only one who had never heard it before.

When I turned to look at him, I realized he was crying, and not just a little bit. Tears were literally coursing down his cheeks as he realized what was going to happen next in this tale, the loss of someone special to Anne. Now if you have read this book, you will understand. If you have not . . . well, you will see. Our girls reached over from the backseat to pat his back kindly. And I realized really just why I had married this wonderful man: he was not only willing to drive us thousands of miles to see Anne's "birthplace," but was also as moved as we had been by her story. There are a few wondrous chapter book read-alouds that, I will be honest, generally girls prefer more than boys, but don't leave your son out. Give the books a try, or let him listen in as you read to your daughters. You may be surprised.

Anne of Green Gables series by Lucy Maud Montgomery (Random House Books for Young Readers)

Little House on the Prairie series by Laura Ingalls Wilder (HarperTrophy)

Little Women by Louisa May Alcott (Signet Classics: 2004)

Historical Tales

Nine-year-olds are listening intently to you as you talk about the daily news and the noise of world events. They can have great conversations with you about history too. There are nonfiction books, and also a few lovely historical novels, you can read aloud that capture different time periods effectively and accurately through the eyes of a child.

Adventures of the Treasure Fleet by Ann Martin Bowler, illustrations by Lak-Khee Tay-Audouard (Turtle Publishing: 2006)
Around the World in a Hundred Years: From Henry the Navigator to Magellan by Jean Fritz, illustrated by Anthony Bacon Venti (Penguin Young Readers Group: 1998)
Betsy and the Emperor by Staton Rabin (Simon Pulse: 2006)
Brothers in Hope: The Story of the Lost Boys of Sudan by Mary Williams (Lee & Low Books: 2007)
Can't You Make Them Behave, King George? by Jean Fritz (Putnam Juvenile: 1996)
Catherine, Called Birdy by Karen Cushman (HarperTrophy: 1995)
Dia's Story Cloth: The Hmong People's Journey of Freedom by Dia Chue, illustrated by Nhia Thao Cha (Lee & Low Books: 1998)
If You Lived . . . series (at all different times in history) by Ann McGovern (Scholastic)
The Midwife's Apprentice by Karen Cushman (HarperTrophy: 1996)
Shh! We're Writing the Constitution by Jean Fritz, illustrated by Tomie dePaola (Penguin Young Reader's Group: 1997)
The True Confessions of Charlotte Doyle by Avi (Orchard Books: 2003)
Viking Ships at Sunrise by Mary Pope Osborne, illustrated by Sal Murdocca (Random House Books for Young Readers: 1998)
We by Alice Schertle, illustrated by Kenneth Addison (Lee & Low Books: 2007)
When Harriet Met Sojourner by Catherine Clinton, illustrated by Shane W. Evans (Amistad: 2007)
Will You Sign Here, John Hancock? by Jean Fritz, illustrated by Trina Schart Hyman (Putnam Juvenile: 1997)
You Want Women to Vote, Lizzie Stanton? by Jean Fritz (Putnam Juvenile: 1999)

Mystery Books

Fourth graders love a good puzzle, a mystery, a discovery. There are many mysteries they can dig into on their own at this age, and so it is really fun to read to them from the same genre. These books are not exactly mysteries of the purest kind, but each has twists and turns and levels of excitement to make all your hearts pound together.

The Mysterious Disappearance of Leon (I Mean Noel) by Ellen Raskin (Puffin: 1989)
Series of Unfortunate Events series by Lemony Snicket (HarperCollins Publishers)
The Westing Game by Ellen Raskin (Puffin: 2004)

Ten Years Old: Exploring New Horizons

Ten is, as Billy Collins the poet once said, "the first big number." It is a year full of wonderings and worries. It is the year you will have the pang of heart for the childhood that is moving from the shores. It is the year you will see the hints of the adult your child will become.

Ten-year-olds like to be seen carrying a big, heavy book around, but if you read aloud to them, they will still snuggle close to you. You can explore heavier themes together through chapter book read-alouds, but do not think you have to give up on picture books at this age. There are in fact many serious picture books for this age level that address all kinds of things your child might be wondering about or struggling with. Books are a bridge from their world to yours, and can help you immeasurably in engaging in deep conversations with your child on matters of grave importance to him. The paintings, photos, or etchings in these sophisticated picture books help to ease the intensity of some of their themes and will often enrich your discussions and philosophical explorations, your child's wonderings and worries about the world.

Extreme Coral Reef! Q&A, Smithsonian Q&A series by Melissa Stewart (HarperCollins Publishers: 2008)
Extreme Planets! Q&A, Smithsonian Q&A series by Mary Kay Carson (HarperCollins Publishers: 2008)
Fox by Margaret Wild, illustrated by Ron Brooks (Kane/Miller Book Publishers: 2006)

Silent Music: A Story of Baghdad by James Rumford (Roaring Brook Press: 2008)
The Man Who Walked Between the Towers by Mordicai Gerstein (Square Fish: 2007)
The Other Side by Jacqueline Woodson, illustrated by E. B. Lewis (Putnam Juvenile: 2001)

Imagination

Ten-year-olds are escaping to their imaginations, and yet they are deeply curious about the "real" world. Children enter their eleventh year with knobby knees and braces, and exit with those intact, but with a new hint of a grown-up fiber, with voices starting to deepen as they enter their adolescence. They are between two worlds, and they know it. Let's ease their transition by giving them books set in imagined lands, with characters similar to themselves. The characters may be fantastical, but their journey into adolescence is nothing if not real.

The City of Ember by Jeanne DuPrau (Yearling: 2004)
Secrets of Droon series by Tony Abbott (Scholastic)
Swordbird by Nancy Yi Fan, illustrated by Mark Zug (HarperCollins Publishers: 2007)

Admiring Great People

The movement at ten is toward friends and the group, and away from parents and teachers. Not too far away, of course, but enough so they feel powerful and independent. They are seeing how far away they can fly without getting lost. This choice to move toward friends and cliques is often fraught with pain and frustration, as maintaining one's desire to be an individual begins to compete with the need to be the same as everyone else. Books celebrating the accomplishments of great people in history will offer them a compelling case for being true to themselves. See Part Three for more books on "heroes," but here are two I love:

Helen Keller: The World in Her Heart by Lesa Cline-Ransome, illustrated by James Ransome (HarperCollins Publishers: 2008)
Ida B. Wells: Let the Truth Be Told by Walter Dean Myers, illustrated by Bonnie Christensen (Amistad: 2008)

Books with Strong Themes

There are some chapter books that are at an independent level for older children and yet are terrific as read-alouds for you and your ten-year-old. You may have to give her some background information on the context of the book, but you will both be swept in. Since your child might not be ready for these books on an independent level, reading together feels sensible and exciting all at the same time. Some of the following books are really intense thematically, so look over the content before reading aloud.

Freak the Mighty by Rodman Philbrick (Scholastic: 2001)
The Giver by Lois Lowry (Laurel Leaf: 2002)
Heat by Mike Lupica (Puffin: 2007)
His Dark Materials series by Philip Pullman (Knopf Books for Young Readers: 2007)

Reimagining the Classics

Ten-year-olds are young and old at the same time, in the same moment. There are several excellent classic stories that have been reimagined with paintings and pictures to support the younger reader.

One fantastic example is *The Canterbury Tales* by Barbara Cohen and Trina Schart Hyman. It begins with: "One sweet day in April in the year 1386 a man named Geoffrey Chaucer mounted his horse . . ." This book, with its magnificent paintings, is a whimsical and extraordinary retelling of Chaucer's classic tale. Phrases like the one above along with descriptions like "a somewhat important man" are so surprising and subtle that the most sophisticated ten-year-old will get a tremendous kick out of all their nuances, while a less sturdy reader will simply enjoy the good tales even if the language is somewhat over his head at times.

The same is true for the meticulously crafted and emotional poem by Walt Whitman, set to gorgeous illustration in the illuminating picture book illustrated by Loren Long.

The Canterbury Tales by Barbara Cohen, illustrated by Trina Schart Hyman (HarperCollins Publishers: 1988)
When I Heard the Learn'd Astronomer by Walt Whitman, illustrated by Loren Long (Simon & Schuster Children's Publishing: 2004)

Discussing the Creative Process

The ten-year-old is immensely curious about how things work and where ideas come from. There are a great number of books which let us into the artist's and author's process and life story and explore what factors influenced their craft. Age ten is a wonderful time to talk about the creative process, and there are some really well written, special books that capture the lively minds of creative people.

Leonardo, The Beautiful Dreamer by Robert Byrd (Penguin Young Readers Group: *2003)*

Boy: Tales of Childhood by Roald Dahl (Puffin: 1999)

Bill Peet: An Autobiography by Bill Peet (Houghton Mifflin Company: 1994)

Magazines for Ten-Year-Olds

Across this year, building confidence and capacity are key for your ten-year-old: we want him to engage with all kinds of new forms and content in a zestful, spirited manner.

Science Magazines

Ask; www.cricketmag.com
Kids Discover; www.kidsdiscover.com
Muse; www.cricketmag.com
National Geographic Explorer; www.magma.nationalgeographic.com/ngexplorer/index.html
Odyssey; www.odysseymagazine.com

Arts & Literature Magazines

Creative Kids; www.prufrock.com/prufrock_jm_createkids.cfm
Cricket; www.cricketmag.com
Highlights; www.highlights.com
New Moon (for girls); www.newmoon.org
Spider; www.cricketmag.com
Stone Soup; www.stonesoup.com

Sports Magazines

Sports Illustrated for Kids; www.sikids.com

Culture Magazines

Faces; www.cobblestonepub.com
Footsteps; www.cobblestonepub.com
Cobblestone; www.cobblestonepub.com
Calliope; www.cobblestonepub.com
Skipping Stones; www.SkippingStones.org

Conventions

Ten-year-olds are serious about conventions. They want to be conventional themselves! They are trying to fit in; they are constantly looking at one another to see how the social group behaves. We want to encourage our children to adhere to certain standards: like having good manners in the real world, using correct grammar will give them a sense of ease and belonging. Then, once those structures are in place, they have the freedom to explore their own distinctly unconventional voices. There are wonderful books that can help you have conversations with your child about some of these techniques of language. Don't be afraid to talk about what you don't know that well either. These books are designed to help guide you, and so you can learn too.

Eats, Shoots & Leaves: Why, Commas Really Do *Make a Difference*! by Lynne Truss, illustrated by Bonnie Timmons (Putnam Juvenile: 2006)
Eats, Shoots & Leaves: The Zero Tolerance Approach to Punctuation by Lynne Truss (Gotham: 2006)
The Elements of Style Illustrated by William Strunk Jr. and E. B. White, illustrated by Maira Kalman (Penguin Press: 2007)
Hairy, Scary, Ordinary: What Is an Adjective? by Brian Cleary, illustrated by Jenya Prosmitsky (First Avenue Editions: 2001)

Poetry

Angels Ride Bikes and Other Fall Poems/Los Ángeles Andan en Bicicletas y Otros Poemas de Otono by Francisco X. Alarcón, illustrated by Maya Christina Gonzalez (Children's Book Press: 2005)
The Butterfly Jar by Jeff Moss (Bantam: 1989)
Doodle Dandies: Poems That Take Shape by J. Patrick Lewis (Aladdin: 2002)

The Flag of Childhood: Poems from the Middle East edited by Naomi Shihab Nye (Simon & Schuster: 2002)

Inner Chimes: Poems on Poetry edited by Bobbye Goldstein, illustrated by Jane Breskin Zalben (Boyd Mills Press: 1992)

Joyful Noise: Poems for Two Voices by Paul Fleischman, illustrated by Eric Beddows (HarperCollins Publishers: 1992)

A Kick in the Head: An Everyday Guide to Poetic Forms edited by Paul Janeczko, illustrated by Chris Raschka (Candlewick Press: 2005)

Love to Mama: A Tribute to Mothers by Pat Mora, illustrated by Paula Barragan (Lee & Low Books: 2004)

In his poem "On Turning Ten," the great poet Billy Collins also wrote: " . . . as I walk through the universe in my sneakers/It is time to say good-bye to my imaginary friends/time to turn the first big number."

Here you are together, in the moment of that turning. I hope the books listed in this chapter will accompany you as you sail upon glorious adventures of the mind with your children.

Now, let us journey into a different realm of time: emotional turning points. These are the moments that transcend age and allow us to talk across generations with our children about all kinds of things. The next chapter is a collection of books around fifty core themes that I have found resonate with children throughout their childhoods. I have found them to be of great comfort to me and to my daughters and to all my students. I hope they will be the same for you.

Part III

The Emotional "When": Fifty Essential Themes

7. How to Make Best Use of the Fifty Themes

What follows are fifty themes that for me are heartbeats under all of my teaching and parenting, fifty themes that truly cross age ranges and can apply to family reading experiences together. These are themes I want to share with children, and also themes I hear from children that preoccupy them in deeply felt ways.

You might want to read through all of the themes now, gathering titles for future reading. Or, you might want to skip directly to a theme that you know will speak to your child at this very moment. Within themed sections, the books are listed with brief descriptions. For certain books, a special "Talk about It" section offers a guide for discussing key ideas from the reading with your child, and integrating it with her day-to-day life. These "Talk about It" sections are recommendations for talking points, but not mandatory. They are guides for you, but you will create your own great conversations as you listen deeply to your child and follow your instincts.

Throughout this list, you will find books that speak to issues in a variety of ways. They are by turns funny, poignant, tender, profound, and silly. They are all deeply reassuring: someone else has felt exactly the same as your child does, no matter the size or scope of the issue.

Each book on this list is annotated so you get a deeply felt impression of the books and can best make your own decision as to which ones would be just right for you and your child to read together.

I have deliberately selected books that will cross a span of ages, from birth to ten. You may be reading these selections to all your children together, and these books cross ages well. You may be spending one-on-one time with one of your children, or with your only child, and these books, though some are designed for older or younger readers, are also able to travel across a time span with you and can be revisited as your child grows.

In this section, I have labeled each book with a code to help you in determining which ones might be best in each section for your particular child. You will see that each book is marked with one of the following initials:

E = emerging
D = developing
M = maturing

The age codes refer more to your child's emotional development than his or her chronological age. Think of *emerging* readers as children as from birth to age four, *developing* children from four to around seven, and *maturing* children from after seven to age ten, but your child may be different, and so while you can use the codes as a guide, don't let them restrict you in your selections.

Please know that I want to encourage you to make your own wise choices for and with your children. You may have a child who really loves to return to the familiar warmth of the slower-paced book, the "easier" text, the simpler story, even when he is eight or nine or ten. This is just fine. Beyond that, there are books I have identified as *E* for emerging, but that is only because they are great for all readers, beginning with the youngest. Don't let the codes stop you from exploring every single book on this list, no matter what the age of your child.

Conversely, you may have a child who is uniquely able to process heavier information and themes and is really ready to talk with you about more sophisticated ideas and to sit through longer, denser text. So then even though the book is coded for the more "mature" reader, you may be interested in reading this book to your five-year-old. That is okay too, if it's comfortable for you and your child.

These codes should serve as a flexible framework for you and for your family. Remember, children are the most forgiving audiences of all. If, as the reading begins, you feel you have not made the right choice for your child, simply stop and say, "Let's save this one for another time." This probably will happen very rarely, as you will build your understanding of what your children like and what works best for you all.

This list was a joy to compile: many of my favorite books over the years are on it, as well as some spectacular and exciting new ones, fresh off the presses.

All together, for me, they represent must-read books that will provoke, entertain, inspire, and move you and your child to what I hope are conversations that nourish your relationship.

Inevitably, you will feel there are some of your favorites, both book titles and themes themselves, that are missing from this list. These are the hazards of creating lists, and also the pleasure. I invite you to add your favorites to the mix by visiting my Web site, whattoreadwhen.com, and adding your own choices.

Find that couch, that nook, and get ready for the journey of a lifetime. Reading aloud is one of the best things you can do to fortify your child, and one of the best things you can do to nurture your relationship. Here are fifty great themes for many precious hours spent together in a world of literature. Enjoy!

8. The Fifty Themes: All the Best Books for the Moments That Matter Most

ADOPTION

There was a time not so long ago when adoption was far more complicated to talk about. Adoptees and their families often felt as if they were traveling on a new terrain on their own, a journey that changed over time and as relationships developed. As a child who grew up in a family with multiple adoptions, I wish very much that there had been books for us to read together while I was growing up. Both for me, as the biological child in a family of multiple adoptees, and for my siblings, as adopted members of the family, it would have helped us so much to have a forum to discuss some of the aspects of adoption more openly. My parents most certainly did their best, but the experience was new for them too. Literature offers a venue for children to express themselves, and for parents to do the same. The best children's literature is about complexity. The story of life is about the poignancy of joy and the poignancy of sorrow too. What are the feelings we face as our family is created? What are the ways we can learn to become a family? In modern children's literature, we are so lucky to have the complex and joyous world of adoption as a story that is not just told, but celebrated. Hold your child tight, be conscious of this complexity, but don't let it consume you. Instead, let it inspire you, and use these words to accompany you on this precious journey.

I Love You Like Crazy Cakes by Rose Lewis, illustrated by Jane Dyer (Little, Brown and Company: 2000) (D)

Read to an adopted child, or any child, to show the love of a mother for her young daughter.

In this book, the mother narrates to her adopted daughter the story of how she traveled to China to bring her home. The book overflows with the love and connection that the mother feels for her new daughter.

Talk about It: You may want to use this book to talk about the relationship between the mother and her adopted daughter. Discuss how their love and connection transcends these differences. This book is intended for a young audience, not for an older child who might have questions about cross-cultural adoption or international adoption. The focus is a mother's love for her new daughter.

- What is adoption?
- Discuss where the mother had to travel to meet her new daughter. Does this help to show the love that the mother feels for her daughter? What is the meaning of family?

Jin Woo by Eve Bunting, illustrated by Chris K. Soentpiet (Clarion Books: 2001) (D)

Read to discuss the feelings of a biological child who will welcome an adopted sibling into his family.

Although his parents are excited to welcome their new adopted baby from Korea, Dave is not excited to meet Jin Woo. At the airport he refuses to believe that this little baby will be his new brother. As Jin starts to become part of the family, Dave moves through an emotional journey toward accepting his new brother and sharing his parents' love.

The Little Green Goose by Adele Sansone, illustrated by Alan Marks (North-South Books: 1999) (E)

Read to introduce the topic of adoption in a fun and unique way.

Mr. Goose always wanted a child, but when he finally gets an egg to take care of, he gets a big surprise when it hatches. His child may look nothing like him, but Mr. Goose loves him the way he is. Little Green Goose, however, has a bit of a harder time realizing where he belongs. After being teased in the barnyard, going on a journey to find his real mother, and enduring a bit of soul-searching, the Little Green Goose finally understands the meaning of love, belonging, and acceptance.

Talk about It: Although this story takes place in a barnyard, it introduces the real challenges an adopted child may face, particularly if he or she looks different than his or her parents. The story teaches us that love is stronger than appearance; use this concept as a basis for further conversation.

- ✦ What is Mr. Goose looking for at the beginning of the story? How do the hens and other animals in the barnyard react to Mr. Goose? Why do you think that Mr. Goose wants a child?
- ✦ Why do the chicks make fun of the Little Green Goose? How would you feel if you were the Little Green Goose?
- ✦ What does the Little Green Goose discover at the end of the story? What is the lesson of the story?

A Mother for Choco by Keiko Kasza (Puffin Books: 1992) (E)

Read when your child wonders about the qualities that make a person a mother.

Choco is a little yellow bird; he has no mother, so he goes in search of a mommy who looks like him. No other animal looks quite right, so he finds himself crying and alone. Finally, Mrs. Bear shows him that the qualities of a mother aren't in the way she looks but in how she loves and cares for her children.

Talk about It: What does Mrs. Bear show is important about being a mother?

- ✦ What happens when Choco asks the other animals if they could be his mother?
- ✦ When Choco is upset, he thinks about the things that he wishes a mother would do for him. What are they? How does Mrs. Bear respond to Choco?
- ✦ When do you think Choco realizes that Mrs. Bear could be his mother and that he could live with her? How does Choco know?

My Family Is Forever by Nancy Carlson (Penguin Young Readers Group: 2004) (D)

Read to discover the many different characteristics that make up a loving family.

The narrator tells the reader that her parents wanted to have a child to love, and so they adopted her. Even though some of her friends have similar physical characteristics to their parents, the narrator knows that her "family is forever" because they love each other, support each other, and enjoy being together.

Over the Moon: An Adoption Tale by Karen Katz (Henry Holt and Company: 1997) (D)

Read to express the joy of adoption.

A couple goes on a magical journey to meet and to bring home the daughter whom they had dreamed of long before she was even born. Beautiful illustrations fill this adoption tale with life and joy.

Pablo's Tree by Pat Mora, illustrated by Cecily Lang (Simon & Schuster Children's Publishing: 1994) (D)

Read this to discuss the love and tradition in three generations of a family.

On the day Pablo's mother adopted him, his grandfather planted a special tree to commemorate the day. Every year on Pablo's birthday, his grandfather specially decorates the tree for him. This year, Pablo wonders how his *abuelo* will decorate the tree. He looks forward to hearing the story of his adoption and seeing his tree, and continuing the birthday tradition.

Talk about It: Use this book to talk about the stories of your child's adoption or birth. Use it as a time to bond with your child; let him ask you questions about important moments in his young life, or moments that you remember from your own childhood.

- The story of Pablo's tree reminds me of when . . .
- Talk about the special bond between Pablo and his grandfather. Does your child have a special bond with a grandparent or another adult?
- Create a ritual like the one Pablo has with your child.

Tell Me Again About the Night I Was Born by Jamie Lee Curtis, illustrated by Laura Cornell (HarperCollins Publishers: 1996) (D)

Read for a deeply respectful and loving story about the importance of story in families to create meaning and identity.

A girl asks her parents to tell her the very special story of her birth and adoption, a story she remembers quite well from having heard it so often.

APPRECIATING THE NATURAL WORLD

Children experience nature with full-force intensity. What we as adults have to remind ourselves to pay attention to, our child is noticing every single day. The turning colors of leaves, the cold crystals of snow, the orange streak of a sunset, the small miracle of the perfect swirl of a clamshell found on the beach: these are the daily signs of magic for a young child.

Literature fosters these small passions, and tells our children that we too feel the beauty of nature and are moved by it. The earliest stirrings of conservation and environmental awareness can be gently nurtured through these conversations. In this era of global warming and a near certainty that we are damaging the Earth, read-alouds of this nature can be not only beautiful and poetic, but also instructive and informative. We do not want to scare our youngest readers with grim forecasts, but we can include older readers in conversations (especially when we are reading to multiage groups in our family). Read on one level to the younger ones by admiring the qualities of the natural world, while at the same time begin a more sophisticated conversation with older children about the implications of what we humans are doing to the Earth. For example, a book like *Welcome to the Ice House* by Jane Yolen can be "read" solely for the extraordinary pictures throughout, or as a way to launch a conversation with an older child about how the Arctic is becoming dangerously warmer, and how this affects us all.

Our children are growing up in a world that is thankfully far more conscious of the effects of our behavior on the natural world, but this awareness can be perceived by your child as quite frightening. While we are familiar with news about global warming and extinction, the decimation of the environment, and the need for green innovation, to a child's ears this can all sound incredibly overwhelming and nightmarish. Literature introduces the child to the possibility for social action and engagement with the real issues of the world through love. We love the gray wolf, so we want to be sure to protect it. We love a tundra or a glacial terrain, so we want to advocate for it. Love leads to action.

An Egg Is Quiet by Dianna Aston, illustrated by Sylvia Long (Chronicle Books: 2006) (D)

Read to learn about many beautiful and purposeful varieties of eggs; relate eggs to the miracle of animal life that comes from within.

This book is a beautiful tribute to a unique part of the natural world. Eggs nurture so many baby animals before they are born. This book uncovers the countless varieties of eggs, and the animals that are born from them. No egg is alike; we learn the similarities and differences between the many types of eggs, and the deliberateness of nature in making sure that they protect the young growing inside.

Talk about It: Use the beautiful colors and textures in the illustrations as a guide to revel in the varieties of nature and why the egg, something we might see as so ordinary, is actually such an important part of the natural world.

- Discuss all of the illustrations of the different eggs. Which egg do you particularly like, which do you think is interesting looking? Research some of the animals that come from these different eggs.
- Pick a page that describes or compares a certain aspect of the egg, such as its shape. Talk about why the shape is important for the different animals (where the animals live, their predators, etc.).

Beetle Bop by Denise Fleming (Harcourt Children's Books: 2007) (E)

Read with a child who loves beetles, bugs, insects, or any variety of these incredible creatures.

This book uses beautiful rhymes to celebrate the natural world right in our own backyard. The author enables her young audience to glimpse the lives of the beetles and bugs they search for on a summer afternoon. Plus, it has gorgeous illustrations.

Extreme Animals: The Toughest Creatures on Earth by Nicola Davies, illustrated by Neal Layton (Candlewick Press: 2006) (M)

Read when you want to understand how humans compare with the "toughest creatures on Earth" in surviving unbelievable conditions. Read if you've been pondering nature and enjoy science.

This humorous book discusses the incredible animals, insects, and plants that can survive in extreme environmental conditions where humans would surely die. It clearly explains the reasons why these extreme creatures are able to survive in the Arctic, hatch eggs in the South Pole, allow their body temperature to drop to 23 degrees Fahrenheit, survive life in the desert, spend years without food, live in the mouth of a volcano or at the bottom of the sea, and thrive under intense air or water pressure. What is the toughest creature on Earth?

Talk about It: This is a great "why" book, with answers to some questions that your child may have wondered, and others that are simply fascinating. Take time to make sure that your child understands the explanations on each page. Celebrate the crazy, and sometimes downright unbelievable, facts about the natural world. Read with an older child; vocabulary and concepts may be too difficult for little ones.

- Discuss the facts that you find most unbelievable. Enjoy the concept that nature can be hard to understand sometimes, but above all so resourceful and deliberate. Share examples from the book.
- Imagine if you were one of these "extreme" creatures. Which would you prefer to be and why?

The Eyes of a Gray Wolf by Jonathan London, illustrated by Jon Van Zyle (Chronicle Books: 1993) (E)

Read to celebrate the regal life of the gray wolf, the intimate connection between animals and nature, and the importance of keeping this connection alive.

Follow the majestic Gray Wolf through the night in this beautiful, haunting story. Notice the reflection of the moon in Gray Wolf's eyes as he leaps a frozen creek, howls toward the far mountains, hunts using the light of the moon, and discovers White Wolf, with whom he will create a new wolf pack. Simple text and simple illustrations make this book very effective.

Gone Wild: An Endangered Animal Alphabet by David McLimans (Walker Books for Young Readers: 2006) (D)

Read to learn more about endangered species, or to pique a child's interest in becoming an advocate for the world's most threatened animals.

Author David McLimans uses art and graphic design to incorporate the alphabet into beautiful images of animals; each letter of the alphabet introduces a new endangered species. On each page is a box with details about the animal, why it is threatened, and ways that the reader can help. The images will fascinate and enthrall older readers, especially those interested in graphic design.

Gorilla Doctors: Saving Endangered Great Apes by Pamela S. Turner (Houghton Mifflin Company: 2008) (M)

Read to experience the adventurous but grave mission of scientists trying to save mountain gorillas in Rwanda and Uganda.

This nonfiction book full of color photographs follows the work of the scientists in the Mountain Gorilla Veterinary Project (MGVP), which is trying to save threatened mountain gorillas in eastern Africa. More important, it offers a glimpse into the life of the majestic and seriously endangered mountain gorilla.

The Great Kapok Tree: A Tale of the Amazon Rain Forest by Lynne Cherry (Harcourt Children's Books: 2000) (M)

Read to learn about the interconnection of creatures in the natural world, the effects of harming nature, and the importance of conserving the rain forest.

This story revolves around a great kapok tree in the Amazon rain forest, and all of the animals that rely on its shelter and nourishment. One day, a man comes into the forest to cut down the tree; before he can do so, the animals take their turns pleading on the tree's behalf.

Hurricanes by Seymour Simon (Smithsonian, Collins, an imprint of HarperCollins: 2003) (D)

Read to learn all about the formation of hurricanes, the destruction they cause, and details of several major hurricanes that have devastated parts of the United States. Talk about the powerful pictures that accompany the text.

What causes hurricanes? How do people forecast hurricanes? Learn the answers to these questions and more in this evocative and informative book on hurricanes. Seymour Simon uses real-life examples and photos to document the effects of these powerful storms. He shows how forecasters use satellite maps to track pending storms. This is a great read for children who are interested in the intersection of current events and science.

Look to the North: A Wolf Pup Diary by Jean Craighead George, illustrated by Lucia Washburn (HarperCollins Publishers: 1997) (D)

Read to understand how wolf families are so inextricably tied to natural cycles.

In this diary, we learn about the life and growth of three young wolf pups; each important moment in their development coincides with an important moment in nature's cycle. As the pups develop, they learn to play, communicate, and create their own personalities, and the reader learns that the wolves' lives follow patterns not unlike our own.

A Mother's Journey by Sandra Markle, illustrated by Alan Marks (Charlesbridge Publishing: 2006) (E)

Read and be fascinated by the journey of the Emperor penguin mother, and touched by the sacrifices she makes for her young.

Follow the journey of a mother emperor penguin who braves the harsh Antarctic winter, traveling to the sea to find food for her baby chick. She then must retrace her steps, walking back across Antarctica, to feed her hungry little one. The story of the emperor penguin is based in facts; however, it is so moving that it becomes a beautiful narrative of lyrical prose.

Snowflake Bentley by Jacqueline Briggs Martin (Houghton Mifflin Company: 1998) (D)

Read after a first snow, to admire the uniqueness of each individual snowflake.

Snowflakes are an amazing testament to the brilliance of nature; children are particularly mesmerized by the idea that every flake is different. This book tells the true story of a boy who was so captivated by snowflakes that he acquired a microscope and camera to document each individual snowflake crystal. As an adult, he used mathematics to calculate their structures. Not only does this book celebrate nature, it also shows how a man dedicated his life to appreciating the natural world.

Stopping by Woods on a Snowy Evening by Robert Frost and Susan Jeffers (Dutton Children's Books: 2001) (E)

Read curled up on a snowy evening, before going to bed,

Memories, wonderings, and observations come together in this well-loved collection of poems. Beautiful illustrations by Susan Jeffers bring Frost's poems to life.

The Sun Is So Quiet by Nikki Giovanni, illustrated by Ashley Bryan (Henry Holt and Company: 1996) (E)

Read to stir a variety of emotions and memories about the seasons and nature.

This collection of poems and its accompanying illustrations will make you smile as you feel winter's chill, a rainbow, and the sun upon your face. Ashley

Bryan is a magnificent illustrator who brings a reverberating energy to these poems through his interpretations.

The Tale of Pale Male by Jeanette Winter (Harcourt Children's Books: 2007) (D)

Read this story to start a discussion about the inevitable conflicts between humans and nature.

Pale Male, a red-tailed hawk, and his mate build a nest on the top of a Fifth Avenue apartment building in New York City. While bird-watchers are enthusiastic to see the family of birds grow, some residents start complaining about the effects of having these hunters in the neighborhood. It all leads to a conflict between different values and beliefs with the lives of the birds caught in the middle. What will be the fate of the birds?

Welcome to the Ice House by Jane Yolen, illustrated by Lauren Regan (G. P. Putnam's Sons: 1998) (D)

Read to learn about the beautiful and intriguing seasons of the Arctic tundra.

Jane Yolen uses poetry to explore the seasons of the Arctic tundra. Her excellent use of language paints a picture of the animals moving about the snowy terrain; the reader will feel the contrast between the cold winter and, finally, the emerging summer.

Winter Eyes: Poems and Paintings by Douglas Florian (Greenwillow Books: 1999) (D)

Read to revisit the winter season with new eyes and ears.

This book encourages readers to take a moment to appreciate all the special and unique things about winter: the struggle and triumph of trudging up a hill pulling a sled, the comfort of smoke coming from a chimney, or the orange sun on the gray horizon. If you enjoy this book, for a different season, read *Handsprings*, *Summersaults,* and *Autumnblings*, also by Douglas Florian.

Wolves by Emily Gravett (Simon & Schuster: 2006) (D)

Read this with a child to learn about wolves in a humorous way.

This entertaining book depicts a rabbit reading an informative book about wolves that he shares with readers. He is so absorbed in the book that he doesn't realize that he is about to encounter a real wolf who is sneaking up behind him! Don't worry, however, there's an alternate ending for more sensitive children.

A BAD DAY

It is so painful when our children have a hard day. It really and truly has the power to break our hearts. Literature gives us a way to take a bad day seriously enough to talk about it; it lets us soothe the wounds of life with tender words. Or sometimes, best of all, books let us just collapse in a fit of giggles when there is nothing else for it but that. Through it all, the best children's literature respects the dignity of a child who is navigating a sometimes deeply problematic world where unkindness and confusion do exist.

The characters in these books are real children: Alexander, Lilly, and Sophie all feel as human as can be. They are not perfect, either, so their bad day may or may not be the result of some of their own actions. And yet, there is no blame. Each of these authors has enormous compassion and respect for the struggles of a child and how human interaction can be painful at times.

Literature helps us to embrace the idea that none of us are perfect. We sometimes handle a bad day with aplomb, while the very next time we handle it not so well. Reading aloud to your child, you can both give one another a break, especially when the bad day had something to do with you together. Great literature does not ignore or deny confusions. It sorts through them, making sense of them by telling a story that everyone can relate to and talk about peacefully and reflectively, after the hard day is done, and there is the promise of a better day to come.

Alexander and the Terrible, Horrible, No Good, Very Bad Day

by Judith Viorst, illustrated by Ray Cruz (Simon & Schuster Children's Publishing: 1987) (D)

Read when your child has had a terrible, horrible, no good, very bad day.

Alexander wakes up to a terrible, horrible, no good, very bad day. He realizes though, that maybe it's okay to sometimes have a very bad day.

Talk about It: Alexander's day just keeps getting worse. But sometimes, what appears to be a very bad day turns out to be not so awful after all.

- Why did Alexander have such a terrible, horrible, no good, very bad day? How did he handle having such a bad day?

- What would you describe as a bad day? How do you handle those days that just keep getting worse?

Bad Day at Riverbend by Chris Van Allsburg (Houghton Mifflin Company: 1995) (D)

Read with your child to discover a town trying to adapt to change.

The quiet town of Riverbend is disrupted one day when "some kind of shiny, greasy slime" appears. As the book progresses, the reader discovers that the town is set in a coloring book, and the "slime" is color, disrupting the peaceful black-and-white town. This book shows how a group of people deals with change through humor and innovation.

How Are You Peeling? Foods with Moods by Saxton Freymann and Joost Elffers (Scholastic: 2007) (E)

Read this book to talk about emotion and learn how to express different feelings.

Colorful pictures depict fruit and vegetables reacting to different situations with emotions ranging from confusion and frustration, to surprise and amusement. Young readers will learn how to articulate their own emotions and to identify feelings in others.

Lilly's Purple Plastic Purse, one in a series by Kevin Henkes (Greenwillow Books: 1996) (D)

Read for a great school story about how to handle not always getting your way.

Lilly loves school and her teacher, Mr. Slinger. So when Lilly gets a new purple plastic purse and movie-star sunglasses, she really, really wants to show her class. But Mr. Slinger asks her to wait, and Lilly does something she regrets later.

Talk about It: This is a wonderful conversation starter on how to handle a situation where you do not get your way. It is very hard to learn how to wait your turn to share something special, or how to sit quietly when all you want to do is talk. Sometimes it takes making a mistake to learn a very important lesson.

- Has someone ever done something to hurt your feelings? How did you respond?

- Have you ever hurt someone's feelings? How did you feel after you hurt their feelings? What did Lilly do?
- What did Lily do when she did not get her way? What do you think about that?

Mrs. Biddlebox by Linda Smith, illustrated by Marla Frazee (Harcourt Children's Books: 2006) (E)

Read with your child to talk about making a bad day into something much better.

Mrs. Biddlebox wakes up on the wrong side of the bed and from there everything goes from bad to worse. The weather is gray, she has a headache, and her morning tea is bitter. With her can-do spirit, however, Mrs. Biddlebox refuses to be discouraged and bakes a delicious cake, turning her day right around.

Penelope Nuthatch and the Big Surprise by David Gavril (Harry N. Abrams Books for Young Readers: 2006) (D)

Read this with your child to talk about making the best of a day that does not turn out the way you expected.

Penelope is excited when her friend Luther tells her he has a big surprise planned. She assumes he means the ballet, but the friends go to Wet and Wild Water World instead. Penelope is upset at first because she does not want to get her nice clothes wet, but, in the end, she discovers that she can adapt to the surprise and enjoy herself.

Rainy Day! by Patricia Lakin, illustrated by Scott Nash (Dial Books for Young Readers: 2007) (D)

Read with your child to see how a boring day can be turned into an adventure.

When four friends are bored of being cooped up inside on a rainy day, they decide to venture out, despite the weather. Decked out in their rainy-day gear, the friends invent games and meet all sorts of interesting creatures. Eventually they end up at the library, reading about adventures like their own.

When Sophie Gets Angry—Really, Really Angry . . . by Molly Bang (Scholastic: 1999) (E)

Read to learn new ways to deal with anger.

When Sophie discovers she has to share her stuffed gorilla with her sister, she gets really, really angry: so angry that the reader can feel her anger escalate.

There are only a few words per page; lots of context cues and illustrations work as scaffolding to help explain the intense emotion of the story.

BATH TIME

Nothing soothes a tired toddler more than a warm bath and the nearness of you. There are magical powers in bath time. It's a great time to read to your child. As he plays and relaxes, you have his attention. Let him always subconsciously connect the warmth of the water and the excitement of playing in the bath to the sounds and playful quality of reading.

When my children were little and they'd had a hard day, I'd put them in the bath with an ice pop and sit on the rim of the tub while they sucked quietly on their pop and soaked in the warm water. I'd sit there and read them familiar books as the water cooled down and the pop disappeared. The bath time was as much for me to regroup and recharge as it was for them. If your child has a low threshold for attention, and does not really love to cuddle up at bedtime with you for reading, the bath may very well be the place he learns to love being read to.

After a long day of work, when you are too tired to do the whole bath, bed, and read-aloud routine that you might have so carefully constructed, feel free to conflate them all into one magnificent bath-time experience. Then whisk them out of the tub, wrap them up in a warm towel, give them a final hug, and off to bed they go. Then you should sit down and have that cup of tea or glass of wine and read your own book.

Bathtime for Biscuit (My First I Can Read series) by Alyssa Satin Capucilli, illustrated by Pat Schories (HarperCollins Publishers: 1999) (E)

Read with your child to talk about taking a bath.

Biscuit is energetic and enthusiastic about doing everything—except taking a bath. When he finds a friend to play with, he gets even dirtier and his owner finally gets him to take a bath, and enjoys one herself.

Do Pirates Take Baths? by Kathy Tucker, illustrated by Nadine Bernard Westcott (Albert Whitman & Company: 1997) (E)

Read to make bath time a fun adventure.

This bouncy jaunt through the daily activities of pirates is presented in the form of thirteen simple questions that you can explore with your child.

Whether your child is in the bath or preparing for one, the pursuits of these seafaring rogues will make any task seem humorous and fun.

Estelle Takes a Bath by Jill Esbaum, illustrated by Mary Newell DePalma (Henry Holt and Company: 2006) (D)

Read to bring new meaning and humor to the idea of bath time.

Estelle is relaxing in her bubble bath after a long day, never suspecting she has the company of a little mouse in the bathroom. When they suddenly notice each other, things start to get just a little bit hectic.

Harry the Dirty Dog by Gene Zion (HarperCollins Children's Books: 2006) (E)

Read this with your child to laugh over the consequences of not taking a bath.

Harry the dog hates bath time so much that he buries his scrubbing brush in the backyard so his family cannot bathe him. Harry then goes out and spends the day playing, having fun getting so dirty that no one can recognize him. Sadly, Harry's family cannot recognize him either—until he uncovers his brush and begs for a bath.

King Bidgood's in the Bathtub by Audrey Wood, illustrated by Don Wood (Harcourt Children's Books: 2005) (D)

Read to learn how even kings love the bath.

King Bidgood refuses to leave his bathtub in order to pursue his kingly duties. When the serious members of the court try to convince him, the king drags them into the bath to conduct business and other matters while soapy, bubbly, and wet. Will the king spend the entire day in the tub?

Talk about It: This book is about bath time, but also about the value of being silly, even as a king. Talk about the contrast between the king and the other characters who try to persuade him to get out of the tub. Talk about times to be serious, but also when to be silly.

- Take some time to look at the detailed illustrations. What do you notice about the king? What do you notice about the members of his court? How do they change throughout the story?
- What part of your day makes you feel silly?

My First Word Bath Book by DK Publishing (Dorling Kindersley Publishing: 1999) (E)

Read with your child to learn new words during bath time.

Learn to name new objects and identify words with this spongy and colorful bath time book.

Splish-Splash: Baby Bundt by Jaime Harper (Candlewick Press: 2007) (E)

Read with your child to learn about a bath-time routine.

The routines of bath time become a recipe for a happy baby in this sweet book. Baby and Big Sister demonstrate the perfect combination of rubber ducks, soap, bath mitts, and toys to create a sparkling clean little one.

Take Me Out of the Bathtub and Other Silly Dilly Songs by Alan Katz, illustrated by David Catrow (Margaret E. McElderry: 2001) (E)

Read to put a spin on popular tunes, which your child will love.

"Take Me Out of the Bathtub," sung to the tune of "Take Me Out to the Ball Game," features a boy who has gone through three bars of soap while bathing. Although "Take Me Out of the Bathtub" is the title song, each page introduces a different well-known tune and new lyrics about an everyday childhood incident.

Touch and Feel Bathtime (Dorling Kindersley Publishing: 2003) (E)

Read with your child for an interactive bath experience.

Bath time comes alive in this touch-and-feel board book. Each page contains a common bath time item, like a towel, to teach your child about taking a bath anytime.

BECOMING SOMEONE WHO LOVES TO WRITE

What I have seen over and over in my work in kindergarten classrooms is that children instinctively love to write. From the most struggling student to the child who enters kindergarten knowing all the letters, children long for the knowledge the alphabet brings. The code of the alphabet is enchanting, mysterious, and beautiful. We may recall some negative experiences about writing from our own school days, but I urge you not to pass that along to your own children. Give them the chance to love language and admire the magic of the alphabet. Perhaps they will guide you.

One of my kindergarten students once said that her favorite memory was when she learned how to write the letter *A*. She said she got a "shiver" when she did it for the first time. Writers of all ages will understand. Long after we know how to write the alphabet itself, we feel that same shiver when we compose a sentence that works, or tell a story that conveys a big idea. Universal literacy will mean that we all get to not only tell our stories, but also to hear the stories of people from all over the world. Language is the architecture by which humanity tells its stories. And stories are what connect us to one another. Give your child a sense of the magic and wonder of what language can do.

The Boy Who Loved Words by Roni Schotter, illustrated by Giselle Potter (Random House Children's Books: 2006) (D)

Read to find the perfect word, the perfect collection of words, or even just to enjoy the beautiful illustrations.

Words, words, words. Selig loves words. He collects new words and words he likes, writing them down on pieces of paper. "He stuffed new ones inside his shirt, down his socks, up his sleeves, under his hat." Selig's practical father and robust mother wonder what Selig will do with all of his words. His classmates tease him and even Selig begins to doubt the usefulness of his word collection, until one night a genie comes to visit and suddenly Selig finds a purpose.

Eats, Shoots & Leaves: Why, Commas Really Do Make a Difference! by Lynne Truss, illustrated by Bonnie Timmons (G. P. Putnam's Sons: 2006) (D)

Read to realize the serious trouble that can ensue with errors in comma placement.

This is a hilarious book that will teach even the most punctuation-reluctant child why commas are so important in writing. Illustrations help the reader to imagine the chaotic and strange things that might occur if we literally behaved according to the meanings of poorly punctuated sentences. Grammatical explanations for each sentence are in the back of the book.

Grass Sandals: The Travels of Basho by Dawnine Spivak, illustrated by Demi (Atheneum Books: 1997) (M)

Read to find writing inspiration from nature in each small moment.

Writing can be so inspired by nature that it begins to resemble the mountains, trees, and rivers; these are the Japanese characters formed into the simple haikus written by the famous poet Basho. This book follows Basho as he journeys through Japan in his grass sandals, writing beautiful haiku about his precious moments with nature. Excellent illustrations propel this introduction to ancient Japanese culture. Notice Basho's use of his senses throughout the story and the dignity with which he conveys his craft and life work.

How I Came to Be a Writer by Phyllis Reynolds Naylor (Aladdin: 2001) (M)

Read when you want practical tips for becoming a writer.

The author of the Shiloh series shares her journey to becoming a writer. Read about a writer's life and the process of writing a book and getting it published. This book will help inspire a dream and foster a gift.

Nothing Ever Happens on 90th Street by Roni Schotter, illustrations by Kyrsten Brooker (Orchard Books, 1997) (D)

Read when you want to discuss how exciting and interesting the world around you can really be.

Eva is convinced that "Nothing Ever Happens on 90th Street." Waiting to fill the pages in her notebook for a school assignment, Eva slowly watches the excitement and mystery of her street unfold before her eyes. Limousines bearing movie stars, cats escaping, and coffee spilling help Eva fill up the blank pages in her notebook. This book honors the life of the imagination and the life of the ordinary world. Great writers savor both.

The Place My Words Are Looking for: What Poets Say About and Through Their Work edited by Paul Janeczko (Simon & Schuster Children's Publishing: 1990) (M)

Read to an aspiring poet, or as an introduction to good poets and their poetry.

In this book, thirty-nine poets share some of their best work, along with commentary on their own writing processes. Carefully selected, this is an anthology with beautiful poetry and great insights for anyone with an itch to write.

BEING YOURSELF

From Fancy Nancy to Madeline to Yoon to Woolbur, children's literature provides a multitude of examples of quirky, eccentric characters who live as themselves and only become *more* themselves in the telling of their story. This is huge to convey as a parent, because oftentimes schools inadvertently (or not so inadvertently) create an atmosphere of sameness through routines and a desire for order.

In the long run, though, I hope we will raise our children to be different, a global community of individuals who effect change and create new ideas. If you think of people you recognize and know from the world of culture, science, history, and the news, they are all people who are really and truly different, who innovate and create. They are speaking their unique voice to the world. They are making change. They are Madelines, Woolburs, Clementines. Let literature inspire you and your children to be yourselves.

Bark, George by Jules Feiffer (HarperCollins Publishers: 1999) (E)

Read to a young child when you are looking for a silly, simple read about identity.

George's mother tries to teach him to bark, like any other normal, well-behaved dog. George can oink, quack, and meow but seems unable to let out even a feeble "arf." George's mother takes him to the vet, who seems to cure George by removing various animals from his stomach . . . or is George cured?

Bintou's Braids by Sylviane A. Diouf, illustrated by Shane W. Evans (Chronicle Books: 2001) (D)

Read to celebrate the uniqueness of each person's appearance.

Everyone is always giving Bintou cornrows, so all she has is four little tufts of hair. She wants braids. Fatou, Bintou's sister, has braids full of colorful beads. Her mother's friends have gold coins attached to their braids and even Mariama, a friend, has braids that hang down to her waist. But Bintou's Grandma Soukeye, who comes for a visit, says, "When you are older, it's fine to want to look your best and show everybody that you have become a young woman. But you are still just a girl. You will get braids when it is time." At night, Bintou dreams of braids. Will her dreams ever come true? This book is a gentle tribute to the beauty of each individual and the details of appearance that enhance beauty inside.

Black, White, Just Right! by Marguerite Davol, illustrated by Irene Trivas (Albert Whitman & Co.: 1993) (M)

Read to notice that skin color is only one, small thing that defines us.

The narrator describes the differences between the likes and dislikes, the characteristics and talents, of her mother and father. She decides that as a combination of them both, she is "just right." A sensitive exploration of a child's inquiry into how people are defined and how their qualities inside and out impact their awareness of themselves.

The Cow Who Clucked by Denise Fleming (Henry Holt and Company: 2006) (E)

Read to teach younger children to celebrate uniqueness through the simple text conveying the unique sounds of different farm animals.

Cow finds out one morning that she has lost her "moo" and that it has been replaced by a "cluck." She trudges about the farm, trying to figure out which animal has her moo. Will she find a way to get back her unique sound?

Eleanor, Ellatony, Ellencake, and Me by C. M. Rubin, illustrated by Christopher Fowler (Gingham Dog Press: 2001) (D)

Read when you want to discuss the power of names and the role they play in self-identity.

Everyone keeps trying to come up with a new nickname for Eleanor! Her mother calls her E, her father calls her Punch, and her grandmother calls her Elle. Eleanor realizes that she should take matters into her own hands and finds herself the perfect new name.

Ella Sarah Gets Dressed by Margaret Chodos-Irvine (Harcourt Children's Books: 2003) (E)

Read this to see creativity and individuality in everyday activities.

Ella Sarah is getting dressed for a tea party and has her own ideas about the sort of outfit she wants to wear. Despite her parents' objections, she wears what she wants, showing off both a bright fashion statement and her individuality.

Fancy Nancy by Jane O'Connor, illustrated by Robin Preiss Glasser (HarperCollins Publishers: 2005) (D)

Read when you need some inspiration to feel frilly and fancy.

Fancy Nancy loves glitz, glitter, and frill. She can't understand why her family doesn't embrace being fancy. Nancy goes on a campaign to fancy up her drab family.

How We Are Smart by W. Nikola-Lisa, illustrated by Sean Qualls (Lee & Low Books: 2006) (M)

Read to embrace all the unique intelligences that different people possess.

This book introduces the eight different kinds of intelligence. Then, it dedicates a spread to twelve unique persons in history, each of whom possessed one of the intelligences. The diverse set of historical figures with unique talents will allow your child to find a bit of herself in each brilliant person.

I'm Gonna Like Me: Letting Off a Little Self-Esteem by Jamie Lee Curtis, illustrated by Laura Cornell (HarperCollins Children's Books: 2002) (D)

Read for the beautiful illustrations and rhymes that help kids make healthy choices.

Jamie Lee Curtis and Laura Cornell teach you that it is okay to like yourself just as you are. Learn how to love yourself, even when you are missing teeth or making mistakes or running just a little slower than everyone else.

Imogene's Antlers by David Small (Crown Books for Young Readers: 2000) (D)

Read to introduce the idea of accepting differences in a hilarious way.

One morning Imogene wakes up to find that she has grown antlers. Although they present some logistical difficulties, Imogene embraces her new and unique look. But will her family learn to accept the large addition coming out the top of her head?

Let's Talk About Race by Julius Lester, illustrated by Karen Barbour (Amistad: 2005) (D)

Read for discussions of race, religion and what makes us all human. This is a heavy topic and should be read aloud and discussed.

This book's illustrations and words provide a powerful exploration of race. It teaches us that we are all made of skin and bones; it is just the small details that differentiate us.

Leo the Late Bloomer by Robert Kraus, illustrated by José Aruego (HarperCollins Children's Books: 1994) (E)

Read to acknowledge that kids bloom at very different times. It is okay to be a late bloomer.

Leo does not read or write or even speak. His dad is worried, but his mom knows that he is just a late bloomer.

In the Fiddle Is a Song: A Lift-the-Flap Book of Hidden Potential by Durga Bernhard (Chronicle Books: 2006) (D)

Read when you want to find the extraordinary in what appears to be just ordinary.

Find the hidden potential in the ordinary objects around you or even in yourself. An acorn "is a tree waiting to grow tall" and wheat is the origin of bread. As you read this delightfully illustrated book, find the possibilities within yourself.

I Want to Be by Thylias Moss, illustrated by Jerry Pinkney (Puffin Books: 1998) (D)

Read when you want to tell the story of all the wonderful things you want to be.

What do you want to be? This young narrator describes all of the delightful things she wants to be. She wants to be in motion, and fast but not too fast, slow but not too slow. Celebrate with this girl as she rejoices in herself and all that she would like to be.

Madeline written and illustrated by Ludwig Bemelmans (The Viking Press: 1939) (D)

Read to enjoy the adventure of being yourself.

Follow this classic heroine as she sets off on her first of many exciting adventures with Miss Clavel and the rest of the twelve girls in that "old house in Paris that was covered in vines." Despite being the smallest of the girls at the school, Madeline isn't afraid to be herself no matter where it takes her, or the trouble it creates.

My Name Is Yoon by Helen Recorvits, illustrated by Gabi Swiatkowska (Farrar, Straus and Giroux: 2003) (D)

Read when you want to discuss the power in a name and in a language.

What is in a name? Yoon, which means Shining Wisdom, loves her name when she writes it in Korean. Yoon has to learn how to write her name in English, but she believes the letters look so lonely on the page. Yoon tries out names like Cupcake and Bird, filling her pages with these new words. As she struggles to find her identity in her new country, Yoon also learns to find the courage to be herself.

Nina Bonita by Ana Maria Machado (Kane/Miller Book Publishers: 2001) (D)

Read when you want to discuss multiracial families and the value of living comfortably with those who look different than you.

A young girl living on the South American coast has darker skin than anyone in her family. A white rabbit sees the girl and her dark skin and begs her to reveal the secret to her beautiful skin. The girl tells the rabbit three made-up explanations that he acts out to no success. Finally, it is revealed that the girl shares her dark skin tone with her grandmother and the rabbit realizes that he should be content with his own color.

Oh No, Ono! by Hans de Beer, translated by Marianne Martens (North-South Books: 2004) (E)

Read when you want to discuss how new experiences, although sometimes scary, can lead to new knowledge.

Ono is a pig whose curiosity always seems to get the best of him. Whether he is doing a cannonball into a mud puddle or tipping a haystack onto a cow, he consistently learns a valuable lesson after following his desire for something new. Ono teaches us all how sometimes giving into our desires for new experiences can lead to an exciting adventure and a useful lesson.

Olivia by Ian Falconer (Simon & Schuster Children's Publishing: 2000) (D)

Read when you want to talk about the power and joy of being confident and being yourself.

Meet Olivia who is "good at lots of things." Olivia is good at singing very, very loudly, terrorizing her brother, and dressing up. What adventures will she have in this fun book?

Sleeping Ugly by Jane Yolen, illustrated by Diane Stanley (Putnam Juvenile: 1997) (M)

Read to think about different kinds of beauty.

Princess Miserella is beautiful but spoiled, whereas Plain Jane is ugly but sweet to everyone around her. When a fairy godmother casts a sleeping spell on Miserella, Plain Jane, and the entire kingdom, only a prince's kiss can wake them. However, whom will he choose to kiss—beautiful Miserella or sweet Jane?

Sylvia Jean, Drama Queen by Lisa Campbell Ernst (Penguin Young Readers Group: 2005) (D)

Read to celebrate dressing up or to teach your child how to find the courage to be herself.

Sylvia Jean is a drama queen. For every occasion, Sylvia finds the perfect outfit. She wears a clown outfit to cheer up her brother, and dresses as the Statue of Liberty to start off the school year. Will Sylvia be able to overcome her fear and find the perfect outfit for the upcoming costume contest?

Tacky the Penguin by Helen Lester, illustrated by Lynn Munsinger (Houghton Mifflin Company: 1990) (D)

Read to appreciate how special it is to be unlike everyone else.

Tacky just does not fit in. When Tacky and his friends encounter a pack of hunters, will he find the courage to be different?

The Whingdingdilly by Bill Peet (Houghton Mifflin Company: 1982) (D)

Read to add some more excitement to your child's life.

Scamp wants a much more exciting life than the one he leads as just a farm dog. When he meets Zildy, a witch living in the woods, he revels in the opportunity to become a Whingdingdilly. During his exciting adventure, Scamp learns the value of loving himself for who he is.

Woolbur by Leslie Helakoski, illustrated by Lee Harper (HarperCollins Publishers: 2008) (D)

Read to celebrate not following the crowd.

Woolbur is a free spirit: he likes to go against the crowd, and is always finding unique ways to make his sheeply duties more fun and interesting. His parents get worried that he is not following the rest of the herd, because that is what sheep are supposed to do. When they tell their son that he must do what the rest of the sheep are doing, Woolbur finds an outside-the-box solution to the problem.

Talk about It: This is an excellent book for a child who feels like he is not like everyone else. In this book, Woolbur embraces his differences and celebrates them. Talk about how being unique is a blessing, and finding the confidence to be yourself is the challenge.

- What are some of the things Woolbur does that go against the crowd? Why do you think that he likes to do things his own way? What does his grandfather think about the way Woolbur acts?
- Why are Woolbur's parents worried? Do you think that Woolbur worries about what the other sheep think of him?
- How does Woolbur deal with the request from his parents at the end of the story? Do you think that the other sheep children like or dislike Woolbur for being different?
- Think about a time when you wanted to, or did, go against what the rest of the crowd was doing. How did you feel about it?

BIRTHDAYS/GROWING UP

Birthdays are joyous occasions, but they can also be fraught with the possibility of disappointment. Your youngest child may not fully understand this celebration while your older child may struggle with the idea of growing up and wishing for things that may not always come true. I worked with a student, age ten, named Marisol. She was a foster child, and she wrote in her notebook that she had never had a birthday party. I had asked the students to write a big wish, and so she wrote all about the birthday party she wished she could have had: with a big white cake and pink frosting and Spanish music and dancing. When the kids heard what Marisol wrote, they decided to throw her a surprise party. They did everything she described in her story: the white-and-pink cake, the Spanish music.

And she cried, with joy and also with, I am sure, her own ten-year-old sorrow for the parties she had missed. Birthdays do, sometimes, make their own kind of magic. Even as adults we feel the magic of birthdays, the candle, the flame, the wish that may very well come true.

Children are exquisitely conscious of growing up. They wiggle their loose teeth; they put their feet out in front of them to see how long they've grown since the night before. And the thing is, you can also sometimes see them grow. Have you ever gone to bed one night and then the next morning had the distinct feeling the baby, the toddler, the child looks different? Growing up happens before our eyes, and theirs too. Your child may be a little bit anxious about growing up. The promise of some freedom is tempered by the worry of what it all means. It can be tough for you too. The child who was your baby yesterday suddenly becomes your "grown-up" kid, an older sibling. In Charlotte Zolotow's *I Like to Be Little*, the girl says, "I have never seen a grown-up do that," wondering if it's worth it to grow up at all. At the same time, she may love the feeling of the two-wheeler and your hand letting go of the seat. She may love the freedom of taking the bus on her own. She may love that you allow her to stay at home alone with her younger brother. These books offer companionship on all of the growing-up journeys.

The Birthday Box by Leslie Patricelli (Candlewick Press: 2007) (E)

Read about loving every part of your birthday present, especially the box.

How exciting a box can be. This toddler discovers the adventure and fun that a box provides. It can be a boat or an airplane. It can even contain a special present!

A Birthday for Frances by Russell Hoban, illustrated by Lillian Hoban (HarperCollins Publishers: 1968) (D)

Read for siblings who sometimes find it hard not to be jealous on birthdays.

When it is time for Gloria's birthday, Frances finds it hard to be generous and nice to her sister.

Birthday Presents by Cynthia Rylant, illustrated by Suçie Stevenson (Scholastic, Inc.: 1987) (D)

Read when you want to celebrate your family's love and to create a special family history.

What do you do on your birthday? On this girl's sixth birthday, her parents recount the parties, cakes, and, yes, presents of her past five birthdays.

Cherry Tree by Ruskin Bond, illustrated by Allan Eitzen (Boyds Mills Press: 1988) (D)

Read about how all living things grow and change.

When Rakhi was six, her grandfather advised her to plant the cherry seed she had left after eating her cherries. She and her grandfather care for the seed; as the small tree begins to grow, it suffers from harsh weather and accidents. Yet, it keeps growing, as does Rakhi, until it is taller than she. She and her grandfather muse about how they have all grown and changed, and about the changes still to come.

Talk about It: This is a simple but beautiful book, with a lovely message about growing and changing. Talk about how the tree changes, along with Rakhi, as the years go by. Talk about how we all grow and change, along with animals and the natural world. Celebrate growing up with your child.

- Discuss what the grandfather means when he says, "Nothing is lucky if you put it away. You must make it work for you."
- Look at the illustrations of Rakhi and the cherry tree as the story goes along. Talk about how they both change.
- Why do you think that Rahki wants to tell her children about the tree? Why should she include her grandfather in the story?

Epossumondas Saves the Day by Coleen Salley, illustrated by Janet Stevens (Harcourt Children's Books: 2006) (D)

Read when you want to have fun with language and illustrations, or when you and your child are preparing for a birthday party.

Coleen Salley retells an old Southern tale of an opossum, named Epossumondas, who saves his friend, a baby gator, his mama, and his auntie from the Great, Huge, Ugly Louisiana Snapping Turtle, after they go to pick up a missing ingredient for his birthday cake.

Talk about It: The language in this book makes it fun to read aloud, and it has joyful illustrations. There are also some fun wordplays and repetitions.

- What is your favorite thing to have for your birthday?
- Epossumondas was courageous in fighting the turtle; when have you or someone you know had to act with courage?

Happy Birthday, Moon by Frank Asch (Aladdin: 2000) (E)

Read for a simple and beautiful story about caring and friendship, on birthdays or any days.

In this timeless book, Bear realizes that no one gives the Moon a gift for its birthday. Because Bear loves the Moon so much, he goes on a journey to find out when the Moon's birthday is and to find a perfect present for the Moon.

Happy Birthday, Sam by Pat Hutchins (Greenwillow Books: 1978) (D)

Read about an innovative way to use a birthday gift.

Sam is a year older. But for some strange reason, he still can't reach his light switch, get his clothes from the closet, or reach the tap in the kitchen. Sam is discouraged until he gets creative with a birthday gift from his grandpa.

Happy Birthday to You! by Dr. Seuss (Random House: 1959) (D)

Read on your child's birthday or when the two of you just want to feel silly.

"I wish we could do what they do in Katroo. They sure know how to say happy birthday to you!" Do you know what they do in Katroo? Discover how they celebrate birthdays in Katroo with the Birthday Honk-Honker, the Birthday Bird, and much more in this silly, rhyming story.

I Like to Be Little by Charlotte Zolotow, illustrated by Erik Blegvad (HarperCollins Publishers: 1990) (E)

Read when you want to enjoy being little and watching the raindrops or running barefoot in the summer.

A little girl explains to her mother exactly why she likes to be little in this sweet celebration of youth. "I can sit at the window and watch the rain run down the pane," says the little girl. "I never saw a grown-up do that." Or maybe it's that she likes to eat snow as it falls, or have birthday parties with candles and cake.

Mr. Rabbit and the Lovely Present by Charlotte Zolotow, illustrated by Maurice Sendak (HarperCollins Publishers: 1962) (D)

Read for a beautiful book about friendship and birthdays and figuring out the perfect gift for mothers.

Mr. Rabbit helps a little girl find the perfect gift for her mother. The walk in the woods together is tender and evocative: a little girl is setting out on her own journey on behalf of someone she loves. Even the smallest child can be the biggest giver.

My Wobbly Tooth Must Not Ever Never Fall Out by Lauren Child (Grosset & Dunlap: 2006) (D)

Read when mixed emotions come along with that very first loose tooth. Read about the other adventures of Charlie and Lola in the other books in the series.

Lola really does not want her tooth to fall out. Or does she? As soon as Lola learns about the tooth fairy, she wiggles, pushes, and pulls until it pops out. Lola is devastated to discover she has lost the tooth before she can leave it for the tooth fairy. Can her brother Charlie help her find a solution?

On the Night You Were Born by Nancy Tillman (Feiwel and Friends: 2006) (E)

Read to discover how truly remarkable it is to be born.

There will never be another time quite like the moment that you were born; the world welcomed a completely new and unique being into existence. In this book, news of the birth is passed throughout the world, and under a glittery moon all of the creatures celebrate.

When I Was Five by Arthur Howard (Harcourt Children's Books: 1999) (D)

Read to remember the fun things your child did when he was five, and to celebrate a best friend.

Six-year-old Jeremy remembers being five. He remembers he wanted to be an astronaut who travels to the moon, or a cowboy. He also remembers playing with his best friend, Mark. At the age of six, Jeremy no longer wants to be an astronaut or a cowboy, but he is still best friends with Mark.

When I Was Little: A Four-Year-Old's Memoir of Her Youth by Jamie Lee Curtis (HarperCollins Publishers: 1995) (D)

Read when you want to celebrate your child and all he can do now that he is a little more grown-up.

"When I was little, I made up words like 'scoopeeloo,' now I make up songs," says this young girl as she expresses her excitement at growing up and learning how to do so many new things.

BUILDING THE WORLD OF FAMILY

No family is the same. We each create the world of our home very, very differently. What might really work for my family may not work for yours, and vice versa. We all have to find our own way toward how we build our concept of family, embracing how the individuality of every member will create a family unit that is extraordinary in its uniqueness.

I remember when I was little reading *The Borrowers* and that I loved how Arrietty was so brave and her mother, Fern, was so worried all the time. And how Pod, Arrietty's father, was so resourceful. They were tiny people, not more than a few inches in height, but what a family they were. The outside world was so big and frightening and they each handled their fears in their own way, yet at the end of the day they'd come back together and sit on their little spools of thread and share all their adventures. They didn't look like a "typical" family by any stretch, but I savored their togetherness and their individuality too and soaked them in. They also taught me a lot about what the members of a family can do for one another, from the smallest family to the biggest, from a family where everyone is somewhat similar to a family where everyone is quite different.

From literature, we can take what we love most and make it our own. But the best thing we can learn from great literature is that together we can create something that has not yet been done, not ever. We are none of us close to perfect. Families are created out of all these imperfections, which, sown together, become a quilt of acceptance, humor, love, and even forgiveness. As your children grow, tell them stories so that you build a history together, so that good and bad, the stories knit together to create an *idea* of who you are. A good friend of mine was diagnosed with cancer. She said to her children: "It's easy to be a close family when times are good. Let's use this as an opportunity to practice how we are that kind of close family when we are facing a challenge." And they did. Name these experiences for and with your children, using literature to help you: "We are the kind of family that . . ." "We always . . ." "Remember when we . . ."

And Tango Makes Three by Justin Richardson and Peter Parnell, illustrated by Henry Cole (Simon & Schuster Books for Young Readers: 2005) (D)

Read to open your child's mind to the many possible ways to create a family.

This is the true story of a very unique family of penguins that live in the Central Park Zoo in New York City. When male and female penguins in the zoo began to couple-off and build homes, Roy and Silo (two males) were only interested in each other. Their keeper notices that the boys "must be in love," and with his help the two have the chance to become a family. Their new chick, Tango, makes three.

Black Is Brown Is Tan by Arnold Adoff, illustrated by Emily Arnold McCully (Amistad: 1973) (D)

Read to enjoy the many colors that can make up a family.

In this book, a mother and father sing to their children about the family members' different colors of skin, about growing up, and about love. In this biracial family, the many colors are to be celebrated. The belief is simple: "That is the way it is for us. This is the way we are."

Blueberries for Sal by Robert McCloskey (Penguin: 1976) (E→D)

Read this to show the power of family and the joy of spending time together.

Through beautiful blue illustrations, McCloskey tells the story of Sal and her mother, who go out blueberry picking one day to make preserves. Sal can't seem to pick as fast as she eats and becomes distracted by the delicious fruit. As the day progresses, Sal gets separated from her mother, trailing a mother bear who is also picking blueberries with her child. In the end, the mothers find their proper children and everyone goes home with pails of blueberries.

The Cousins by Judith Caseley (Greenwillow Books: 1990) (D)

Read when you want to talk about making friends and how people who might seem very different can become very close.

Jenny and Jessica are first cousins. Jenny likes to paint and Jessica likes to dance—the two girls are completely different, even down to their hair color. Yet they see beyond those differences and become close friends, showing that friendship can transcend differences.

Daddy's Roommate by Michael Willhoite (Alyson Wonderland, 1994) (D)

Read when a parent has a new relationship.

In this accessible and straightforward book, a boy describes a new relationship his father has with a man named Frank after his parents divorce. The young narrator shares the daily life of Frank and Daddy and provides a simple, honest explanation of what it means to be gay as he goes on various outings with this new branch of his family.

Families by Susan Kuklin (Hyperion: 2006) (D→M)

Read when you want to get a glimpse of the many different kinds of families.

In this unique book, Kuklin interviews children from all over the country, and from many different families. Read about how children feel growing up with two fathers, with a twin, as an adopted child, with Down syndrome, in a religious family, in a biracial family. Accompanying photographs are poignant.

Fathers, Mothers, Sisters, Brothers: A Collection of Family Poems by Mary Ann Hoberman, illustrated by Marylin Hafner (Little Brown and Company: 1991) (D)

Read when you want to celebrate your family, whether big or small, composed of aunts or uncles, stepparents or adopted babies.

This collection of poems explores all kinds of families: some families have babysitters, others have uncles, and some even have brothers and sisters. As you read this treasure chest of poems, discuss the emotions that arise in families, whether from sibling rivalries, a mother's admonition, or fun with a babysitter.

Hairs/Pelitos by Sandra Cisneros, illustrated by Terry Ybáñez (Random House Children's Books: 1997) (D)

Read this when you want to savor the small moments and details that define us.

Taken from her book *The House on Mango Street,* this beautifully illustrated book paints portraits of the unique hairstyles and tenderly rendered qualities of the members of one family. Written in Spanish and English, it is lyrical and moving in its simple intimacy and appreciation for each family member.

In Daddy's Arms, I Am Tall: African-Americans Celebrating Fathers written and illustrated by Javaka Steptoe (Lee & Low Books: 2001) (E→D)

Read when you want to celebrate fathers everywhere.

This collection of poems beautifully illustrated by Javaka Steptoe explore and rejoice in the special bond between fathers and children.

King & King by Linda de Haan and Stern Nijland (Tricycle Press: 2000) (D)

Read this when you want to talk to your child about different kinds of love and relationships.

The queen decides that it is time for her son, the prince, to get married and together they begin to search for a suitable princess. Many princesses come from around the land hoping to catch the prince's eye, but none of them do. Finally, he follows his heart and finds someone who makes him happy.

The Luckiest Kid on the Planet by Lisa Campbell Ernst (Bradbury Press: 1994) (D)

Read this to teach about the importance of a positive outlook on life, especially during a difficult situation, such as an illness in the family.

Lucky Morgenstern knows he is the luckiest kid on the planet—how could he not be, with a name like Lucky? One day, however, he learns that his real name is Herbert; Lucky was just a nickname. Herbert has to rediscover his luck while his grandfather, who is his best friend, is sick in the hospital. He learns the importance of optimism, especially when it comes to luck.

Neeny Coming, Neeny Going by Karen English, paintings by Synthia Saint James (BridgeWater Books: 1996) (M)

Read when you want to talk about the bonds that tie families together, even when they seem hard to imagine.

Essie, who lives on an island off the mainland, cannot wait until her cousin Neeny, who is living on the mainland, comes to visit. But when Neeny arrives, Essie thinks that Neeny no longer cares about the island way of life. Can Neeny help Essie remember "her family on the island"?

Papá and Me by Arthur Dorros, pictures by Rudy Gutierrez (HarperCollins Publishers: 2008) (D)

Read when you want to celebrate the love between a father and a son.

A father and his son set off for a special day together. They walk through the park, hold each other's *manos,* or hands, and spend the day in the park climbing trees and stepping in puddles. Although father and son may have some differences, such as the father wants eggs and the son pancakes, the father speaks Spanish and the son speaks English, they manage to have a wonderful time.

Pitching in for Eubie by Jerdine Nolen, illustrated by E. B. Lewis (Amistad: 2007) (D→M)

Read when you want to support members of your family and think about ways that everyone can help out during times of need.

When Eubie wins a scholarship to college, her family is so proud. The family pulls together to earn the rest of the money. Lilly really wants to help her big sister, but everyone says she's too young. That is, until she finds the perfect solution.

Talk about It: As Lilly discovered, sometimes it is hard to figure out how to help out in a family during a time of need. Talk about the ways that everyone can chip in, no matter how young they are.

- Why do you think Lilly wanted to help Eulie so much? How did she end up helping her sister?
- Have you every really wanted to help someone and had a hard time finding a way to do so? What did you do?

The Relatives Came by Cynthia Rylant, illustrated by Stephen Gammell (Aladdin: 2001) (E)

Read when visiting with family or missing family that is far away.

When the relatives come to visit from Virginia, the house is full of people, food, and fun.

Talk about It: There are all kinds of relatives, and they live all over. Children hearing this story will love the excitement of the relatives all sleeping over at the house, talking in groups of two and three, and eating around the table.

- What is a strong memory you have of relatives visiting?
- How did the family have to adjust when the relatives came? Did they seem to mind having to share their beds and house?

When We Married Gary by Anna Grossnickle Hines (Greenwillow Books: 1996) (M)

Read to discuss a change in a family.

Sarah lives with her sister Beth and her mom; she doesn't remember when her father left them, because she was still a baby. It's always been the three of them, doing everything together. When Gary enters into the family, things change, but the girls realize that he is the missing piece to a beautiful family puzzle.

BUILDING, MAKING, AND CREATING: THE WORLD OF MECHANICAL THINGS

There was a wonderful teacher at my daughters' elementary school named Lenny Levine. He brought in broken clocks and telephones and during choice time the children would rebuild those things, or reinvent them the way they imagined they would go. I love the idea that a child can look at something broken and fix it in a way an adult could never even begin to imagine. It's possibly a metaphor for childhood itself.

These books are wonderful partners for active learning and active reading. Especially for children who do not love to sit still, these books honor the idea that things on the go are also of value. Sit amid a pile of toy cars or shout your read-aloud over the din of the train going around its tracks, and use literature as a way to genuinely value and honor your child's budding passions.

Cars and Trucks and Things That Go by Richard Scarry (Golden Books: 1998) (E)

Read for an interactive book for the very young one who loves machines and transportation.

The classic Richard Scarry book is oversized and filled with favorite characters, lots to look at, and plenty of new vocabulary words to read. In this book, the pig family takes a road trip and discovers the many different modes of transportation.

Freight Train by Donald Crews (Greenwillow Books: 1996) (E)

Read this board book for exciting information about freight trains.

Learn about each of the cars on the freight train and the tracks that the train follows as it races through cities and countrysides all day and night.

I Stink! by Kate and Jim McMullan (Joanna Cotler Books: 2002) (E)

Read when you want to follow the fun nighttime adventure of a very stinky garbage truck.

Discover the exciting trip that this very smelly garbage truck takes, as it eats an alphabet soup of garbage: "apple cores . . . banana peels . . . candy wrappers . . . dirty diapers" and much more. This garbage truck loves eating your trash, smelling like garbage, and helping keep neighborhoods clean.

Lightship by Brian Floca (Simon & Schuster Children's Publishing: 2007) (D)

Read all about how a lightship, a floating lighthouse, does its job by keeping its "one sure spot." Learn how a machine can be used to save lives, with nice diagrams of a lightship.

Although lightships are no longer used, they served an important purpose in history. The author explains how the ship and its crew worked tirelessly to keep it anchored to her "one sure spot," waiting to guide other ships home to safety.

Rescue Vehicles: Big Books by Robert Gould and Eugene Epstein (Big Guy Books: 2005) (E)

Read to answer those everyday wonderings about rescue vehicles.

What do rescue vehicles look like? How do they sound? Find the answer to all of your child's questions about police cars, ambulances, fire trucks, and more, using this brightly colored and informative book.

Robots Everywhere by Denny Hebson, illustrated by Todd Hoffman (Walker & Company: 2004) (E)

Read to imagine a world with robots in charge.

Imagine a world of robots that live like humans. Follow the quirky adventures of the colorful robots as they go to school.

Sky Boys: How They Built the Empire State Building by Deborah Hopkinson, illustrated by James Ransome (Random House Books for Young Readers: 2006) (D)

Read to explore Depression-era construction.

Despite the hardships of the Depression, Pop and his son watch in awe as the workers construct the Empire State Building. Learn how the hundreds of "sky boys," or builders, brought in the steel and bricks, leveled the ground, dug a foundation, and finally created a building so tall and so thin it seems to reach the sky. Finally, when the building is completed, Pop and his son race to the top of the tallest building in the world.

Smash! Crash! by Jon Scieszka, illustrated by Keytoon, Inc. (Simon & Schuster Books for Young Readers: 2008) (E→D)

Read if your child loves trucks, big machines, smashing, and crashing.

Meet the mischievous Jack Truck and Dump Truck Dan. They are always smashing and crashing, getting themselves into trouble, escaping at the last minute, and even using their destructive ways to do good. Explore truck town with this crazy duo; learn about the different kinds of work being done by the heavy machinery.

Trains: A Pop-up Railroad Book by Robert Crowther (Candlewick Press: 2006) (D)

Read if your child loves trains, locomotives, and steam engines.

How do locomotives run? How do steam engines work? Learn all of this and more as you open the pages of this pop-up book and see the fastest and longest locomotives in the world. Explore the tunnels and stations through which the locomotives race and study the top, bottom, and sides of the trains.

Trucks by Anne Rockwell (Puffin: 1992) (E)

Read to learn about the many different kinds of trucks. If you enjoy this book, read the other books in Rockwell's series: Boats, Planes, Big Wheels, and Trains.

For the young child, this book explores the many different types of trucks and discusses how they are used. Nice, simple illustrations help your child to visualize examples of trucks she sees every day.

BUILDING PEACE, CONFRONTING WAR, AND TALKING WITH YOUR CHILD ABOUT WORLD EVENTS

Even from a very young age, our children are negotiating peace, with friends, with siblings, even with adults. Very early on, they listen to the world around them and worry about it. When adults argue, it feels wounding and hurtful. Children understand the pain of the absence of peace.

The absence of peace is far more typical than the presence of it, but a child can recognize the presence of peace instantly. The coziness of an evening spent playing a game together, or a world in which people are taking care of one another, makes its own big sound. It reverberates, and children adore it. Through these stories, we can talk with them about peace: identifying moments as peaceful, discussing ways we too can bring a sense of peace to all the days of our lives, whether we are in school or at home or out in the larger world. We can acknowledge the absence of peace too, and ask our children to help us create a sense of peace both at home and in all the places they go throughout their lives. "Peace is when we feel at ease with one another." "Peace is really knowing each other and feeling safe." "Peace is when I am playing with my cars and you are doing your work at the table." By naming peace simply, we can begin to scaffold some larger conversations for how those peaceful moments will translate throughout the world in a wider scope. Through these stories, even beyond the immediate conversation, I believe literature can truly help us raise our children to be agents for peace in all aspects of their lives, always.

A Little Peace by Barbara Kerley (National Geographic Society: 2007) (M)

Read this book to show your child that peace is possible, and that he can play a role in promoting it. This is a better discussion book for older children.

This book communicates the belief that when simple actions—a wave, a smile, a dance—are shared, we have the power to "spread a little peace." The photos by brilliant *National Geographic* photographers are the foundation of the book. Through the photos, the reader sees these acts of peace at the market in Guatemala, in a bus in Sudan, at a meditation in Bhutan, at Carnivale in Brazil, at a crosswalk in Japan, and many other places across the world where people come together.

Talk about It: This book is so powerful because the act of reading it can be a strong step toward creating a more peaceful and understanding world. Talk with your child about how small actions can actually promote peace every day. Talk about how we can all create tolerance by understanding our similarities and differences.

- Talk about the differences and similarities of the places, colors, and people in the photos. How does seeing these photos help us to want to promote peace?

- Talk about the prospect of peace. Why does it seem difficult to achieve? How can you help to promote peace?

The Butter Battle Book by Dr. Seuss (Random House: 1984) (D)

Read with a child to talk about reconciling differences in opinion, belief, or custom.

The Zooks and the Yooks are two different societies—the Zooks eat their bread with the butter side down and the Yooks eat theirs with the butter side up. The two groups find their difference irreconcilable and begin a fierce battle to determine which group is superior. The battle becomes a frenzied arms race, until both groups are almost destroyed by the other—all over buttering bread.

Brothers in Hope: The Story of the Lost Boys of Sudan by Mary Williams, illustrated by R. Gregory Christie (Lee & Low Books: 2005) (M)

Read when you want to talk about the impact of war on children and to learn about the lost boys of Sudan.

Garang lived with his parents, grandparents, and sisters in a hut in Sudan. His family tended cattle and by the age of eight, Garang had learned to tend to the cattle on his own. While out in the field with his cattle, Garang heard far off in the distance the sounds of his village being attacked. Upon returning home, Garang discovered he had lost everything and everyone. Banding together with other boys orphaned by the violence, Garang found the courage to survive and the power of hope. Garang and thousands of other lost boys walked from Sudan to Ethopia and then to Kenya in search of refuge from the violence and destruction.

One City, Two Brothers by Chris Smith, illustrated by Aurelia Fronty (Barefoot Books: 2007) (D→M)

Read for a great story about two brothers. It is a delightful tale with an important message about the need for peace in Jerusalem. This is a high-interest book for budding historians.

Two brothers travel to King Solomon to resolve a dispute over land, only to learn the mythical story of the founding of Jerusalem and the magic of brotherly love.

Silent Music: A Story of Baghdad by James Rumford (Roaring Brook Press: 2008) (D→M)

Read when you want to talk about a boy's love of words and to introduce a discussion about the effects of conflict on children living in war-torn nations. This book focuses on the boy's passion for language, so the element of war is muted and thoughtfully, carefully shared.

Ali loves writing calligraphy, celebrating the beauty of words. For Ali, practicing calligraphy serves as a refuge from the war and violence in his city of Baghdad. "I wrote all night and many nights of bombing that followed. I filled my room with pages of calligraphy. I filled my mind with peace." Ali's mother calls him Yakut, the name of the most famous ancient calligrapher who also lived in Baghdad during a time of war.

Snow in Jerusalem by Deborah da Costa, illustrated by Cornelius Van Wright and Ying-Hwa Hu (Albert Whitman & Company: 2001) (M)

Read to introduce the topic of overcoming differences in order to achieve peace and friendship.

In a city divided into quarters, two boys, Avi, who lives in the Jewish Quarter, and Hamudi, who lives in the Muslim Quarter, find a common thread between them: a beautiful white cat.

BULLYING AND HURTFUL PEOPLE

People of all ages are hurt by wounding friends at times. We want to both help our children manage the tough times by standing up for themselves, and also help them develop a kind of empowered empathy toward those who might be harming them. This sometimes feels almost contradictory. When do we encourage our children to stand firm, and when do we help them to be as loving as possible so as to diffuse the harmful impact of a bullying behavior? There are really no easy answers, but literature can help us to have those conversations and to shed some light on the gray areas. I would like for all children to be armed with strength and the conviction that no one is allowed to be hurtful toward them. But I also know that so many times the reason children bully and hurt others is because they have been hurt themselves. If our children can grow up feeling some empathy for even the most wounding offender, perhaps they will create a new world of kindness and acceptance in which no bullies will exist.

On the other side of things, you may have a child who is bullying others. Let the read-aloud be a place of safety for you to explore the "why" of this and not just lecture your child, but also to set really firm boundaries. The child who bullies or hurts others often has huge reservoirs of hurt inside him or her. Take a quiet moment with your child to set new boundaries and to model your own acceptance. Show that each day is a brand-new day of reinvention. The hardest part may be that your child has become associated with this behavior and it's very hard to start fresh. Help give her or him strategies for how to begin tomorrow in a new kind of way, and how to get the outcomes he wants in a kindly manner.

Finally, as bullying often is a sign of serious trouble within a human spirit, you may want to consider getting outside support as early as possible. Child therapists can help your child negotiate his own inner turmoil so he can develop a capacity for kindness toward others. And do not underestimate the pain of bullying on your child. Do not hesitate to talk with the principal, with teachers, or with a therapist to ensure that the behavior being done to your child is stopped, immediately.

Bully by Judith Caseley (Greenwillow Books: 2001) (M)

Read to understand the story behind a bully's behavior.

Mickey feels terrible when his friend Jack suddenly begins being mean to him. He talks to his family about how to solve the problem; in the meantime, the reader discovers some of the reasons behind Jack's behavior. Will the boys be able to solve their problems?

Enemy Pie by Derek Munson, illustrated by Tara Calahan King (Chronicle Books: 2000) (D)

Read when you want to talk about how hurtful friends can be sometimes, and how sometimes when friends are hurtful, they're just misunderstood.

A young boy is planning out the perfect summer, but his plans are ruined when a bully named Jeremy Ross moves near him. His father offers him a solution: bake an enemy pie that guarantees the elimination of enemies. But the boy's father requires that the boy must spend a day with Jeremy first. After a day spent with his would-be enemy, the boy realizes that Jeremy isn't that bad after all, but what will happen when Jeremy eats the enemy pie?

Help! A Story of Friendship by Holly Keller (Greenwillow Books: 2007) (D)

Read for a story about gossiping friends.

Mouse, Hedgehog, Rabbit, Squirrel, and Snake are all good friends. Then one day, Mouse hears some gossip that he should be careful of Snake because "snakes are very dangerous to mice." But when Mouse falls into a hole, the only animal that can help him is Snake. Will Mouse be able to disregard the hurtful gossip and trust that Snake will save him?

Talk about It: This is a great story for introducing the challenges of friendship. Talk about Mouse's feelings and whether or not he should have trusted the gossip of others. Talk about whether actions speak louder than words.

- How does believing the gossip from Fox and Skunk hurt Mouse? Have you ever believed the gossip someone tells you about your own friends? What happened?
- How does Snake prove that the gossip is wrong? How does Mouse feel when he realizes that he was wrong about Snake? How would you feel in Mouse's position?

Hooway for Wodney Wat by Helen Lester, illustrated by Lynn M. Munsinger (Houghton Mifflin Company: 1999) (D)

Read when your child needs the courage to overcome a class bully.

Rodent Rodney Rat cannot pronounce Rs. His classmates tease him and make fun of the way he says his name, "Wodney Wat," and how he calls himself a Wodent. It takes the arrival of a big, mean bully, Camilla Capybara, for Rodney to find the courage to help his classmates and save the day.

How to Lose All Your Friends by Nancy Carlson (Penguin Young Readers Group: 1994) (D)

Read this when you want a funny way to talk about friendship.

Sometimes it is hard to be a good friend; especially when it means sharing or taking turns. This child explains how to lose all your friends by refusing to share, throwing temper tantrums, and more.

Let's Be Enemies by Janice May Udry, illustrated by Maurice Sendak (HarperCollins Publishers: 1988) (E)

Read when you want to discuss the importance of compromise in friendships.

John and James are the best of friends. They share everything, but when James takes the best spoon, hoards all the crayons, and carries the flag in their make-believe army, John decides that James must not be his friend. He is his enemy. This charming story tells of how the forces that bind friends together can overcome even the strongest desire to become enemies.

My Secret Bully by Tracy Ludwig, illustrated by Abigail Marble (Ten Speed Press: 2005) (D→M)

Read this with a child who is dealing with a subtle bully, especially one who used to be a friend, at school.

Katie used to be one of Monica's closest friends, but lately she has started making fun of Monica in front of other children and excluding her from playground games. While this bullying is not physical, it has the same effect—Monica feels hurt and sick and dreads school. Monica turns to her mother for advice and learns that while there are no easy answers, she has a supporter in her mother.

Nobody Knew What to Do: A Story about Bullying by Becky Ray McCain, illustrated by Todd Leonardo (Albert, Whitman & Company: 2001) (M)

Read to talk about how to handle bullies and stand up for what is right. Use this book to talk about the importance of finding an adult who can listen and support children against the force of a bully.

Ray is bullied by some of his classmates. When he stays home from school, the bullies plan actions for the next day. One student, though, has had enough. He finds a teacher who will listen to him and learns how to stand up for himself and his classmates.

The Recess Queen by Alexis O'Neill, illustrated by Laura Huliska-Beith (Scholastic: 2002) (D)

Read when you want to talk about the recess bully.

Mary Jean, the Recess Queen, did everything first: she bounced, kicked, and swung first. Anyone who tried to kick, swing, or bounce before Mary Jean quickly learned not to. When a new girl arrives at school, she stands up to Mary Jean and changes the rules of the playground.

CARING FOR SOMEONE

Look how toddlers carry around baby dolls. They cradle them and hold them and give them a pretend bottle. That early, the innate desire to love and care is right there. It is profound in its passion, even for inanimate things. In *Hug a Bug,* Eileen Spinelli implores us to hug a book, hug "your friend who's feeling blue," hug "a bug—be gentle, please." And she writes: "Hug your darling." Tenderness and openness, generosity and care are values we convey very early on in a multitude of ways. We can point to these values as we read, through all the ways characters care for one another. The act of reading aloud itself signals to your child a form of nurturing and care that is unparalleled. And then they will do the same for their own child someday.

Aggie and Ben: Three Stories by Lori Ries, illustrated by Frank W. Dormer (Charlesbridge Publishing: 2006) (E→D)

Read when you're searching for the perfect pet.

Ben's father takes him on a surprise trip to the pet shop. At the store, Ben searches for the perfect pet. Will it be a mouse, a cat, or even a snake? How will Ben ever choose? When he sees Aggie, a sweet puppie, Ben knows he has found the perfect pet and his new best friend.

Duck and Goose by Tad Hills (Random House Children's Books: 2006) (E)

Read to discuss how important it is to care for others, even when they are different. This is part of the Duck and Goose series.

Duck and Goose stumble upon an egg (or is it?). Whose egg is it? With a little bit of squabbling, Duck and Goose care for it together.

Elizabeti's Doll by Stephanie Stuve-Bodeen, illustrated by Christy Hale (Lee & Low Books: 1998) (E)

Read about a unique way that a little girl celebrates the birth of her baby brother.

Elizabeti has a new baby brother. When she watches her mother care for the baby, it makes Elizabeti want to take care of her own baby. Elizabeti finds a rock outside that is the perfect size and names her new baby Eva. Elizabeti's baby is much better behaved than her brother, Obedi, until one day Elizabeti leaves Eva by some other rocks so that she will have company and later discovers her to be gone. Will Elizabeti find her doll so that she can take care of her?

Guess How Much I Love You by Sam McBratney, illustrations by Anita Jeram (Candlewick Press: 2006) (E)

Read when your child wants to tell someone how much he loves him or her.

Little Nutbrown Hare looks to Big Nutbrown Hare just before falling asleep and asks, "Guess how much I love you?" Through the book, discover how much Little Nutbrown Hare loves Big Nutbrown Hare.

Hello, Biscuit! by Alyssa Satin Capucilli, pictures by Pat Schories (HarperCollins Publishers: 1998) (E)

Read when you want to talk about caring for a pet. This is one of the Biscuit series; it is an I Can Read book.

Biscuit finds everything he could possibly want or need: "You found your bed, and your bone, and your biscuits." But his young owner only wants to find him a name. Will she ever be able to choose a name for this very special puppy?

Julio's Magic by Arthur Dorros, collages by Ann Grifalconi (HarperCollins Publishers: 2004) (M)

Read when you want to talk about ways of helping people who are in need.

Julio and his teacher, the best wood carver, named Iluminado, go to the forest to find wood for their sculptures. The lizards, dragons, and angels inspire Julio and Iluminado. Julio searches for the perfect wood for his sculpture, wood that would talk to him so he could win an upcoming contest. When Julio finds out that his friend can no longer see very well, he wants to find a way to help him. Will Julio find a way to help Iluminado?

Mama, Do You Love Me? by Barbara M. Joosse, illustrated by Barbara Lavallee (Chronicle Books: 1991) (E)

Read when your child needs reassurance that a parent's love is unconditional. This book, about an Eskimo mother and child, also teaches a little bit about Inuit culture and the wildlife of Alaska.

A mother tells her curious daughter, "I love you more than the raven loves his treasure, more than the dog loves his tail, more than the whale loves his spout." The young daughter wants to know if her mother will still love her if she makes a mistake, turns into a walrus, or tests her limits in any other way. This book is a beautiful testament to a parent's unconditional love and a child's need for reassurance.

Mommy, Carry Me Please! by Jane Cabrera (Holiday House: 2006) (E)

Read to learn the ways that all mothers in the animal kingdom care for their babies.

On each page of this book, a young animal asks his mother to carry him. For each animal, this means something different and the reader learns how various mothers carry their babies. On the last page, a little boy asks his mommy to "carry me please" and she picks him up, giving him a big hug.

My Father's Hands by Joanne Ryder, illustrated by Mark Graham (HarperCollins Publishers: 1994) (D)

Read about the special bond a father and his daughter share over their love for nature.

A daughter is mesmerized by the amazing creatures her father finds in his green garden. He reaches out his "earth-stained hands" and calls to his daughter to share his love of nature through the beautiful beetles and worms he digs up.

Owl Moon by Jane Yolen, illustrated by John Schoenherr (Philomel Books: 1987) (D)

Read for a beautiful story about how nature can help create ritual and special moments between a father and his daughter.

The night woods create the backdrop for this special time between a father and his daughter: the tradition of going owling. This is the narrator's first time going with Pa to see the owls; she describes how their "feet crunch the crisp snow" in the still, dark night. Although they see no owls at first, she doesn't call out to disturb them; the only thing you need for owling is hope.

Pierre in Love by Sara Pennypacker, pictures by Petra Mathers (Scholastic: 2007) (D)

Read to show your child how to find the courage to tell someone you love them.

Pierre is a poor fisherman and Catherine is a ballet teacher. Pierre loves Catherine but is too afraid to tell her for fear that she will not love him back. Can Pierre find the courage to let Catherine know how he feels?

Won't You Be My Kissaroo? by Joanne Ryder, illustrated by Melissa Sweet (Harcourt Children's Books: 2008) (E)

Read this with a child to show the joy found in giving and receiving kisses.

A little lamb wakes on her birthday to kisses from her mother. As she walks around her neighborhood, she sees other parents and children exchanging kisses as signs of their affection for one another. At the end of the day, the little lamb receives an affectionate good-night kiss—the perfect way to end her birthday.

THE CHALLENGES AND JOYS OF SIBLINGS

My colleague Patty was one of nine children growing up. She remembers standing around the stove with her father as he cooked pasta sauce, with eight other faces peering in the pot and trying to wedge in to get her spot too. Sibling relationships can be intense, frustrating, joyous, loving, hilarious, close, distant. There is no way to generalize. Respect your children as they navigate the waters of their own relationships. Try not to be too quick to jump in to manage the nuances of these growing relationships, but also don't leave them completely alone to figure things out. It is their first big relationship and it will determine some of how they trust and interact with others for the rest of their lives.

Literature leaps to the rescue so you are not alone in setting this foundation: offering images, stories, values, and possibilities for the child's growing sense of himself in relation to the other: his sister or brother. You may worry when you see conflict. Some measure of conflict is normal; your children have to be able to have some without feeling too guilty about it. But the important thing is how the day ends. In a physical sense, reading thematically as we are doing here is the perfect way to bring your family together at certain points in the day, gathering everyone on or near your lap as a book soothes the ruffled edges of the day. On a metaphoric level, literature also grants the chance to help build empathy by having children see and hear another point of view. There are many faces around that pot: they all matter; they are all beloved.

Amber Was Brave, Essie Was Smart: The Story of Amber and Essie Told Here in Poems and Pictures by Vera B. Williams (Greenwillow Books: 2001) (M)

Read for a sometimes funny and sometimes sad exploration of the love and the bond between siblings.

Many poems and pictures tell the story of Amber and Essie, two sisters whose father is in jail and whose mother works all day.

The Big Alfie and Annie Rose Storybook by Shirley Hughes (Red Fox: 2007) (D)

Read when you want to discuss the many ways in which siblings can help each other.

This is a collection of stories about a brother and sister, Alfie and Annie Rose, who share adventures and undertakings both big and small. They are a compassionate, affectionate pair who work together to overcome obstacles and have fun. While their mother makes many appearances in the stories, their father is never seen or mentioned, so this would be a good book to read if you are raising your children in a single parent household.

Big Sister and Little Sister by Charlotte Zolotow, pictures by Martha Alexander (HarperTrophy: 1966) (D)

Read to siblings.

Big Sister is always taking care of Little Sister and teaching her new things. One day, Little Sister gets tired of hearing Big Sister tell her what to do, so she runs away. Each sister learns that roles can change and both need to comfort and take care of the other.

Talk about It: This is a wonderful book about the joys and tensions in a relationship between two sisters. Use it to spur discussions on the challenges in sibling relationships.

- Do you help each other? Does it ever feel like someone helps you "too much"?
- What are your favorite things to do with your sister/brother?

- Do you think Little Sister imagined that her big sister would cry when she left?
- Did you ever make someone unhappy when you didn't mean to? Did you do anything to help them afterward?

Do Like Kyla by Angela Johnson, illustrated by James Ransome (Scholastic: 1993) (D)

Read when your child wants to celebrate the joys of doing things like her older sister, or maybe even like her younger sister.

A little girl loves imitating her big sister, Kyla. Whether eating oatmeal or making steps in the snow, this younger sister loves doing like Kyla. Though by the end of the evening, Kyla too learns that it can be fun to do like her younger sister.

Do You Know What I'll Do? by Charlotte Zolotow, illustrated by Javaka Steptoe (HarperCollins Publishers: 2000) (D)

Read when you want to celebrate the special bond between a sister and her brother.

This little girl asks her brother: "Do you know what I'll do?" She proceeds to tell him all of the special things that she will do for him: bring him birthday cake, tell him her dreams, and, most importantly, hug him. As you read, enjoy the beautiful illustrations.

Hello Twins by Charlotte Voake (Candlewick Press: May 2006) (E)

Read to show your child that even the most different siblings can be close friends.

Simon and Charlotte are twins, but they have nothing in common. Despite their differences, the twins are close friends and love each other for who they are.

Jitterbug Jam: A Monster Tale by Barbara Jean Hicks, illustrated by Alexis Deacon (Farrar, Straus and Giroux: 2004) (D)

Read about making friends and finding that special person to play hide-and-seek with.

Bobo, the young monster, is too scared to sleep because of the boy hidden under his bed, in this book that will challenge all your notions about monsters.

Julius, the Baby of the World by Kevin Henkes (Greenwillow Books: 1990) (D)

Read on those days when it is hard not to be jealous of the new baby.

Lilly finds it hard to adjust to her new brother, until one day something happens to change her mind.

The One in the Middle Is the Green Kangaroo by Judy Blume, illustrated by Irene Trivas (Yearling: 1992) (D)

Read for a great introductory chapter book on being in the middle.

Freddy is always in the middle. He is the middle sibling and sometimes feels like the peanut butter in a sandwich. It all changes when Freddy gets to be the Green Kangaroo in the school play.

Sayonara, Mrs. Kackleman by Maira Kalman (Penguin: 1991) (D)

Read to talk about fun adventures that a brother and a sister can share.

Alexander suggests to his big sister, Lulu, that she avoid her dreaded piano lesson with Mrs. Kackleman by joining him on a trip to Japan. Together, Alexander and Lulu set off on a wonderful adventure to Japan. Visit Japan through the eyes of these two excited and observant young people.

Sheila Rae, the Brave by Kevin Henkes (Greenwillow Books: 1987) (D)

Read to see how a younger sister can save the day.

Sheila Rae is so brave that she walks on all the cracks in the sidewalk, giggles when the principal walks by, and rides her bike with no hands and her eyes closed. Sheila Rae's sister Louise is the scaredy-cat in the family. Then, one day, Sheila Rae takes an unfamiliar route home from school and finds herself alone and lost and scared. Luckily, little Louise is there to save the day.

Stevie by John Steptoe (HarperCollins Publishers: 1986) (D)

Read to discuss how difficult it can be to adjust to new people and situations.

The young narrator of the story has a young boy named Stevie move into his house for a week. At first he really dislikes having Stevie live with him:

Stevie breaks his toys and leaves footprints on his bed. But when Stevie has to go home, the young boy realizes that he will miss his new friend.

Two Is for Twins by Wendy Cheyette Lewison, illustrated by Hiroe Nakata (Penguin Young Readers Group: 2006) (D)

Read for a great tale about twins.

This is a celebration of twins and the numeral two.

Where's the Baby? by Pat Hutchins (Greenwillow Books: 1988) (E)

Read this book when your child feels mischievous and silly.

Hazel, her mom, and her grandma track the baby by following the mess he left behind.

Zelda and Ivy: The Runaways by Laura McGee Kvasnosky (Candlewick Press: 2006) (D→M)

Read this with a child to explore the power dynamics between sisters. This is one story in a series about Zelda and Ivy.

When their dad serves cucumber sandwiches for lunch again, Zelda and Ivy pack up and run away to the backyard. They spy on their parents, who don't seem to miss them at all. Eventually they return and find that Dad has saved lunch for them.

THE COMPLEXITY OF SHARING

Sharing is hard, even for us adults. Or shall I say, especially for us! Grown-ups do a fine job of lecturing to children on the benefits of sharing, but we struggle with it too. Sometimes just the glint of hurt in a child's eye as we rip a treasured toy out of his hands for the benefit of a playdate is enough to give us pause: is sharing always necessary? We do want to help our children negotiate the realm of play confidently and generously. Sharing is sometimes about objects, but it is also about sharing ideas later on too, as well as sharing relationships. The early forays into sharing are practice for the harder kinds of sharing that come as we grow. Acknowledging the challenge while savoring the benefits can be discussed through some of these great read-alouds below.

Lilly's Big Day by Kevin Henkes (HarperCollins Children's Books: 2006) (D)

Read to talk about how hard it is to share the limelight.

Lilly thinks that she is going to be the flower girl in her favorite teacher Mr. Slinger's wedding. When Lilly finds out that she must be the assistant flower girl for Mr. Slinger's niece, she is devastated at being second in the show. Will Lilly make the best of a frustrating situation?

Mama, I'll Give You the World by Roni Schotter, illustrated by Susan Saelig Gallagher (Random House Books for Young Readers: 2004) (D)

Read to talk to your child about sharing something special.

Louisa visits her mama at Walter's World of Beauty every day after school. While Mama saves money for Louisa to go to college, Louisa does her schoolwork and creates portraits of the clients.

Talk about It: This can generate a conversation about generosity and doing something nice for a special person, whether a friend or a brother or a sister.

- Would you like to do something kind for someone?
- Can you remember a time when giving someone a special gift made you very happy? Can you remember a time when someone did something very nice for you and made you happy?

The Pigeon Finds a Hot Dog! by Mo Willems (Hyperion Books for Children: 2004) (E)

Read when your child doesn't feel like sharing something that is hers. This book is best for younger children who are learning the concepts of ownership and sharing.

The pigeon has found a glorious hot dog to eat and is about to bite into it when a duckling arrives on the scene. The duckling has never tasted a hot dog before, and asks the pigeon what it tastes like; this makes the pigeon nervous because it is his hot dog, and he has no intention of giving it to the duckling. How will they resolve this problem?

Pinky and Rex by James Howe, illustrated by Melissa Sweet (Simon & Schuster: 1990) (D)

Read this when your child has trouble sharing his favorite dinosaur or stuffed animal.

Pinky and Rex are best friends. Pinky has twenty-seven stuffed animals and Rex has twenty-seven dinosaurs. When they go on a trip to the museum, they both want the same pink dinosaur from the museum shop. Amanda, Pinky's sister, helps Pinky and Rex find a solution.

Talk about It: This is a great book to read when the issue of sharing comes up. The book provides an opportunity to discuss how hard it can be to share, sometimes, but how much fun it can be too.

- Have you ever had to share something very special?
- How did Amanda help Pinky and Rex find a solution to their problem? Was it a good solution?

COPING WITH ILLNESS

I once worked as a visiting literacy consultant in a classroom with a nine-year-old whose name was Kim. Her sister had AIDS. Kim wrote every day about her sister's health. She wrote about how she brushed her sister's thinning hair and bathed her sensitive skin. Sometimes my hand brushed over damp spots on the page as I read. I knew these were Kim's tears. This past year, I received a letter from the woman who had been Kim's teacher the year I was at her school. "Pam," she said, "Kim's sister, is still alive. And Kim has just gotten engaged and has a baby herself." It was fifteen years ago when I first met Kim. And I picture Kim today, holding and caring for her new baby, as she did and probably still does for her own sister, brushing her hair, bathing her tender skin. Children possess vast and extraordinary reservoirs of love and caring.

If your child, or a child you know, is experiencing an illness in the family, there are countless ways that the family energy is given over to the sick child. The well child may be in the position of struggling with his wonderings alone or imagining the worst. And an intuitive, sensitive child may contain a lot of that worry and it manifests itself as irritability or grouchiness. The read-aloud tempers those worries with conversation and shared moments, reminders that as a family you will get through this.

Elvis the Rooster Almost Goes to Heaven by Denys Cazet (HarperTrophy: 2004) (D)

Read to discuss the impact of grief on our actions and how to manage it.

Just as Elvis prepares to open his mouth to crow in the new day, a bug flies down his throat and the crow cannot come out. When the sun still rises without him, Elvis believes that life is not worth living if he cannot crow at the morning sun. He begins to say his humorous farewells to all he knows, until his friends form a plan to cure his case of the blues.

Miz Berlin Walks by Jane Yolen, illustrated by Floyd Cooper (Philomel Books: 1997) (D)

Read to address the sadness that arises when a loved one falls ill, and we miss all that we used to do with them when they were well.

Miz Berlin walks by Mary Louise's house every day, carrying a big black umbrella and telling stories to no one. One day, Mary Louise summons up her courage and walks next to Miz Berlin. Each day, she walks farther and farther with the old woman, and each day Miz Berlin has a new story to tell. One day, Miz Berlin does not walk past Mary Louise's house, and Mary Louise faces the difficulty of dealing with the illness of someone she cares about.

Now One Foot, Now the Other by Tomie dePaola (Puffin: 2006) (D)

Read this with your child to help him understand the changes in someone close to him who is sick.

Bobby is close to his grandfather Bob, who suffers from a stroke. At first Bobby is afraid of the changes he sees in his grandfather and cannot understand why his grandfather doesn't recognize Bobby. Over time, however, Bobby learns that his grandfather is the same person and helps him recover from his stroke.

Remember, Grandma? by Laura Langston (Penguin: 2004) (D)

Read when you want to discuss how creating new memories can be just as important as remembering old ones.

Margaret lives with her grandma, and they spend their time going on long walks and baking apple pie. But soon, Margaret's grandmother begins to lose her memory, and eventually cannot even remember Margaret's name. Margaret faithfully supports her ailing grandmother; on each page she asks, "Remember, Grandma?"

Remembering Grandpa by Uma Krishnaswami, illustrated by Layne Johnson (Boyds Mills Press: 2007) (D)

Read after the death of a family member or close friend, or when you want to talk about loss.

Daysha's grandmother is sad after the death of Daysha's grandfather a year before. Daysha does not remember her grandfather as being sad, and she sets out to gather happy memories of him for herself and her grandmother. The memories bring joy to her grandmother, helping her sadness with "hugs and the right kind of remembering."

Special Kids in School (Taking Diabetes to School, and more) by Kim Gosselin, illustrated by Moss Freedman (Jayjo Books: 1998) (D→M)

Read this to a child who has been diagnosed with diabetes or knows someone with diabetes.

This book is told from the perspective of an elementary-school student who has diabetes. He explains to his classmates and teachers how he copes with the illness and, ultimately, how diabetes doesn't make him any different from other kids.

Wilfrid Gordon McDonald Partridge by Mem Fox, illustrated by Julie Vivas (Kane-Miller Book Publishers: 1985) (D)

Read when you want to talk about memory loss and how to cope with an elderly friend who is experiencing it.

A boy named Wilfrid Gordon McDonald Partridge lives next to an "old people's home" and knows each person who lives there. One day, he discovers that his favorite friend, Miss Nancy Alison Delacourt Cooper, who has four names just like him, is losing her memory. He proceeds to collect things that he considers memory and places them in a small basket in an effort to help Miss Nancy protect the important and magical substance that is memory.

COURAGE

What may seem commonplace to you is perhaps awesome for your child. The courage needed to make our way through life takes many forms—physical, social, emotional. We barely notice some of the many forms of courage. Children may need to summon courage to walk on a ledge for the first time, to ride a two-wheeled bike, or simply to fall down and get back up again. A child needs courage to be herself in a group—to navigate the first days of school or an awkward moment on the playground, to find someone to sit with at lunch, to go home to an empty apartment after school. A child may need to find courage to see himself in relation to the world: to deal with feeling different because of the color of his skin, his religious background, or even his name. Children find themselves in situations that require courage every day. The following books are both windows and mirrors for courage; read them with your child and discover what is possible in terms of courage in the outside world, as well as how to find courage within.

Alfie Gets in First by Shirley Hughes (Lothrop, Lee & Shepard Books: 1981) (E)

Read when your child is afraid of being alone, feels bad about a mistake he has made, or when he needs to get himself out of a tricky situation. This book is one of a series about Alfie, his sister, and their family.

Alfie runs ahead of his mother and sister because he wants to get home. But when he gets inside his apartment, he closes the door by mistake and locks himself in. All the neighbors come over to try to help him. While everyone is getting more and more worried, Alfie figures out a way to open the door.

Talk about It: There are acts of courage well suited to every child's age. Toddlers hearing this story will appreciate the warm outcome (everyone comes in for tea in the end) and also appreciate the attention Shirley Hughes gives to a young child's first experience with independence.

- When was a time you felt good about figuring something out? Did it require courage?
- What would you have done if you were Alfie?
- Alfie seems to have a very warm relationship with his family. Does courage come from love? Where do you think courage comes from?

Brave Charlotte by Anu Stohner, illustrations by Henrike Wilson, translated from German by Alyson Cole (Bloomsbury: 2005) (D)

Read when your child needs the courage and inspiration to help someone.

Charlotte has always been different from all of the other sheep in the herd. She is a very adventurous sheep who climbs trees, swims in the river, roams through the countryside at night, and is not afraid of Jack, the sheepdog. The other sheep are amazed by Charlotte's courage. Late one afternoon, the herd's shepherd falls and breaks his leg. What will the sheep do? Jack is too old to go back by himself, and no sheep has ever passed through the valley alone. Will Charlotte be able to save the day?

Chrysanthemum by Kevin Henkes (Greenwillow Books: 1991) (D)

Read when somebody hurts your child's feelings or when your child feels sad about being different.

Chrysanthemum loves her name until she starts going to school. There, everyone teases her about how long her name is and how many letters it has. But when Chrysanthemum meets her music teacher, Mrs. Delphinium Twinkle, things start to look up. Henkes captures Chrysanthemum's realization that while being different is sometimes very difficult, it can also be tremendously fun.

Talk about It: This book is a wonderful conversation starter on how to handle difficult social situations, and also how to be open to kids who seem different. Being open to differences oftentimes takes courage too.

- Have you ever needed courage because you felt different? Can you tell me about that?
- When has feeling different felt good for you? When has it been difficult?
- Do you know anyone who seemed different to you when you first met them? Did it take courage for you to talk to that person or befriend them?

Cyrus the Unsinkable Sea Serpent by Bill Peet (Houghton Mifflin Company: 1982) (D→M)

Read about when it takes courage to stay true to your values.

Cyrus, the friendly and shy sea serpent, does not want to sink ships. But a mean shark tries to pressure him into sinking a passing ship. Despite the pressure he feels to listen to the shark, Cyrus discovers that by finding the courage to be himself, he can become a hero and save a foundering ship during a storm.

Doña Flor: A Tall Tale about a Giant Woman with a Great Big Heart by Pat Mora, illustrated by Raul Colón (Knopf Books for Young Readers: 2005) (D)

Read this wonderful folktale, which has Spanish words tucked throughout, to begin a conversation about the courage it takes to be different and how good it feels to help other people.

Doña Flor, a very, very tall lady, loves to help the neighbors and animals in her village. Doña Flor carries the village children to school on her very, very broad shoulders, allows the birds to build nests in her hair, and "when her hands, wide as plates, started pat-pat-patting tortillas, everyone in the village woke up." One morning, when none of her friends arrive to eat her tortillas, she knows something is wrong. Doña Flor discovers that her friends are scared by a loud noise they hear during the night. Can Doña Flor save her friends from the source of the noise?

The Forest by Claire A. Nivola (Farrar, Straus and Giroux: 2002) (D)

Read to teach your child about finding the courage to face his fears.

A small mouse begins a journey of self-discovery as he gathers the courage to enter the forest that seems so scary. Step by step, he coaxes himself to face the forest, and his overwhelming fears become lessened as he realizes the bigness and beauty of nature.

Talk about It: Use this book to start a conversation about overcoming fears. Although he is very scared, when the mouse faces his fear, he realizes that it is small in comparison to the wonderful sky and the beauty of nature. Discuss how fear can seem to overtake and even cloud our ability to notice the goodness and beauty of things. Discuss the value and rewards of facing your fears.

- What were some of the mouse's specific fears as he began entering the forest? Do you think that it was okay for the mouse to have those fears?

- Although he is terrified, the mouse still enters the forest. What happens first? Then, what does he experience when he opens his eyes?
- How do you think the mouse feels at the end of the story?
- Think about something that frightens you. Talk about how you might try to face this fear and be like the mouse in the story.

Halibut Jackson by David Lucas (Knopf Books for Young Readers: 2004) (M)

Read when your child needs courage to overcome his shyness.

Halibut Jackson is so shy that he tries to blend into his surroundings so that no one will notice him. He makes clothing for himself that matches the background of the place to which he is going. When he goes to the library, he wears a suit covered in books and when he goes to the park, he wears a suit peppered with flowers. When Halibut Jackson receives an invitation to attend a party at the palace, he designs a palace suit. However, the party is actually in the garden. Will the people at the party be able to help Halibut Jackson overcome his shyness?

I'm Not Going Out There! by Paul Bright, illustrated by Ben Cort (Good Books: 2006) (D)

Read for a fun way to coax any child who decides that she is not coming out from under the bed.

The young narrator will *not* come out from under his bed. It isn't because he is scared of all the creatures he imagines are in the house: a dragon, a ghost, dancing monsters. Instead, it is because of something very real, very angry, and her name is Kate.

The Man Who Walked Between the Towers by Mordicai Gerstein (Roaring Brook Press: 2003) (M)

Read to teach your child about finding the courage to try something hard.

Based on the true story of Philippe Petit, who walked on a tightrope between the World Trade Center towers in 1974, this book is about having the courage to pursue a dream. When Petit gets ready for the walk, he looks "not at the towers but at the space between them and thinks, what a wonderful place to stretch a rope."

Talk about It: Explore the idea that courage takes work and is not accidental. In the end, Petit walked, ran, and danced on the wire. He was eventually arrested, but his punishment was to perform his tightrope feats for the schoolchildren of New York City. The avenues of conversation here are many: talk about the loss of the World Trade Center, the spaces left by things that are lost, and the courage it takes for all of us to go on after difficult times. Petit's sheer determination combined with the tremendous loss we now feel after September 11 creates a deeply moving reading experience.

- What kind of big dream can you imagine for yourself?
- Discuss September 11, if it's appropriate for your child. Can you remember a time when it took courage to keep on after something sad happened to you or someone you know?

Mercy Watson Fights Crime by Kate DiCamillo, illustrated by Chris Van Dusen (Candlewick Press: 2006) (D)

Read to talk about a scary event. Other popular titles by Kate DiCamillo include Because of Winn-Dixie *and* The Miraculous Journey of Edward Tulane, *two books that appeal to readers ages eight to twelve. Because they are fans of DiCamillo, older children in the family may actually enjoy read-alouds of the Mercy series, while younger siblings will naturally have a ball with Mercy's adventures.*

Mercy Watson is a pig who loves buttered toast. One night, she hears the sound of the toaster and wakes to discover a man in a big hat stealing it. Mercy solves the problem of the burglar in a most gutsy way. The book addresses real fears children have in a way that is just lighthearted enough to quell them.

Mirette on the High Wire by Emily Arnold McNully (G. P. Putnam's Sons: 1992) (D)

Read to talk about when you doubt that you can accomplish something or need encouragement to recognize your own value and importance.

When Mr. Bellini, the world-famous tightrope artist, comes to stay at her mother's boarding house in Paris, Mirette is enthralled by the idea of walking across the sky on a rope. Finally, she convinces Mr. Bellini to teach her the art of tightrope walking. Although it seems as though Mr. Bellini is fearless, by the end of the story, Mirette actually has the chance to repay Bellini for his kindness by helping him to overcome some of his fears.

Talk about It: Even a world-famous tightrope walker has moments of doubt. Use this book to talk about when you feel doubtful and discouraged about yourself. Also, recognize that young people can help grown-ups to overcome their fears as well.

- Mirette must practice long and hard to walk across the tightrope without falling. Why didn't she give up? What is something that you worked hard to achieve?
- Why do you think that Mr. Bellini might have been fearful of the rope? Has there ever been a time when you were suddenly scared to do something that you used to find easy? What did you do?

Pancakes for Supper by Anne Isaacs, illustrated by Mark Teague (Scholastic: 2006) (D)

Read to talk about when you need daring and creativity to get yourself out of a bind, or when you have to solve a problem and your family isn't there to help guide you.

Toby sets out to Whisker Creek with her family in a wagon. Suddenly she is thrown from the wagon and lands in the middle of the forest. She has to use her courage and ingenuity to make it safely out of the forest and back to her parents.

Silly Billy by Anthony Browne (Candlewick Press: 2006) (D)

Read this story when your child is feeling worried.

Billy worries about everything. When Billy visits his grandma's house, he worries so much he can't sleep. But his grandma has the perfect solution.

Small Knight and George by Ronda Armitage, illustrated by Arthur Robins (Barron's Educational Series: 2007) (D)

Read this to talk about being faced with a daunting task.

Small Knight must set out to fight a dragon, but he does not feel very brave. Along the way, as he hears stories about fierce dragons, he feels even less brave, until he finds a reassuring ally.

Thunder Cake by Patricia Polacco (Philomel Books: 1990) (D)

Read for a fitting story for those stormy days.

As a grandmother and a granddaughter bake Thunder Cake together, the granddaughter learns that she is really very brave. The grandmother gently fosters the granddaughter's independence. This is a beautiful story about overcoming fear, and trusting in a relationship.

CREATING COMMUNITY

Great children's book authors recognize that children have extraordinary power to shape their own worlds. Fern reaches out and saves Wilbur the pig, with the help of a spider who knows how to spell. Lucy rescues Mr. Tumnus from the grips of the White Witch. Anna teaches Amber how to read. Early on, through the read-aloud, you can give your child a sense of his or her own power in shaping and creating a powerfully loving community, in the family, at school, in the larger communities of sports and friendship. He does not have to wait to become a grown-up to impact his world.

Amber on the Mountain by Tony Johnston, illustrated by Robert Duncan (Dial Books for Young Readers: 1994) (M)

Read when you want to discuss the role of community in shaping our world.

Amber lives high up on a lonely mountain where people live far apart from one another; she yearns for company. One day, a man comes with his daughter, Anna, to build a road on the mountain. Amber wants to learn to read almost as much as she wants company, and so Anna sets her mind to teaching her the skill. When Anna leaves the mountain, Amber dedicates herself to learning how to write to keep in contact with her faraway friend.

The Bookshop Dog by Cynthia Rylant (Scholastic: 1996) (D)

Read this book when you want to discuss how communities rally to care for their members.

When the bookshop owner falls ill, she has to decide who will care for Martha Jane, her beloved dog. The whole town loves Martha Jane, but one special person comes to her rescue.

A Chair for My Mother by Vera B. Williams (HarperCollins Publishers: 1982) (M)

Read when you want to talk about how to help others.

The main character, her mother, and grandmother have been saving their extra coins in a jar for a year, ever since their apartment burned down. They are saving to buy a comfy chair to add to all of the furniture that families, friends, and neighbors gave to them when they lost everything in the fire. Finally, they are able to add the chair they had dreamed about to an apartment furnished through the kindness of others.

Talk about It: This is a good book to begin a conversation about the importance of helping out others who are in a difficult situation. You may want to discuss ways that your child could help out others in your own community. You may also use this book to talk about the value of working hard and saving for something special.

- Why was the main character saving her money? Do you think that saving her own money made the chair even more special? Why or why not?
- How did their friends and neighbors react when the family's apartment burned in the fire? What would you have done if you were friends with the main character?

Come on, Rain! by Karen Hesse, illustrations by Jon J. Muth (Scholastic: 1999) (D)

Read this book when celebrating with your community.

After a long, hot, dry spell, Tess pleads for rain. When the rain finally comes, Tess and her friends rejoice.

For You Are a Kenyan Child by Kelly Cunnane, illustrated by Ana Juan (Simon & Schuster Children's Publishing: 2006) (D)

Read to learn about a day in the life of a child in a Kenyan village, to appreciate this boy's inextricable connection to the natural world, and to find similarities and differences in your child's life.

As he rises in the morning, a Kenyan child prepares for a day in which he will watch his grandfather's cows in the pasture. But there are so many beautiful things to see and do in his village that it is easy to get distracted; he might stop at the tea shop, chase the black monkeys, explore a garden of green onions, or kick a rag ball with friends. In the meantime, what is happening to his grandfather's cows?

In the Forest by Marie Hall Ets (Puffin: 1976) (E)

Read this to explore the power of a child to create a community of his own.

A young boy is celebrating his birthday with his new horn. On a magical journey through a forest of his imagination, he meets animals who come with him on his adventure. More and more animals join him as this enchanting story progresses.

Miss Rumphius by Barbara Cooney (The Viking Press: 1982) (D)

Read this with a child who is pondering creative ways to better the world.

As a child, Miss Rumphius promises her grandfather she will do three things: go to faraway places, live beside the sea, and make the world a more beautiful place. After accomplishing the first two, Miss Rumphius, growing old, is at a loss for how to make the world more beautiful. That is, until one winter, when she is suffering from illness and comes up with a simple and creative plan.

Move Over, Rover! by Karen Beaumont, illustrated by Jane Dyer (Harcourt: 2006) (E)

Read with a younger child for a silly story about companionship.

Rover is alone in his doghouse, feeling lonely. As it begins to rain, other animals venture into the doghouse because they are looking for a dry place. "Move Over, Rover!" But when a skunk decides he wants to find shelter from the rain, the animals disperse into the oncoming sunshine.

Mr. Gumpy's Outing by John Burningham (Henry Holt and Company: 1970) (E)

Read when you want to talk about the importance of working together with people.

When Mr. Gumpy decides to go for an outing on his boat, all of the animals in the barnyard and two neighborhood children beg to join him. Mr. Gumpy makes them promise to behave, but when they don't, everyone gets a little wet.

Out of the Egg by Tina Matthews (Houghton Mifflin Company: 2007) (E)

Read when you want to discuss the importance of sharing in fostering a sense of community.

This book provides a fresh take on the familiar story of the Little Red Hen. She toils and toils to help a new tree to grow out of a seed that she found. She lays a little white egg under the tree, and soon a new Little Red Hen hatches. The little hen teaches its mother a valuable lesson about sharing and inclusion.

The Problem with Chickens by Bruce McMillan, illustrated by Gunnella (Houghton Mifflin Company: 2005) (D)

Read this with your children to explore community through a funny and lighthearted book.

A group of women decides to buy chickens so their community will have an endless supply of eggs. What they do not anticipate, however, is that the chickens start acting like women—they have teatimes and go to parties—until they are too busy to lay eggs. The women must find a resourceful solution to their problem before the eggs run out.

The Rain Came Down by David Shannon (The Blue Sky Press: 2000) (D)

Read when you want to discuss how frustrations can lead to rifts within the community, and how often the simplest solution can be the most effective.

When the rain begins, it triggers a series of events that travel throughout the animals and people in the town. Frustrated with the rain, the town fills with commotion and anger. Just when the storm threatens to tear the community apart, the skies clear and the sun shines down.

Rainbow Fish by Marcus Pfister (NorthSouth Books: 2006) (D)

Read to discuss the role of community in helping solve a problem.

Filled with colorful illustrations, this book tells the story of an independent fish who gets swept away by a powerful storm while he is focused on collecting shiny blue pebbles. He finds himself in an unfamiliar world with no fish that have glittery scales like him. It takes teamwork and help from his new friends to get the Rainbow Fish home again.

Stone Soup by Jon J. Muth (Live Oak Media: 1987) (D)

Read when you want to discuss the role of working together in creating happiness for all.

This book, featuring beautiful watercolor illustrations, tells the story of three monks, Hok, Lok and Siew, who travel down a mountain road to find what makes people happy. They come across a village where the townspeople have experienced hard times and do not trust one another. The monks devise a way to teach the villagers the value of working together as they all combine their efforts to concoct the perfect stone soup.

Wild Lives: A History of People & Animals of the Bronx Zoo by Kathleen Weidner Zoehfeld, photographs by Wildlife Conservation Society (Knopf Books for Young Readers: 2006) (M)

Read to learn about the large and caring community found at the Bronx Zoo.

This book documents the evolution of the famous Bronx Zoo, and the lives of its zookeepers and animal inhabitants. Photographs of the zoo and its zookeepers accompany the story, which spans more than a century.

CREATIVE THEATER: MAKING PLAYS AND SCENES TOGETHER

As you read this book, I hope you feel how strongly I care about finding ways to make the read-aloud just right for you and your child. Some children love to be active and moving around. They are not ones to sit and snuggle for very long. The read-aloud can be done standing up, twirling around, and in motion. Let your voice inspire your children to create live action through theater and the oral tradition.

In the first class I ever taught, we performed "Free to Be You and Me" for the neighborhood. I had read it aloud to them so many times that they knew it by heart and had the idea to perform it for the elderly people who lived on the same block as the school. Everyone brought cookies and lawn chairs and my second graders belted out the songs, with no music background, no costumes. Just their joyous smiles, all around.

Amazing Grace by Mary Hoffman, illustrated by Caroline Binch (Dial Books for Young Readers: 1991) (D)

Read to celebrate taking on different characters.

Grace loves acting out stories. "She was Hiawatha, sitting by the shining Big-Sea-Water . . . and Mowgli in the backyard jungle." Grace was so excited when she learned that her class would be performing *Peter Pan*; she knew she could play the lead. Grace feels discouraged when her classmates doubt that she will be able to be Peter Pan, but her warm and wise mother and grandmother teach Grace that she can be whoever she wants to be.

Free to Be You and Me by Marlo Thomas and Friends (Running Press: 2002) (D→M)

Read to celebrate individuality.

Through this collection of stories, songs, and poems, Marlo Thomas celebrates the importance of individuality and of not adhering to stereotypes.

Good Masters! Sweet Ladies! Voices from a Medieval Village by Laura Amy Schlitz, illustrated by Robert Byrd (Candlewick Press: 2007) (M)

Read aloud or act out when you want to learn about many of the exciting characters who lived on or near a medieval manor.

This collection of seventeen monologues depicts the lives of the men and women who lived by a medieval manor. Learn all about Piers, the glassblower apprentice, or Nelly, the sniggler, or Thomas, the doctor's son, through these riveting portraits.

How to Eat Like a Child: And Other Lessons in Not Being a Grown-up by Delia Ephron, illustrated by Edward Koren (HarperCollins: 1977) (M)

Read to perform the sections aloud as monologues.

Learn how to eat like a child or how to tell a joke or how to torture your sister in these short and delightful snippets.

Really Rosie: Starring Nutshell Kids by Maurice Sendak (Harper Trophy: 1986) (D)

Read to learn about Rosie through song.

Join the ever-energetic Rosie as she sings. This Maurice Sendak book contains the script to *Really Rosie* along with sheet music for a child to create his or her own scenes from the popular TV show.

CREATIVITY

There are many ways to be creative. What may seem to you like eccentricity or even a sign of a slightly worrying difference may really be the early stirrings of a deep potential for creative thinking. Keep a dress-up box in a central location for your child, even through the age of ten and beyond. At that point, though, you may want to move the dress-up box to their bedroom or to a more private place, as creative play becomes less "cool" then and they may need more privacy to continue to live in a world of imagination. Support this. It all contributes to a lifetime of literacy. Have paints and markers available day and night. Put a low table in your kitchen so that while you are cooking your child can be engaged with some form of creativity alongside you. When I was about seven, my grandmother brought my brother and sister and me to the beach and we all built a car out of the sand, down to every last detail. It is something I still remember: she took the most obvious materials and made something very surprising. We stayed in a state of delight over it for a long, long time. When my brother and sister and I reminisce about it, I still feel those flickers of the same delight. I know they do too.

Creativity is the energy source for a doctor's discovery, a writer's great story, a chef's perfect recipe. It is an essential part of raising your child, this support for her creativity. It's part of literacy development too. Stories are the manifestation of an author's creative mind, as is great art. Here are some books that will help you stoke the creative spirit in your child.

Building an Igloo by Ulli Steltzer (Henry Holt and Company: 1999) (D)

Read this book to teach your child about the Inuit in the Arctic and how igloos are made.

Tookillkee and his son Jopee build a new igloo for themselves in the cold Arctic winter. They outline and cut the blocks of snow, fit them into a spiral, put the pieces together, and after hours of working, the result is one of the warmest places in the Arctic.

Talk about It: Use this book to talk about how often you have to think outside the box in order to find a solution. Jopee and his dad work hard to build a warm home using the snow and ice that is available to them.

- ✦ How did Jopee and his dad build their igloo?
- ✦ How did teamwork make the project easier?

Emma's Rug by Allen Say (Houghton Mifflin Company: 1996) (D)

Read this when you want to discuss how often being creative means using your imagination and believing in yourself.

Young Emma, a talented artist, believes that the inspiration for all of her paintings and drawings comes from the rug she received when she was a baby. But one day, after her mom washes the special rug, Emma discovers where her creativity really comes from.

How the Ladies Stopped the Wind by Bruce McMillan, illustrated by Gunnella (Houghton Mifflin Company: 2007) (D)

Read to inspire your children to solve difficult problems, and to teach them about legends and the questions they are meant to answer.

Why aren't there trees in the countryside of Iceland? The ladies in Iceland know how challenging walking in the wind can be. With the help of the chickens, sheep, and cows, can the ladies find a way to stop the wind?

Talk about It: Use this beautifully illustrated and funny book to explore how the Icelandic women come up with a solution to nature's challenge by thinking creatively and working together, both with the members of their community and with the animals around them. Also, use this book to discuss what a legend is and how legends explain the story of natural phenomena, like the absence of trees in Iceland.

- ✦ Have you had a situation in which traditional solutions did not solve the problem? What did you do to solve the problem?
- ✦ Have you ever worked with a group of people (your friends, classmates, family, or neighbors) to solve a problem? Was the solution different than it would have been had you worked to solve the problem on your own?
- ✦ What is a legend? How does this legend explain why there are no trees in Iceland? Can you think of a legend you could create to answer a question you have?

I'm in Charge of Celebrations by Byrd Baylor, illustrations by Peter Parnall (Aladdin: 1995) (M)

Read this book to talk about creating new forms of entertainment, or when you want to celebrate the beauty of nature.

A girl who lives in the desert explains her daily celebrations of nature, like Dust Devil Day and Coyote Day.

Talk about It: This is a great story about how a girl entertains herself in a desert some might call lonely. Allow the book to become a conversation starter about finding ways to entertain oneself by celebrating the beauty of nature and the power of imagination.

- Have you ever used your imagination to create a new game? What was the game?

Mike Mulligan and His Steam Shovel by Virginia Lee Burton (Houghton Mifflin Company: 1939) (D)

Read to explore the determination and creativity sometimes necessary to solve a problem that seems overwhelming.

When steam shovels become outdated, Mike Mulligan and his steam shovel Mary Anne dig their way to a new home.

Not a Box by Antoinette Portis (HarperCollins Publishers: 2006) (E)

Read in celebration of the creativity and imagination of children.

In this story dedicated to "children everywhere sitting in cardboard boxes," the narrator continuously asks (as any adult might) what the child is doing with *that* box. The creativity is in the child's simple response that it is not a box. Instead, the box is respectively a race car, robot suit, mountain, hot-air balloon, and elephant.

Pie in the Sky by Lois Ehlert (Harcourt: 2004) (D)

Read to learn about how, with a little creativity and a lot of patience, the buds on a tree can become a delicious dessert.

Have you ever seen a Pie Tree? As the seasons change, a child studies the tree next to the house, trying to understand why dad calls it a Pie Tree. It's not until spring that the child learns the exciting and tasty answer.

Talk about It: This book is a wonderful way to learn about how trees grow and change over the seasons, some even producing delicious cherries. When you read this book, talk also about how to follow a recipe and bake a delicious pie.

- Have you ever studied the trees around you? How do trees change over the seasons?
- Why did this child's dad call the tree a Pie Tree? How did the child in the book have to think creatively to turn the tree into a Pie Tree?

The Pot That Juan Built by Nancy Andrews-Goebel, illustrated by David Diaz (Lee & Low Books: 2002) (M)

Read to talk about the inspiration provided by your surroundings, heritage, and traditions.

This book about Juan Quezada's pottery is composed of both a poem about how he creates his beautiful pots, and a historical account (both genres of text are on each page). Reading the flowing rhymes on the left-hand page, the reader learns of all the beautiful, local materials that Juan carefully picks to create his beautiful pottery. On the right-hand page, you can read in more detail about the history and process of making the pottery that Juan first discovered in the village of Mata Ortiz in the Chihuahua plains of Mexico.

Soul Looks Back in Wonder compiled by Tom Feelings (Puffin Books: 1999) (D)

Read this collection of poems accompanied by poignant illustrations to discover the work of thirteen African-American poets. With your younger children, enjoy the beautiful pictures and words; with your older children, discuss the importance of creativity and community building.

This is a captivating collection of thirteen poems by thirteen writers, including Maya Angelou, Walter Dean Myers, and Mwatabu Okantah. The poems and accompanying illustrations provide insight into the rich and deep history of African creativity.

Talk about It: Talk about what these poems teach you about creativity, about the strength and power of African culture, and the impact that culture has on one's writing.

- Where does creativity come from?
- How is creativity passed on from generation to generation?
- How does art or music or literature draw a community together?

CULTIVATING A SENSE OF TIME AND PLACE

A sense of the textures of time and place is a critical anchor for the growing child. The places he returns to with you again and again, the grocery store at the end of the street, a grandparent's house, become etched into his growing brain and heart. Talk together about what anchors you both to this world and why.

So too, by learning about the times and places that others experience, we become more understanding of the fluidity of the human experience and the universality of human emotion, no matter where or when we live.

Whether it is Harlem or Appalachia, San Francisco or Nairobi, we experience a love for place, and also a desire to escape it at times. As our children grow, we want to help them both love and appreciate where they come from, and also develop a love and appreciation for all the places they might go.

The Great Blue House by Kate Banks, illustrated by Georg Hallensleben (Farrar, Straus and Giroux: 2005) (D)

Read with a child to use your imagination to explore the changing seasons from a new perspective.

The Great Blue House is the happy summer home of a family, who leaves when fall comes. However, the house is not alone—it welcomes many creatures as fall turns to winter, spring, and summer again. As the seasons change, the house finds its guests shifting, but it is never alone.

Harlem by Walter Dean Myers, illustrated by Christopher Myers (Scholastic: 1997) (D)

Read this colorful poem to teach about the rich history of Harlem and explore the importance of appreciating a special place and community.

"Harlem" is a poem that brings to life the streets, people, and history of a very special neighborhood. Celebrate the well-occupied fire escapes, the uptown A train, and the smell of summer barbecue in this delightful book.

Knoxville, Tennessee by Nikki Giovanni, illustrated by Larry Johnson (Scholastic: 1994) (D)

Read to honor the time you and your child spend with your extended family.

Giovanni's warm poem celebrates summer in a rural community in the South.

Mei-Mei Loves the Morning by Margaret Holloway Tsubakiyama, illustrated by Cornelius Van Wright and Ying-Hwa Hu (Albert Whitman & Company; 1999) (D→M)

Read to explore the power of a grandparent's relationship with a child, as well as the wonderful things to be found around your child in her everyday life.

Mei-Mei and her grandfather enjoy breakfast together before setting out on a midmorning bicycle ride through their home city. As they ride, they affectionately greet many friends, whose company, along with that of her grandfather, makes it easy for Mei-Mei to love the morning.

Meteor! by Patricia Polacco (Putnam Juvenile: 1987) (D)

Read to learn all about the aftermath of a meteor crash and how an occurance that alters your hometown can transform a sense of time and place.

Based on a true event, this book explores the excitement and magic that surrounds the surprise crash of a meteor into the front lawn of the Gaw family.

My Little Island by Frané Lessac (HarperCollins Publishers: 1987) (D)

Read to delve into traveling and exploration.

A young boy and his best friend, Lucca, travel to the special island in the Caribbean where he was born. "My cousins and I gobble up pumpkin soup, pigeon peas, goat-water stew, red snapper fish, and fried bananas topped with guava ice cream," explains the young boy. The two boys visit the market, the seashore, and the island's very own volcano. Learn all about the island and its wild animals and vibrant traditions through the bright eyes of these two boys.

The Seashore Book by Charlotte Zolotow, paintings by Wendell Minor (HarperCollins Children's Books: 1994) (D)

Read when you want to use your imagination to visit somewhere you and your child have never been, or to remember why a day on the beach is so special.

A little boy asks his mother to describe the seashore. She brings the feel of the sand, the warmth of the sun, and the fading claw prints of the sandpipers to her son by cultivating his vivid imagination.

Talk about It: What makes a place very special? Is it the sounds or the smells that you remember about a place? Talk about how you can use you imagination to journey to the seashore or even to a mountaintop or outer space: that is the power of imagination.

- Do you have a very special place you love to visit? What makes that place so special?
- Have you ever used your imagination to travel to a new place? Where could you go and visit using your imagination?

Time of Wonder by Robert McCloskey (Penguin: 1957) (D)

Read to transport your child to a special place full of memories.

An island in Maine comes alive as children explore the sea, the shore, the forests, and harbors. With beautiful illustrations and fun alliterations, this story celebrates the wonders of nature and summertime.

What You Know First by Patricia MacLachlan (HarperCollins Children's Books: 1998) (D)

Read as you prepare to leave a place and want to be alive to all its details.

A child is deeply saddened when her family must leave their home in the prairie. Her mother suggests that she collect memories of the things she loves about the prairie—the grass, the sky, the trees—so she can tell her baby brother about it when he grows up. As her family prepares to leave, this young girl finds a way to collect mementos.

When I Was Young in the Mountains by Cynthia Rylant, illustrated by Diane Goode (Penguin Young Readers Group: 1993) (D)

Read for an intimate portrait of the joys and hardships of life in the mountains and the importance of family. This book will transport you to a time and place unlike any other.

A young girl remembers her life growing up in the mountains with her brother and grandparents. She recalls eating her grandmother's dinners, heating water for a bath, going to church at the schoolhouse on Sundays, and sitting with her family on the porch in the evenings. She remembers feeling complete and satisfied.

DEATH

Even now, years later, I still wake up in the middle of the night, anguished, and tears come to my eyes as I think of my grandparents and others in my family who are gone. The wide-awake child perceives the love around him and understands loss better than we can even imagine. Often, our own grief is so strong that it is very hard for us to provide the kind of comfort we want for our child. Rest your burden on the backs of these books. Find some measure of relief in using them to explore the mystery of death in gentle and unafraid ways with your child. There will never be one book that will speak to all the layers of our perception of what death is: but we can open up the conversation so our children are not afraid, and know they can always begin one with you. Children's book authors such as the ones here are gentle guides into this unfathomable journey. They cherish the spirits of those who have passed on, and cradle what could be a really scary topic into one of acceptance and understanding.

Tasnim Nagrath was Charlotte's first-grade teacher. When their frog, named March, died, the class wrote poetry for him and had a ceremony in the garden behind the school. Tears were shed. "Dear March," one of the children wrote, "You changed our lives." Now to us this might seem silly, that little frog changing the lives of six-year-olds, but you know what? It is entirely possible. Those compassionate little folks were practicing separations, safely, with their beloved teacher, a set of poems, and the memory of a frog to guide their way.

Annie and the Old One by Miska Miles, illustrated by Peter Parnall (Little, Brown and Company: 1972) (D)

Read with a child who is asking about death or if someone close to your child is dying.

Annie discovers that her grandmother is dying and tries everything she can to stop it from happening. However, after talking to her grandmother about dying and her grandmother's beliefs, Annie no longer tries to stop death and finds strength in her family's support.

Badger's Parting Gifts by Susan Varley (HarperCollins Publishers: 1984) (D)

Read this with a child who has lost someone close to her.

Badger's friends are heartbroken by his death. Soon, however, they realize that Badger is not truly gone—he lives on through his friends' memories of him and his kind, caring, and helpful nature.

Beyond the Ridge by Paul Goble (Simon & Schuster: 1993) (D)

Read when you need to discuss death with a child.

This book tells the story of a grandmother who hears the call of her long-dead mother while she lies dying. She climbs up a steep mountain ridge to follow the mysterious voice that continually beckons her forward. The grandmother can hear the sorrow of those she is leaving behind, but she travels onward beyond the ridge, to a world of natural beauty inhabited by those who left the physical world long before her.

Dog Heaven by Cynthia Rylant (The Blue Sky Press: 1995) (D)

Read when you want to imagine together what might happen to dogs after death.

Telling the story of what happens to dogs when they go to heaven, this book provides a lighthearted take on what heaven would be like for man's best friend. Filled with fields to run in, geese to chase, children to play with, and an infinite amount of biscuits to eat, *Dog Heaven* shows that those we love and share our lives with are rewarded with an idyllic sanctuary.

Each Little Bird That Sings by Deborah Wiles (Gulliver Books: 2005) (M)

Read to address the desire to avoid dealing with the emotions of a funeral and how confronting issues can be the most effective way to solve them.

Young Comfort Snowberger is accustomed to death, since her family owns the town's funeral home. She thinks that she knows the ins and outs of funerals until her own great-great-aunt Florentine dies. Will she skip Florentine's funeral to avoid confronting her problems?

A Grand Old Tree by Mary Newell DePalma (Arthur A. Levine Books: 2005) (D)

Read when you want to talk about death and how the memory of those who have died still lives on.

There was a grand old tree that lived for many, many years. "Her roots sank deep into the earth, her arms reached high into the sky." Every year she flowered and become home to many animals and insects. After a long time, she grew old and died, leaving behind the roots for many new beginnings.

Talk about It: Use this book to talk about how, like this tree, all people leave their roots, even after they die. Discuss how when the tree died, her memory and the children she left behind continued to flourish.

- How did the tree bring happiness to many creatures?
- When the grand old tree died, how was it also a new beginning for her grandchildren?
- How will the grand old tree's memory still live on even after she has died?

I Miss You: A First Look at Death by Pat Thomas, illustrated by Lesley Harker (Barron's Educational Series: 2001) (D)

Read this book with a child who is asking questions about death, or has experienced the death of someone close to him.

This book helps explain death to a child who may not understand what it means or how a death will change her life. This book also poses questions for talking to children regarding death and feelings associated with death.

Lifetimes: The Beautiful Way to Explain Death to Children by Bryan Mellonie (Bantam: 1983) (M)

Read this with a child who is asking about death or who has recently experienced someone's death.

In this book, Mellonie explores the life and death of many different types of creatures—from people and animals to plants. The book strives to show that birth and death are part of the life cycle, encompassing all that is known as "living."

Michael Rosen's Sad Book by Michael Rosen, illustrated by Quentin Blake (Candlewick Press: 2004) (M)

Read to a child who is feeling depressed by or coping with the loss of a friend or parent.

Michael Rosen describes the feelings associated with the loss of his son. He discusses his lingering feelings of sadness and the emptiness he feels because his son and mother are no longer with him. Yet, in the end, he remembers simple and happy memories that help him cope.

The Mountains of Tibet by Mordicai Gerstein (HarperTrophy: 1989) (M)

Read to explore a reflective, Buddhist view of death.

A young boy looks up at the sky and dreams of all the different worlds he wants to see in his lifetime. When he grows up and becomes a woodcutter in the mountains of Tibet, this dream seems farther and farther away. When he dies, a voice tells him that he may choose to live another life in any world he chooses. He chooses to come back to life in Tibet as a young girl who loves to fly kites as much as he did. This book is magical and also profoundly reassuring for a child who has recently experienced loss.

My Grandson Lew by Charlotte Zolotow, illustrations by William Pène du Bois (HarperTrophy: 1974) (D)

Read about special times with grandfathers and about remembering people who have died.

Lew remembers his grandfather's scratchy beard and how he came in during the night when Lew called out. But Lew was only two when his grandfather died. Together, Lew and his mom remember Lew's grandfather. It may be of great help to a child to know that adults also mourn and grieve and that together, grieving is tempered by the shared memories.

Talk about It: Use this book to talk about how to remember someone very special who has died. Discuss how his mother helps Lew remember his grandfather and the times they shared together.

- ✦ How does Lew's mother help him remember his grandfather?
- ✦ What makes Lew ask his mother to help him remember his grandfather?
- ✦ How does talking to his mother make Lew feel better?

Nana Upstairs & Nana Downstairs by Tomie dePaola (Puffin: 1973) (D)

Read this moving story about the death of a grandparent.

Tommy loves his Nana Upstairs and his Nana Downstairs and eagerly awaits his weekly visits with them. When he arrives at the house of his Nana Upstairs and his Nana Downstairs, Tommy runs between the two, sharing special traditions. One day, Tommy learns that his Nana Upstairs has died and he has to learn how to deal with the loss of someone he loves.

Rattlesnake Mesa by EdNah New Rider Weber (Lee & Low Books: 2004) (M)

Read this with a child who has recently changed schools or settings. The book also deals with the difficult death of a grandparent and the changes that children face as they grow up.

EdNah must go live with her father on a Navajo reservation after the death of her grandmother. Just as she is adjusting to her new surroundings, EdNah is sent away to a strict government school and must rely on a new community of friends for support. The book is both sad and humorous as it describes a Native American girl growing up in America.

Rudi's Pond by Eve Bunting, illustrated by Ronald Himler (Clarion Books: 1999) (M)

Read this beautiful story when attempting to cope with the death of a young person.

A small girl tries to cope with the death of her best friend, Rudi. At school, she uses her memories of Rudi to help create a lasting memorial, and the class comes together to celebrate Rudi's life.

The Tenth Good Thing About Barney by Judith Viorst, illustrated by Erik Blegvad (Atheneum Books for Young Readers: 1987) (D)

Read when you want to discuss the death of a pet, or how things we believe are lost forever can still impact our lives.

When a young boy's cat, Barney, dies, the boy has trouble dealing with his grief. His mother tells him to think of ten good things to say about his beloved cat, but he can only think of nine. When his father asks for the boy's help with planting seeds in the garden, the boy thinks of a tenth thing: Barney is helping the small seeds grow into beautiful flowers. This is a "pretty nice job for a cat."

The Two of Them by Aliki (Greenwillow Books: 1979) (D)

Read to discuss the death of a close grandparent or caregiver, and how it is okay to grieve.

This moving tale and its beautiful illustrations speak to anyone who has ever lost a grandparent. A young girl is raised by her grandfather, whom she calls "Papouli," and they pass through life together. One day, he falls ill and although she prepares herself for his death, "she hurt[s] inside and out."

DIVORCE

Separations are intense for the growing child. He is trying to understand what is permanent and what is temporary. Divorce disrupts the pattern of everyday life in ways that might be relatively invisible or unimportant to an adult experiencing this loss on an entirely different level. Literature offers a way to heal the rupture: bring the separations back together again by talking about them. Though it may be difficult, the child will accommodate to his new environments and these changes, because children are extraordinarily resilient. But literature can help prepare the path and ready the child for a different kind of journey. Remember also how every family is so different. The joy you create together in a new vision of your family can be as joyous as the vision from before the separation. The child is full of hope, and literature makes it possible to not only hope again but also to construct new ideas of what hope can look like. I promise.

Dinosaurs Divorce: A Guide for Changing Families by Lauren Krasny Brown and Marc Brown (Little, Brown and Company: 1986) (D→M)

Read when you want to talk about the many issues that arise when your parents or your friends' parents go through a divorce.

Written in the form of a comic book, this book explains words associated with divorce. It addresses issues that kids face during a divorce and after a divorce, like telling your friends or visiting your parent. It also discusses issues that might arise later, such as meeting parents' new friends or living with stepparents. In a light manner, this book provides talking points for both parents and children.

Good-Bye, Daddy! by Brigitte Weninger, illustrated by Alan Marks (North-South Books: 1997) (D)

Read when discussing the difficulty of saying good-bye to a parent or loved one, even temporarily.

Tom spends the day with his daddy and when he gets home to his mother's house, he does not want to say good-bye. Tom's teddy bear helps him understand how hard divorce is when he tells him a very special story.

Talk about It: This is a wonderful book to use to discuss the difficulty of adjusting to divorce. Learning how to shuffle between two houses or how to say good-bye to one parent, even for a short time, takes time and courage. Talk to your child about how Tom finds comfort in his teddy bear's story.

- Why is Tom feeling sad? Have you ever felt sad when you had to say good-bye to someone? What did you do?
- What story does Tom's teddy bear tell him? Why does the story make Tom feel better?

I Live with Daddy by Judith Vigna (Albert Whitman & Company: 1997) (D)

Read when you want to talk about how difficult it is to navigate the terrain of parents living separately.

Olivia's parents are divorced and she lives with her daddy because her mother is a reporter and travels a lot. Olivia must choose a topic to write about for Writer's Day and decides to write about her mother. But when her mother misses Olivia reading her story at school, Olivia wishes she had written about her daddy, who always comes to her school events. Through her struggles, Olivia learns how to include both her parents in her life.

It's Not Your Fault, Koko Bear: A Read-Together Book for Parents & Young Children During Divorce by Vicki Lansky (Book Peddlers: 1998) (D)

Read when you want to talk about divorce with a young child. Use the accompanying information to help guide your talk.

When KoKo Bear learns that MaMa and PaPa Bear are getting divorced, KoKo Bear is very sad. He does not want to live in two houses or say good-bye to MaMa Bear or PaPa Bear. KoKo does not know what to do when he has to draw a picture of his family. How does KoKo Bear learn to cope with his parents' divorce?

Priscilla Twice by Judith Casely (Greenwillow Books: 1995) (D)

Read when you are having a hard time accepting the changes in your life due to divorce.

Priscilla is having a hard time accepting her new family. She has two sets of books and two sets of toys, but she still finds it hard to adjust to her parents' divorce.

Was It the Chocolate Pudding?: A Story for Little Kids about Divorce by Sandra Levins, illustrated by Bryan Langdo (American Psychological Association: 2005) (D)

Read this with your child to talk about why parents divorce.

Told from the perspective of a young child, this book examines why parents divorce, emphasizing that it is not the child's fault. The narrator also discusses some of the things that accompany a divorce, such as joint custody and single-family homes.

FALLING ASLEEP

Falling asleep can be a complicated journey. From light to dark, from togetherness to separation, from comfort to aloneness, the child does not always want to travel this path. Words can provide comfort. Better than counting sheep, reading a lovely book before bed, or at any time of day when a child wants to discuss the long journey from bedtime to sleep, will help ease the way. You may have a child who struggles with sleep, and you may struggle with your child around bedtime. Don't be too hard on your child, or yourself. Breathe deeply before engaging in the nighttime rituals if they have gotten problematic. Try some of these titles if you haven't already. Keep them in a basket near your child's bed. Don't rush. And if you need to rush, read something short. The soothing rhythms of rhymes carry a child along like a soft boat bobbing on the sea. Sometimes a story of a child trying for sleep, like Frances, is just what your child needs to know he is not alone.

Bedtime for Frances by Russell Hoban, illustrated by Garth Williams (HarperCollins Children's Books: 1995) (E)

Read when strange shapes and sounds make it very hard for your child to fall asleep.

As Frances prepares for sleep, she gets a glass of milk, nighttime kisses from mother and father, and her favorite toys. But then, she sees tigers, giants and moths. Will Frances ever fall asleep?

Biscuit by Alyssa Satin Capucilli, illustrations by Pat Schories (HarperCollins Publishers: 1996) (E)

Read this when many distractions keep your child away from sleep. This is one of the Biscuit series; it is an I Can Read *book.*

Will Biscuit, the new puppy, ever fall asleep? A little girl helps him prepare for bed.

Good Night, Good Knight by Shelley Moore Thomas, illustrated by Jennifer Plecas (Penguin Young Readers Group: 2002) (E)

Read when your child has so many things you want to do before going to bed.

One night, a knight hears the loud roar of a dragon coming from the woods. The knight bravely searches for the dragon, but what he finds instead are three baby dragons preparing for bed. The knight helps these three dragons prepare for sleep. He gets them water, tucks them in, and even reads to them before they will fall asleep.

Goodnight Moon by Margaret Wise Brown, illustrated by Clement Hurd (Harper: 1947) (E)

Read when your child is having trouble falling asleep or any other time when a bit of comfort is in order.

This rhyming book is written through the eyes of a young bunny, who is in bed and just ready to go to sleep. He acknowledges all of the unique and wonderful things that he sees or feels or hears both in his room and outside of his window. He then says an individualized good night to each of these wonderful things . . . ending with a good night to noises everywhere.

Talk about It: This is a beautifully written classic, which will soothe a child to sleep. Discuss the deliberateness of the main character as he recognizes and bids good night to things large and small, seen and unseen.

- ✦ What was your favorite thing in the bunny's room, to which he said good night?
- ✦ What do you notice in your own room that you would like to say good night to before you go to sleep?
- ✦ What is the difference between saying good night to the items in the room and saying good night to something like the air and the stars? Can you still say good night to something, even if it can't say good night back to you?

Hush: A Thai Lullaby by Minfong Ho, illustrated by Holly Meade (Orchard Books: 1996) (E)

Read this lullaby to help your child to fall asleep as she listens to the sounds of the animals outside.

A mother sings a lullaby to try to quiet the animals so her baby will stay asleep. "Can't you see that baby's sleeping?" she says to the mosquitoes, lizards, and other summer animals as they peep and beep outside her window. But in the end, the baby too is wide-awake.

I Will Hold You 'Til You Sleep by Linda Zuckerman, illustrated by Jon J. Muth (Scholastic: 2006) (E)

Read this beautiful story about the love between a parent and child when cuddling before bed, or when you just want to say "I love you."

Bask in the comfort of these beautiful illustrations and poignant words, which wish for a child a life bursting with love. "I will love you all your life/ Whether you are near or far." Celebrate your love for your child.

Kheru Nefer (Beautiful Night): A Khamitic (Ancient Egyptian) Lullaby by Obi Shaaim Maa, illustrated by Peter Fasolino (Spirit Publishing: 2006) (D)

Read before bed or for a soothing story about the ancient Egyptian angels, the Khamitic. Listen to the beautiful nighttime lullaby sung on the accompanying CD.

Ancient Egyptian angels of unity, joy, love, and intelligence travel around the world, visiting children as they sleep.

Little Night by Yuyi Morales (Roaring Brook Press: 2007) (D)

Read when your child is preparing for bed.

Mother Sky prepares a bath for Little Night, who is hiding. Is Little Night in the blueberry field or down the rabbit hole? Drift off to sleep with this beautiful and gentle bedtime story.

Lullaby Raft by Naomi Shihab Nye, illustrated by Vivienne Flesher (Simon & Schuster Books for Young Readers: 1997) (E)

Read when you want to be soothed into sleep by the soft sounds of this lullaby.

Journey on the Lullaby Raft as a mother sings a lullaby to her child. Find yourself rocked into sleep as this mother says good night to the animals and to her child. "He was busy all day long/ But the night gives back his song/ My lizard sips the sweetest tune/ From the sleepy ground." Or even sing along to the lullaby by following the musical score Nye provides at the end of the book.

The Napping House by Audrey Wood, illustrated by Don Wood (Harcourt Children's Books: 2000) (E)

Read at bedtime, naptime, or as a waking-up story. Use this book to encourage reading skills in your child, as she remembers the repetitive phrases and uses the illustrations to predict the events in the story. Also, use it to encourage napping, with the promise of waking up refreshed and ready to play.

In this story, with its soothing and repetitive phrasing, everyone sleeps peacefully, until one bite wakes the household. Even though the members of the house were sleeping peacefully, by the end of the story, the sun has come out and they're wide-awake.

Nocturne by Jane Yolen, illustrated by Anne Hunter (Harcourt Brace & Company: 1997) (D)

Read before bedtime to talk about the magical sights you can observe as you walk through nature at night.

A little boy and his mother watch the night unfold around them as they prepare for sleep. "A big moon balloon floats silent over trees," and moths flutter and bats fly around them, as this mother and son observe the beauty of nature together.

The Noisy Way to Bed by Ian Whybrow, illustrated by Tiphanie Beeke (Scholastic: 2004) (D)

Read when your child is having trouble falling asleep.

When one little boy decides to go to sleep, his friends the sheep, the duck, the horse, and the pig have other plans. Their oinks and quacks prevent the boy from falling asleep. Will he ever get to bed?

Once Upon a Time, The End (Asleep in 60 Seconds) by Geoffrey Kloske, illustrated by Barry Blitt (Simon & Schuster Children's Publishing: 2005) (D)

Read when you have a hard time finding the perfect short book to read before bed.

It may not be exactly under a minute, but this book is short and sweet.

Poems to Dream Together by Francisco X. Alarcon, illustrated by Paula Barragan (Lee & Low Books: 2005) (D)

Read when you want to explore the world of poems that focus on dreams.

This collection of poems written in Spanish and English describes a wide variety of dreams, including daydreams: "Daydreaming/another way/of brainstorming." Each poem is accompanied by a beautiful illustration that adds color to the text.

Sleepy Boy by Polly Konevsky, illustrated by Stephanie Anderson (Simon & Schuster Children's Books: 2006) (D)

Read at bedtime after a very exciting day.

At bedtime, after an exciting day visiting the lions at the zoo, this very sleepy boy cannot fall asleep. As his father holds him, the young boy revisits the lions at the zoo.

So Sleepy Story by Uri Shulevitz (Farrar, Straus and Giroux: 2006) (D)

Read on a sleepy night in a sleepy bed.

A sleepy boy lies in a sleepy bed in a sleepy house. As soft music begins to waft into the sleepy house, it wakes up the sleepy chairs, the sleepy dishes, and especially the sleepy boy. They rock, shake, and open their eyes until the soft music disappears and the sleepy house once more falls asleep.

There's a Nightmare in My Closet by Mercer Mayer (Penguin Young Readers Group: 1992) (D)

Read when you want a silly story about nightmares.

What happens when you befriend the nightmare in your closet? This little boy finds out.

When Sheep Sleep by Laura Numeroff, illustrated by David McPhail (Abrams Books for Young Readers: 2006) (D)

Read when you're looking for a perfect read before bed.

What happens when you try to count sheep to fall asleep, but the sheep, cows, and cats are already asleep?

When the Wind Stops by Charlotte Zolotow, illustrated by Stefano Vitale (HarperCollins Children's Books: 1997) (D)

Read this before going to sleep, especially after a very exciting day that your child does not want to end.

After a fun day of playing with friends, a boy asks his mother why the day has to come to an end. His mother explains that nothing ends, not even the wind, the mountains, or the day; they just begin somewhere else or look a little different.

Talk about It: Explore the idea of beginnings and endings. Right before bedtime, sometimes it is very difficult to understand why such a fun day has to come to an end, and it is good to remember that the next morning the "sun will begin a new day."

- Have you ever not wanted a day to end?
- This little boy wonders why the day had to end; what have you wondered about?

FEELING A SENSE OF JUSTICE: CHANGING THE WORLD

Children of all ages can effect change. If they know from a young age that their actions can affect others, they see themselves as purveyors of change from a very early time. The child who reaches a hand to an elderly person, or the child who recognizes inequality is, like little Ruby Bridges who walked alone into a school to desegregate it, courageous in her simple response to a world that is often unfair, but where the possibility for redemption and the dawn of a new day seem right around the corner.

What is really great about these books is that they convey the sense that a small gesture can create a huge impact. Miss Rumphius plants lupines all over her island. Clover sits beside Annie, ignoring the racial boundary that divides their town. Read one of these books, and then make a list with your child of all the ways you could change the world together. Maybe you will plant purple lupines like Mrs. Rumphius, or maybe you will take a stand on something like Martin Luther King Jr. Maybe you will together go read to someone who needs your company. The boys at Children's Village go once a month to read to the elderly. Each group feels they are doing social action for one another. It is a win-win. At the end of each session, they thank one another for being together. And peace fills the room, a happy and loving peace.

Chicken Sunday by Patricia Polacco (Penguin Young Readers Group: 1998) (D→M)

Read to talk about how bonds between people can extend beyond racial differences and generational boundaries.

Three young children want to buy their friend Miss Eula a beautiful Easter hat to show their appreciation for her Sunday chicken dinners. These children need to find a way to earn money to buy Miss Eula the hat. They decide to sell decorated eggs. However, after they are accused of throwing eggs at Mr. Kodinski's shop, their plans are foiled. Will they ever be able to prove their innocence and earn enough money to buy the hat for Miss Eula?

Fly Away Home by Eve Bunting, illustrated by Ronald Himler (Clarion Books: 1991) (M)

Read to discuss the importance of a safe home for all.

A young boy and his father are homeless and live in an airport, sleeping in a different terminal every night. The father teaches his son the importance of blending into his surroundings by wearing clean blue clothing that does not stand out. The boy has closely watched a small bird trapped in the same terminal. When the boy sees the bird fly out of the terminal to freedom, he feels an overwhelming sense of hope.

Talk about It: Please note that this book discusses homelessness. Talk about how reading the book impacted you or how it made you feel, in order to begin a discussion about the impact of homelessness on children. Use the powerful illustrations to guide your conversation.

- Talk about the boy and his father's experiences living in the terminal. How do they blend into their surroundings? Why?
- Look at the illustrations and talk about what you can learn about the boy and his father by studying them closely.
- Why does the boy feel hopeful when he sees the bird escape the terminal?
- What can we do to end homelessness?

The Forbidden Schoolhouse: The True and Dramatic Story of Prudence Crandall and Her Students by Suzanne Jurmain (Houghton Mifflin Company: 2005) (M)

Read when you want to talk about a woman's struggle to change the world, in a world resistant to change.

Villagers threw rotten eggs and rocks at her school; they filled her well with manure and prevented her from shopping in town; and they even jailed her. They tried to prevent her from changing the lives of young African-American girls who only wanted to attend school. Prudence Crandall set up one of the first schools for African-American girls and had to struggle to keep it open. Read this powerful book to talk about the adversity Prudence Crandall faced and how she fought against the forces of bigotry and racism to bring about a positive change in the world.

I Can Make a Difference: A Treasury to Inspire Our Children by Marian Wright Edelman, illustrated by Barry Moser (HarperCollins Publishers: 2005) (D)

Read when you want to talk about how you can make a difference in the world.

Marian Wright Edelman compiled a collection of poems, folktales, quotations, songs, and stories about how people can and do make a difference in the world. Find inspiration to act in a moral way and to bring about positive change from these rousing selections.

Let the Celebrations Begin! by Margaret Wild, illustrated by Julie Vivas (Orchard Books: 1991) (M)

Read when you want to show how, by building a sense of community and working together, people can hold on to their will to survive and their sense of hope for the future in the face of overwhelming adversity.

Miriam, who is twelve years old, lives in the Belsen concentration camp. Despite the hardships of her current situation, Miriam, the women, and the other children make toys out of scraps and rags to give to children after they are liberated from Belsen.

Talk about It: This book depicts the impact of life in concentration camps on women and children. It is a very difficult topic to discuss with children.

- Talk about how the will to survive drew these women to plan the party for the children, and how, even in the most difficult of situations, hope and community can help people to overcome great adversity.

Martin's Big Words by Doreen Rappaport, illustrated by Bryan Collier (Hyperion Books for Children: 2001) (D)

Read this to read to learn about civil disobedience and the civil rights movement. It is moving and rich, with quotations from Dr. King and beautiful illustrations.

Through his own words, this beautifully written book tells the story of Martin Luther King Jr.'s life growing up in the segregated South and the influence of words in his life.

The Other Side by Jacqueline Woodson, illustrated by E. B. Lewis (G. P. Putnam's Sons: 2001) (M)

Read this with your child when you want to discuss the essence of friendship.

Clover knows that the fence dividing her town separates the white neighbors from the black neighbors. She wants to understand why this fence splits the people in her town. Her curiosity grows when she sees a young white girl, Annie, sitting on the fence. Will Clover find the courage to sit on the fence next to Annie? Despite the fence and the racial tension in their town, Annie and Clover discover the beauty of friendship.

The Story of Ruby Bridges by Robert Coles, illustrated by George Ford (Scholastic: 1995) (M)

Read this to discuss having courage in the face of impossible situations.

Ruby Bridges is a young girl starting a new school. The parents and neighbors of her new fellow classmates are not accepting of Ruby and try to dissuade her from attending. However, Ruby does not allow herself to be intimidated and goes to school every day to learn to read and write. Ruby's teacher admires her courage and, eventually, the community begins to accept Ruby's presence.

The Wednesday Surprise by Eve Bunting, illustrated by Donald Carrick (Houghton Mifflin Company: 1989) (D→M)

Read when you want to talk about adult illiteracy and the importance of helping other people.

Anna loves Wednesdays, when she can spend the night with her grandma and the big bag of books her grandma reads. Together, Anna and her grandmother read book after book as they prepare a secret present for Anna's father.

Who Was the Woman Who Wore the Hat? by Nancy Patz (Penguin Young Readers Group: 2003) (M)

Read this powerful book to talk about the Holocaust and injustice.

Inspired by a woman's hat seen in the Jewish Museum in Amsterdam, poetic lyrics and beautiful illustrations reflect on who the woman behind the hat was. When did she wear the hat? Did she wear it as she was captured? Through gentle musings about the hat, Patz brings to light the devastation and loss brought about by the Holocaust. Life is in the details, someone once said. The hat without its wearer conveys great sorrow and respect.

FEELINGS ABOUT SCHOOL

School, oh, school. Be a sanctuary. We so hope, as we send our child off on the bus or walk her down the road, that school will take care of her, that she will learn most joyously, that she will make friends. We cannot always control these variables, of course. But at least we can be there, story in hand, to welcome back the traveler, and inspire him to tell his own stories of his own journeys that day.

We often get frustrated when we ask: "How was your day?" and our child replies simply: "Fine." Remember that the day for him is long and complex. A question like that is so open-ended he almost can't figure it out. You might be better off asking: "How was recess today? What did you do there?" Or: "What did you learn in science today?" Practice asking very focused questions that are fairly objective (rather than, of course: "Were you a good boy today in school?"), questions that you really don't know the answers to, and that may help your child be more specific in his response. Books about school help foster that conversation too. Each person reacts to school differently. Pay special attention to your child who does not seem to be thriving in school. The read-aloud will often help to uncover some of the mysteries about what may be holding him back and help you to advocate for your child effectively.

Children dream of school. When they are very young, they pretend to put their backpacks on. They play school, imagining themselves as teachers for a circle of stuffed animals. My daughter used to pretend she was "Mrs. England," and would gather her animals and dolls all around her as she gently gave her alphabet lessons. How I miss Mrs. England, and how grateful I am to the wonderful teachers she had in her life who inspired her to create her own image of the perfect teacher.

Use the read-aloud as an opportunity to talk about what feels good in a classroom and what feels good about learning, what feels good about going away, and what feels good about coming home. Use the read-aloud to celebrate learning and to acknowledge that the place your children go to learn houses countless stories of its own.

Barney Is Big by Nicki Weiss (Greenwillow Books: 1988) (E)

Read this great book when you want to talk about growing up, starting school, and becoming just a little bit more independent.

The night before Barney begins nursery school, he remembers what it was like to be a baby and shows his mom how big a boy he is now.

Ella the Elegant Elephant by Carmela D'Amico, illustrated by Steven D'Amico (Scholastic: 2004) (D)

Read when your child is apprehensive about starting school.

Far, far away on the Elephant Islands, which are in the middle of the Indian Ocean, lives a young elephant named Ella. Ella is very scared about beginning school and especially about making friends. Ella's grandmother gives her a red hat, a gift for the first day of school. Ella is sure that this red hat will be her lucky charm, but Belinda, one of the other elephants at school, makes fun of Ella's hat. She calls Ella "Ella the Elegant Elephant" until Ella's bravery and red hat save the day.

A Fine, Fine School by Sharon Creech, illustrated by Harry Bliss (HarperCollins Children's Books: 2003) (D)

Read when you want to talk about how much fun it is to go to school, just not all the time.

Mr. Keene, the school principal of this fine, fine school, knows that his school is superb and decides that students and teachers should go to school on Saturdays, Sundays, during vacations, and even over the summer. Will Mr. Keene soon make students and teachers go to school during the night too? Tillie, who loves her fine, fine school, needs to show Mr. Keene that while going to school is great, maybe there is such as thing as too much school.

Here Comes the Bus! by Carolyn Haywood (William Morrow: 1963) (E)

Read when you want to talk about riding the school bus and all the fun you can have, and, yes, the mischief you can find.

When he first starts to take the bus to school, Jonathan gets himself into sticky situations with the help of his new friend Melissa. Luckily for Jonathan, his bus driver, Mr. Riley, is kind to all the kids and is able to help Jonathan. Little does Mr. Riley know that he will be faced with his toughest challenge yet when all the children bring their pets to school for the pet show!

I Am Absolutely Too Small for School by Lauren Child (Candlewick Press: 2005) (D)

Read right before beginning school, when it seems very hard to want to be big enough for school. This is one of the Lola and Charlie *series.*

Lola insists that she is "absolutely too small for school." She has no need to count to ten or learn how to write letters. Or does she? Charlie must convince Lola and her best friend, Soren Lorensen, that school really is fun.

If You're Not Here, Please Raise Your Hand: Poems about School by Kalli Dakos, illustrated by G. Brian Karas (Aladdin: 1990) (M)

Read when you want to talk about your own experiences in school.

This collection of thirty-eight poems captures the essence of the school experience. It depicts the fun had in school, the wistful longing to be outside, and the pleasure of sharing time.

Look Out, Kindergarten: Here I Come by Nancy Carlson (Penguin Young Readers Group: 2001) (D)

Read to untangle the expectations that surround beginning kindergarten.

Henry is very much looking forward to beginning kindergarten. He will learn to paint and sing and count. However, when Henry walks into school, he starts to get very nervous. Will he really like school as much as he'd hoped?

My Kindergarten by Rosemary Wells (Hyperion Books for Children: 2004) (D)

Read this book to your child before she starts kindergarten or throughout the exciting year.

Join Miss Cribbage's kindergarten class, where the students learn to count, sing, and study the leaves and holidays.

Sammy the Seal by Syd Hoff (HarperCollins: 2000) (E)

Read when you want to talk about the fun things you can do in school.

During feeding time at the zoo, Sammy the Seal escapes for an adventurous day. He finds himself in a school, where he sees the children learning many new things, and even learns to read himself.

Sumi's First Day of School by Joung Un Kim and Soyung Pak (Viking Juvenile: 2003) (D)

Read this with a child who is nervous about his first day of school.

Sumi is scared of starting school in a new place, where she does not know anyone. At first she thinks school is scary; the kids are mean and she is terribly lonely. However, soon she realizes that her teacher is nice and, while some kids are mean, most are friendly, and things start to look up.

Things I Learned in Second Grade by Amy Schwartz (Katherine Tegen Books: 2004) (D)

Read when you want to share all of the exciting things you have learned in school. Use this book to begin a discussion about all of the things your child has learned so far in school.

How much we learn each year in school! Andrew reviews all of the exciting things he learned to do in second grade. He learned to spell the word "should," wrote poems, made friends, and much more.

Timothy Goes to School by Rosemary Wells (Penguin: 1981) (D)

Read this with a child who is having trouble adjusting to a new school or who is intimidated by other children.

Timothy is starting a new school and can't seem to wear the right clothes, as pointed out by his classmate Claude. Even worse, Claude seems to be good at everything: sports, school, the saxophone, *and* he's popular! Timothy never wants to go back to school—until he meets Violet.

Will I Have a Friend? by Miriam Cohen, illustrated by Lillian Hoban (Aladdin: 1989) (D)

Read to talk about the very scary fears about making new friends that emerge before starting a new school.

Jim is very worried he will have no friends at school, but his father tries to convince him that he will find a friend. It is not until nap time, when Jim realizes that someone else shares his very same fears, that Jim feels better.

FEELING SILLY

The "feeling silly" books listed here are not only for the times you are all just genuinely feeling goofy, they are also great for when your child is not feeling well, or when you want to defuse a tough moment. Also, the development of a sense of humor is a joyous thing to nudge along. It requires some of your time and support too. By reading together some very silly books, you model the pleasures of laughing, of how words are not only meant to inspire, they are meant to amuse. Keep your "feeling silly" books in a special basket, for emergencies or for a ticklish everyday routine.

Behold the Bold Umbrellaphant and Other Poems by Jack Prelutsky, illustrated by Carin Berger (Greenwillow Books: 2006) (E)

Read to imagine the silliest creatures possible.

In this collection of poems and great wordplays, Jack Prelutsky introduces us to the Umbrellaphant, the Alarmadillos, the Pop-up Toadsters, and the Clocktopus; we even get a glimpse into a day in each of their crazy lives. See what crazy creatures you can invent when you put together real animals and everyday objects.

The Best Pet of All by David LaRochelle, illustrated by Hanako Wakiyama (Penguin Young Readers Group: 2004) (D)

Read when your child really, really wants a pet.

This is the story of a boy who really, really wants a dog. His mother agrees to let him have a dragon, if he can find one, but no dog. But the dragon turns out to be very loud, very messy, and very disagreeable. Will this boy ever be able to get rid of the dragon and find a dog instead?

Don't Let the Pigeon Drive the Bus! by Mo Willems (Hyperion Books for Children: 2003) (E)

Read for a fun tale about being mischievous, and trying to convince others to join in.

When a bus driver leaves his bus unattended to take a break, he gives specific instructions: "Don't Let the Pigeon Drive the Bus." But the mischievous pigeon tries to weasel his way into getting permission to drive by bribing, conjuring sympathy, and using other tricks. Will the pigeon get behind the wheel before the bus driver gets back?

The Dumb Bunnies by Dav Pilkey (HarperCollins Publishers: 1994) (D)

Read when you want to laugh at the silly adventures of one crazy family.

The Dumb Bunnies sure do some silly things, like eating lunch in a car wash or bowling in a library. But the Dumb Bunny family has a very good time—that is, until they get home and find Little Red Goldilocks making herself comfortable.

Frankenstein Makes a Sandwich by Adam Rex (Harcourt: 2006) (M)

Read to have a good laugh about the everyday life of some very quirky monsters.

Have you ever wondered what would happen if Frankenstein, also known as Frankie, just wanted a ham-and-cheese sandwich on wheat bread, but ran out of the meat, cheese, and bread? He'd go next door, of course. Read about the hilarious daily adventures of famous ghouls like Count Dracula, the Invisible Man, Godzilla, and, of course, Frankenstein.

Gimme Cracked Corn & I Will Share by Kevin O'Malley (Walker & Company: 2007) (D)

Read to kids who love jokes and wordplays. It is funny and silly.

When Chicken has a dream about a buried treasure of cracked corn, he and George set out to recover the treasure. Chicken and George go on to have an adventure filled with wit and humor.

The Great Fuzz Frenzy by Janet Stevens and Susan Stevens Crummel (Harcourt Children's Books: 2005) (E)

Read for a funny story about how prairie dogs might react to the arrival of a tennis ball.

When the dog, Violet, drops a tennis ball down a prairie dog hole, a great fuzz frenzy begins. Try as they might, the prairie dogs in the town cannot figure out what the furry item is.

This Is the House That Jack Built by Simms Taback (G. P. Putnam's Sons: 2002) (E)

Read this as a fun, colorful play on a traditional children's chant.

This book uses the traditional rhyme or repetition, "This is the house that Jack built." The crazy illustrations and anecdotes that fill the very busy pages make it unique, fast-paced, and fun. Children with short attention spans will like this book.

Minnie and Moo, the Case of the Missing Jelly Donut by Denys Cazet (HarperCollins Publishers: 2005) (D)

Read when you've had a fun and silly adventure with a friend. Continue reading about the adventures of Minnie and Moo with the other books in the series.

Minnie and Moo, the two cow friends, set off after a donut thief. Will Minnie and Moo ever find out who stole Minnie's donut?

The Perfectly Orderly House by Ellen Kindt McKenzie, illustrated by Megan Lloyd (Henry Holt and Company: 1994) (D)

Read when you want a silly story about organization. This book also celebrates the alphabet.

The old woman could throw nothing away. So she had her brother Sam build her a new, perfectly orderly house with twenty-six rooms each assigned a letter in the alphabet. However, when the old woman tries to match her belongings to a room, she encounters a few problems.

Thirteen O'Clock by James Stimson (Chronicle Books: 2005) (D)

Read when you want to enjoy a spooky, eerie telling at thirteen o'clock. If you have a child who frightens easily, this might not be the best choice.

This is the story of a young girl who lives in a house that "had an old clock whose numbers counted not twelve . . . but a spooky number thirteen." Enjoy the alliterations and wordplays as you find out what happens at thirteen o'clock.

Today I Feel Silly and Other Moods That Make My Day by Jamie Lee Curtis, illustrated by Laura Cornell (Joanna Cotler Books: 1998) (E)

Read for an amusing celebration of all our moods.

Some days, this young girl feels silly, other days she feels lucky or excited, or even sad. This book celebrates all her moods.

Talk about It: Moods come and go and this book helps us embrace all kinds of moods. This is a great book for discussing the range of emotions: silly or sad, worried or lonely. The words in the book rhyme and there is a movable picture at the end to match a mood to a facial expression.

- How did the girl act when she felt silly? How did she act when she felt excited? How do you act when you feel silly or excited?
- How do you know when someone is feeling sad or lonely or joyful? How do you let other people know how you are feeling?

Why the Banana Split by Rick Walton, illustrated by Jimmy Holder (Gibbs Smith: 2005) (E)

Read this funny story full of wordplay and vivid imagination.

Why did the banana split? Find out why the banana split the minute a Tyrannosaurus rex came to town.

HEROES

You are a hero to your child. And so is a superhero. A child's heroes can be both very near and familiar, and also very distant and exotic. Literature that illuminates some kind of heroism provides an excellent opportunity for us to talk about all the ways we admire the people who motivate us. Someone once said that to have heroes is not to want what they've got, but to seek what they dream. I love that, and I hope that by reading about people who really took chances and had the courage to be different, we can inspire our children to be and do the same.

Brother Eagle, Sister Sky: A Message from Chief Seattle speech by Chief Seattle, paintings by Susan Jeffers (Puffin Books: 1991) (M)

Read to admire Chief Seattle's fierce passion for the natural world.

American Indian Chief Seattle gave this speech about the importance of respecting nature and celebrating all living creatures over a hundred years ago. His message is still deeply relevant today and his powerful, clear message can spark great discussion.

Crazy Horse's Vision by Joseph Bruchac, illustrated by S. D. Nelson (New York: Lee & Low Books: 2000) (M)

Read to inspire your child to set off on his journey and find his own heroic deeds.

How did Crazy Horse, the brave and dedicated leader of the Lakota Indians, earn his name? Curly, as he was known, proved to be a natural-born leader, who tamed wild horses and joined the other men on buffalo hunts. When settlers threatened the Lakota's way of life, Curly ignored his family and traditions and set off on a spiritual quest to seek a vision to guide him. Will Curly's vision help him save his people?

Dad, Jackie, and Me by Myron Uhlberg, illustrated by Colin Bootman (Peachtree Publishers: 2005) (M)

Read this moving book when you want to discuss how, through determination, teamwork, and practice, you can overcome obstacles.

During the summer of 1947, when Jackie Robinson joins the Brooklyn Dodgers, a young boy and his deaf father bond over the game of baseball. The boy teaches his father all about baseball and, like Jackie Robinson, the boy and his father find a way to overcome their obstacles together.

Eleanor Roosevelt: A Life of Discovery by Russell Freedman (Houghton Mifflin Company: 1997) (M)

Read when you want to find inspiration from the experiences of Eleanor Roosevelt.

Learn all about the life of Eleanor Roosevelt before her journey to the White House, during her husband's presidency, and after his tragic death. Discover how Eleanor Roosevelt fought to preserve her independence and showed great courage during difficult times. This is an excellent photobiography for young historians who want to find inspiration from the actions and life mission of an influential woman.

Ellington Was Not a Street by Ntozake Shange, illustrations by Kadir Nelson (Simon & Schuster Books for Young Readers: 2004) (D)

Read to learn about how the actions of W. E. B. Dubois, Duke Ellington, Paul Robeson, and many other influential men impacted the life of a young narrator.

Told through the eyes of a young girl, this book is a tribute to the many important African-American men who brought change to their country, despite restrictions on where they could live, go to school, or even sit on a bus. The beautiful paintings give life to the walls of the house in which these groundbreaking men met to talk and change the world.

Freedom Walkers: The Story of the Montgomery Bus Boycott
by Russell Freedman (Holiday House: 2006) (M)

Read when you want to talk about how the actions of a few people changed the world forever.

Learn about what life was like for African-Americans living in the South during the 1950s, and how through the work of leaders like Martin Luther King Jr. and Rosa Parks a giant movement was born. Read about the Montgomery bus boycott and talk about the power of holding on to a sense of justice. The personal accounts of the people who experienced the Montgomery bus boycott bring to life this revolutionary time in American history.

Henry's Freedom Box by Ellen Levine, illustrated by Kadir Nelson (Scholastic: 2002) (M)

Read this book to discuss the effects of slavery. Henry's story shows how it often takes determination and perseverance to overcome very difficult times.

Henry was born a slave on a plantation. After his wife and children were sold into slavery far away from him, he used courage, determination, and creativity to find his way to freedom and back to his family.

Talk about It: This book offers a powerful way to start a conversation on the devastating effects of slavery on the men, women, and children who endured its horrors. Use this book to explore how ordinary people can become heroes by fighting for what is right.

- How did slavery affect Henry's life and the lives of so many other men and women? How did Henry find a way to escape the horrors of enslavement?
- Have you ever been in a situation where you have had to overcome a difficult challenge? What did you do to overcome the challenge?

The Librarian of Basra: A True Story of Iraq by Jeanette Winter (Harcourt Children's Books: 2005) (M)

Read to provide a new perspective on the war in the Middle East, and to show the incredible capacity of books to inspire heroism.

This work is based on the true story of a heroic librarian, Alia Muhammed Baker, in Basra, Iraq, who struggled to save her library's valuable collection of books. With the war on its way, Baker worried that the library and its books would be destroyed. She took matters into her own hands to save the precious volumes, all while spreading her message of hope.

Lou Gehrig: The Luckiest Man by David A. Adler, illustrated by Terry Widener (Voyager Books: 2001) (D→M)

Read when you want to talk about what it means to be a hero.

Find out why Lou Gehrig was known as the Iron Horse and how he became a legendary player for the New York Yankees. Also, learn about how he found the courage to face a debilitating illness. As you read this book, think about what it means to be a hero.

The Man Who Went to the Far Side of the Moon: The Story of Apollo 11 Astronaut Michael Collins by Bea Uusma Schyffert (Chronicle Books: 2003) (M)

Read to learn about the heroic actions of Michael Collins, an astronaut on Apollo 11.

On the famed voyage of Apollo 11, Neil Armstrong and Buzz Aldrin left the perceived safety of the spacecraft to walk on the moon, but Michael Collins stayed on the spacecraft and maneuvered it fourteen times around the moon. While on the other side of the moon, Collins was completely out of radio contact with the outside world and further away from the Earth than anyone else had ever been. Learn about the courage it takes to venture where no one else has before.

Mighty Jackie: The Strike-out Queen by Marissa Moss, illustrated by C. F. Payne (Simon & Schuster: 2004) (D)

Read to find inspiration from the story of a seventeen-year-old girl who made baseball history.

For as long as she can remember, Jackie Mitchell has loved baseball. She becomes such a good baseball player that she outplays all of the boys in her neighborhood. Jackie has a very special pitch—a dropping curve ball. But is Jackie really good enough to pitch against the New York Yankees in an exhibition game? Find out how Jackie became the first female pitcher in the history of baseball.

My Name Is Gabito/Me llamo Gabito by Monica Brown, illustrated by Raúl Colón (Luna Rising Books: 2007) (M)

Read this with your child to learn about the life of Gabriel García Márquez and the power of imagination. The book is written in both English and Spanish.

This book traces the life of the brilliant writer Gabriel García Márquez, or Gabito, focusing on his childhood and his expansive imagination. From his grandfather, Gabito learns about magic and finds inspiration for writing stories. By pushing the limits of imagination, these stories would become the works Márquez is famous for.

Nobody Particular: One Woman's Fight to Save the Bays by Molly Bang (Henry Holt and Company: 2001) (M)

Read to discover how one person can change the world.

Diane Wilson, a shrimp fisher from Texas, battled the large chemical plants that were polluting the water she and many others depended on for survival. Find out how one woman fought against an entire industry to bring about change and save her bay.

Odd Boy Out: Young Albert Einstein by Don Brown (Houghton Mifflin Company: 2004) (D)

Read to learn how it can take courage and perseverance to become a hero.

Young Albert Einstein never fit in—he had few friends and looked rather unusual. However, during his childhood, young Albert learned that he loved solving scientific problems, a trait that continued through his whole life. Learn about how Albert Einstein came to be a person who changed the way people saw the world.

Out of the Ballpark by Alex Rodriguez, illustrated by Frank Morrison (HarperCollins Publishers: 2007) (D)

Read when you want to learn how Alex Rodriguez became a world-famous baseball player.

Alex was a child who loved playing baseball. But he also knew he had to work very hard and practice for many, many hours in order to become a great baseball player. Read about how he woke up early to practice and struggled for many years to become the superstar that he is today.

JOURNEYS

There are internal journeys and there are external journeys. An author once said that there are only two classic stories told in literature: the story of the stranger who comes to town and impacts a community, and the story of a character setting off on a journey. I have selected several different kinds of journey books here. If you want to encourage your child toward a life of open adventuring, of curiosity, of the journey as possibility, these books begin those conversations. If you sense your child may be making an internal journey or a transition, you can use these books as levers to start conversations about how those kinds of journeys feel. I believe in the power of the imagination to help us transcend, to take us on journeys we might never have imagined otherwise. The children I work with at the Children's Village find escape every day in the pages of a book. They may have never had the opportunity to leave their school or their town, but they fly all the time with words as their guides. And like the mother taking her baby ducks for a walk in *Make Way for Ducklings*, even the smallest journey should not be underestimated. For your child, and for you too, it can be huge.

The Arrival by Shaun Tan (Scholastic: 2007) (M)

Read when you want to talk about the feelings of loneliness, fear, hope, and courage that accompany a journey from one's home country to a new land.

This wordless picture book depicts the journey of a man from his homeland to a new place. The pictures evoke the emotions that this man experiences as he leaves his family behind and immigrates to a new country. Tell aloud the story of this man's journey by using the vibrant and powerful pictures as your guide.

Calabash Cat and His Amazing Journey by James Rumford (Houghton Mifflin Company: 2003) (D)

Read to explore the excitement of searching for the answers to wonderings.

Calabash Cat sets off from his home in Chad to find where the world ends. With the help of a camel, tiger, whale, horse, and eagle, Calabash Cat finds a surprising answer to his question.

Talk about It: Let this book help you begin a conversation about the importance of searching for knowledge and wisdom. As you follow the adventure of the Calabash Cat, talk about how his journey to find the end of the world began with a wondering and led to a journey across a desert, through a grassland, into a jungle, over an ocean, and finally into the sky. Think together about the questions you wonder about. This story is also written in Arabic, the native language of Chad.

- What do you wonder about? How do you search for answers to your questions? Have you ever used travel to seek answers?
- What did the Calabash Cat discover was the answer to his question? How did he come to that realization?

Captain Raptor and the Space Pirates by Kevin O'Malley and Patrick O'Brien, illustrations by Patrick O'Brien (Walker & Company: 2007) (D)

Read to enjoy a fantastical adventure with Captain Raptor.

Sinister pirates from space are invading the planet Jurassica. "A mob of misshapen mutants and reptilian cyborgs flow like a river out of the ship, screaming and shouting and waving their laser swords," as they set off to raid the imperial palace. Can Captain Raptor and his fearless crew save the day? Find out in this exciting book written in the style of a comic book.

Come with Me: Poems for a Journey by Naomi Shihab Nye (Greenwillow Books: 2000) (D)

Read when you want poems to take you on a journey with your child.

Journeys can be imaginary, like a young girl's trip to the moon. They can take you from place to place, like a ride on an airplane. Take many types of journeys through this wildly beautiful collection of poems, and begin a discussion of how journeys can take a minute or a lifetime, can take you from place to place, or through your imagination into an entire new world.

Jamberry by Bruce Degen (HarperCollins Publishers: 1983) (E)

Read to appreciate the joy of a berry-picking adventure.

A boy and a bear set of on a wonderful adventure in a berry-filled world. Laugh with them as they rush off to gather delicious berries.

The Journey That Saved Curious George: The True Wartime Escape of Margret and H. A. Rey by Louise Borden, illustrated by Allan Drummond (Houghton Mifflin Company: 2005) (M)

Read this book when you want to talk about how war forces some people to flee their homes to seek safety elsewhere.

Margaret and H. A. Rey, authors of the Curious George series, lived in Paris in 1940. As the Nazis approached the city, Margaret and H.A. fled Paris, traveling by bicycle and carrying with them only a few possessions, including a very important manuscript. Read about their harrowing journey and their incredible courage.

Kami and the Yaks by Andrea Stenn Stryer, illustrated by Bert Dodson (Bay Otter Press: 2007) (D)

Read to find inspiration from the incredible courage of this little boy and the beautiful language of his mesmerizing story.

Kami, a young deaf boy, and his family live high in the Himalaya Mountains. Like many Sherpa people, Kami's family leads treks through the mountain ranges. Early one morning before a trek, Kami's family realizes their prized yaks are missing. Can Kami overcome his fear during an approaching storm and find the yaks?

Make Way for Ducklings by Robert McCloskey (The Viking Press: 1969) (E)

Read this classic story when you want to celebrate the joys of childhood and the excitement of new journeys.

Mr. and Mrs. Mallard look long and hard for the perfect place to raise a family of ducklings. After flying for many miles, Mr. and Mrs. Mallard discover the pond in the Boston Public Garden. Will the Mallards be able to raise their family there? Oh no, it is far too dangerous for young ducklings. But soon after, the Mallards discover a perfect little island in the Charles River. Mrs. Mallard teaches her ducklings to swim and dive. One day, with the help of some policemen, she leads the ducklings through the busy streets of Boston back to the pond in the Boston Public Garden.

The Mitten by Jan Brett (Putnam Juvenile: 1989) (E)

Read when your child wonders what might happen to things that get lost during the course of a journey.

After Nicki drops one of his new white mittens in the snow, it seems like it will blend into the snow and be forgotten. However, the mitten takes an exciting journey, providing warmth to all of the animals out and about in the snow. Will Nicki find the mitten his grandmother knitted for him? As you follow the mitten's journey, check in with little Nicki, or make predictions, by looking at the illustrations in the page margins.

Night Driving by John Coy, illustrated by Peter McCarty (Henry Holt and Company: 1996) (D)

Read when your child begins a memorable journey, or when he wants to bond with his father.

A father and his son set off for a drive to the mountains where they are planning to camp. As they drive all night long, they look out for night animals, change a flat tire, and watch the sky change color. The father tells his son stories about his own dad and his childhood, and the son helps his dad stay awake for the long drive. Enjoy this portrait of the unique relationship between a father and his son as they journey through the night.

Shortcut by Donald Crews (HarperCollins Publishers: 1996) (D)

Read to show when taking a shortcut can become a dangerous and exciting journey.

Although they have been warned of its danger, a group of children decide to take a shortcut home along the train tracks. Too far along the track to turn back, the children hear the whistle of an approaching train. Will they be able to get to safety before it is too late?

A Small Tall Tale from the Far Far North by Peter Sís (Farrar, Straus and Giroux: 2001) (M)

Read when you seek a story about a long and rewarding journey of self-discovery.

This is a story of a Czech hero, a story that weaves fact and fiction and explores one man's journey from his home to the Far North. Jan Wetzl left his home and set off on a riveting thirty-year adventure through the Far North, where he found a sled pulled by reindeer, bonded with the native population, and became a true explorer. Maps and pictures accompanying the text add even more excitement to this enjoyable read.

Stringbean's Trip to the Shining Sea by Vera B. Williams and Jennifer Williams (HarperCollins Publishers: 1999) (D)

Read to talk about recording your experiences during a special journey by sending postcards home.

Stringbean and his older brother Fred travel across the country in Fred's pickup truck with the little house they built in the back. Fred and Stringbean send postcards home to their mom, dad, and grandfather of what they see along the way. Follow their journey from Kansas to the Pacific Ocean by reading their postcards.

Tar Beach by Faith Ringgold (Random House Children's Books: 1996) (M)

Read when you want to talk about how journeys can take you places where anything is possible.

Travel with Cassie as she soars over New York City in this beautifully illustrated story. "Lying on the roof in the night, with stars and skyscraper buildings all around me, made me feel rich, like I owned all that I could see." Cassie takes off from Tar Beach, her magical rooftop. On her journey, she sees the George Washington Bridge on which her father works, and the building that houses the union that will not accept her father. Cassie dreams of helping her family as she conquers the city below.

Tibet Through the Red Box by Peter Sís (Farrar, Straus and Giroux: 1998) (M)

Read this poignant story about a man's journey through Tibet and China, told through the eyes of his son.

A red box, holding his father's journals from the two years he was lost in Tibet and China, had always been forbidden to Peter Sís. So when his father asked Peter to return home to Prague to take possession of his special red box, Peter quickly returned. When Peter was young, the Soviet government sent Peter's father, a documentary filmmaker, to Tibet and China for a short visit. His journey ended up lasting two years, during which he trekked through Tibet, met the Dalai Lama, and witnessed events he could not speak about upon his return. Peter tells the story of his father's journey using his father's journal entries and the stories he secretly told Peter.

Traveling Man: The Journey of Ibn Battuta 1325–1354 by James Rumford (Houghton Mifflin Company: 2001) (M)

Read to learn about the journey of a man who traveled throughout the world during the fourteenth century.

Ibn Battuta traveled more than seventy-five thousand miles between 1325 and 1354. He traveled from Northern Africa to Asia, passing through parts of Europe. Using maps and illustrations that depict the places Ibn Battuta traveled, Rumford tells the story of this well-traveled man.

LEARNING NEW THINGS

This section is about the powerful act of learning, and engaging in something deeply. I am fascinated by how children learn. When they are connected to something, they will study it intensively. I have seen children watch a beetle travel along a stick as intently as any scientist. I have seen children play a song over and over until they are sure they know it by heart, and all because they love it. Children know better than anyone that in order to do something well, you must love to do it. Read some of these books and talk with your child about work you love, and what you have learned that has inspired you. Keep a small notebook together of "daily learnings." Let them be the smallest things too: learning to stir the soup, learning to whistle, like Ezra Jack Keats's Willie, learning how many hours are in a day.

Becoming Butterflies by Anne Rockwell, illustrations by Megan Halsey (Walker & Company: 2004) (D)

Read this to learn all about butterflies.

Have you ever wondered how a caterpillar becomes a butterfly? Miss Dana's class watches as their caterpillars magically transform into monarch butterflies.

Diary of a Wombat by Jackie French, illustrations by Bruce Whatley (Houghton Mifflin Company: 2003) (D)

Read when your child is curious about how some animals interact with their human neighbors.

Have you ever wondered what the cuddly Australian wombat eats, or how much it sleeps? In this book, you can learn all about how the wombat eats, sleeps, digs holes, and even befriends some human neighbors.

Talk about It: As you read this very funny story about the day-to-day life of a wombat, which will surely leave everyone laughing, talk about how exciting it can be to learn about animals and their daily life.

- Have you ever written a diary of your daily activities? How different is your day than the day of the wombat?
- What did you learn about the wombat? Where does it live? What does it eat? Where does it sleep? Have you ever encountered a wombat?

Dino Wars: Discover the Deadliest Dinosaurs, the Bloodiest Battles, and Super Survival Strategies of the Prehistoric World by Jinny Johnson and Michael J. Benton (Abrams Books for Young Readers: 2005) (D→M)

Read this book to learn about many different types of dinosaurs.

If pitted against each other, who would win, a tyrannosaur or a triceratops? Find out this and much more about the strengths and weakness of each dinosaur in this book, which brings the prehistoric creatures to life through colorful illustrations and fascinating statistics.

Floating Home by David Getz, illustrated by Michael Rex (Henry Holt and Company: 1997) (M)

Read this with a child who wishes to gain a new perspective on home and the Earth.

When Maxine is asked to draw her home for a school project, she decides she wants a truly new perspective of her home—one from outer space. She travels with NASA and becomes the world's youngest astronaut. As she looks down on the Earth, she cannot see the lines that divide the world into states and countries. Instead, she sees "just one Earth" and gains a new perspective on the meaning of "home."

How to Be by Lisa Brown (HarperCollins Publishers: 2006) (E)

Read to learn how to just love being yourself.

What do monkeys do? What do dogs do? What do people do? Learn how to be a monkey, fish, or snake in this fun book that explores how to be so many things.

A Second Is a Hiccup: A Child's Book of Time by Hazel Hutchins, illustrated by Kady MacDonald Denton (Arthur A. Levine Books: 2007) (E)

Read to learn about time spans.

Learn how long a second, a minute, a day, and a year are in this fun, exciting book about time.

Voices in the Park by Anthony Browne (Dorling Kindersley Publishing: 1998) (M)

Read to learn about different voices and perspectives.

As a bossy woman, a sad man, a kind girl, and a lonely boy walk through the park, we see the park and their experiences through each of their eyes. How do the bossy woman, the sad man, the kind girl, and the lonely boy describe their experiences? How are their descriptions different?

Whistle for Willie by Ezra Jack Keats (Penguin Young Readers Group: 1977) (E)

Read this delightful story about really, really wanting to learn something new. Discuss how the learning process can be frustrating sometimes, but rewarding in the end.

Peter wants so badly to learn how to whistle for Willie, his dog, just like the big kids do. Can he learn how to whistle?

Yum! Yuck! A Foldout Book of People Sounds by Linda Sue Park, Julia Durango and Sue Rama (Charlesbridge Publishing: 2005) (D)

Read with your child to explore the different sounds and faces people make to express emotions.

All over the world, in every culture, people make faces and noises to express their feelings of joy, disgust, and sadness, among others. Park, Durango, and Rama explore these sounds in many languages, including English, Farsi, and Korean, to show the different ways people express similar feelings.

LONELINESS

Loneliness can creep in, or it can hit hard. A child sits by the window during class time and feels a pang. A child goes to lunch and squeezes in at the end of a table, and no one really makes room for her. You go out for dinner and the babysitter does not know your rituals for bedtime. A walk to school, a long bus ride. All of these are occasions for loneliness to rear its waiting head. Our job as parents is not to eliminate loneliness, but to help our children navigate its terrain. We want them to know that they are going to be able to manage those feelings, and even embrace them on the occasions when they must face them. Reading together and talking about loneliness is a salve: you, by your presence and the presence of your voice reading aloud, stave off the loneliness that is part of the human condition for all of us.

Beegu by Alexis Deacon (Farrar, Straus and Giroux: 2003) (E)

This is a fun read about how sad it is to be lonely, and how nice it is when you finally make friends.

Beegu is a little, friendly alien lost on Earth. "Beegu didn't like being alone." Lonely, she sets out to find some friends. Who will be her friend? Will it be a pile of leaves or a box of puppies or a playground full of children?

Best Friends for Frances by Russell Hoban, illustrations by Lillian Hoban (HarperCollins Children's Books: 1976) (E)

Read this on one of those days when your child feels left out and lonely.

When Frances's friend Albert won't let her play in an all-boy's baseball game, Frances feels lonely, until she finds a new best friend in her younger sister.

Crow Boy by Taro Yashima (Penguin: 1976) (D)

Read with your child to discuss loneliness and feelings of isolation.

Chibi is shy and is teased for being different from his classmates, leading him to feel isolated and rejected. As he confronts his feelings, Chibi grows to accept his differences and uncommon talents.

My Best Friend by Mary Ann Rodman, illustrated by E. B. Lewis (Penguin: 2007) (D)

Read this with your child to discuss fitting in and feeling left out.

Lily desperately wants to be friends with Tamika. She tries everything she can think of to impress Tamika, but Tamika teases and ignores her. Eventually Lily learns that she doesn't want to be friends with someone who doesn't want her, and finds someone special with whom to spend her time.

The Name Jar by Yangsook Choi (Dragonfly Books: 2003) (D)

Read to explore when the process of trying to find your identity is a lonely experience.

Unhei has just arrived in the United States from Korea. She is very scared about making friends and about how other children will pronounce her name. On the first day of school, Unhei decides that she will find herself a new name. But how? With the help of her classmates, Unhei learns how friendship runs deeper than surface differences like names.

The Old Woman Who Named Things by Cynthia Rylant, illustrated by Kathryn Brown (Harcourt: 1996) (D)

Read when you want to discuss the importance of letting new people into your life.

A very old woman has named the major objects in her life: her house, car, bed, and chair. She appreciates the company that they provide for her, and is very content until one day a puppy enters her yard. She is initially reluctant to let a new element into her life that might not provide the same constancy as the others, but when the dog goes missing, she realizes the importance of creating relationships.

Tupelo Rides the Rails by Melissa Sweet (Houghton Mifflin Company: 2005) (D)

Read to explore feeling lonely on a journey and wanting to find a place to fit in.

Read about the adventure of Tupelo, the lonely abandoned dog, and his favorite sock toy, Mr. Bones, who must find a new home. Will Tupelo ever find a place to live? Will it be with the birds, or the rabbits, or the pack of dogs known as the Boneheads?

The Very Lonely Firefly by Eric Carle (Penguin Young Readers Group: 1999) (E)

Read with your child to discuss feelings of loneliness and the joy of finding company.

A newly born firefly sets off to find a friend in this Eric Carle classic. However, all the firefly manages to find are other sources of light—a candle and a lantern, for example. Finally, the firefly finds a group of his kind, much to his overwhelming delight.

LOVING ART

When our girls were young, we used to go to the museums to visit one work of art. I did not want to tire them, or to have them remember museums as a place of dread, long walks, and boredom. So we'd look at a catalog or art book and decide which kind of art we'd want to see, and then, luckily for us, living so close to New York City, we could visit that one piece or something like it. The girls used to ask if they could "visit" the little dancer, Degas' masterful work, or Georgia O'Keeffe's clouds. As they got older, their stamina was stronger and we could spend more time browsing and discovering surprises along the way. The beautiful thing about children is that they see art everywhere. You do not need a museum to teach your children about art. Share with them stories of artists as children, imagining Picasso looking at the world and finding shapes and colors everywhere. Develop the artistic eye in your child not by lecturing but by valuing his own artistic eye: the attention to patterns in a leaf, the awareness of color when he looks at the sky, or when she admires the steely silver glint of a train as it goes by.

Children are highly attuned to art, which is made completely clear when you let one loose in an art store. In a museum, children want to touch the paintings, climb onto the sculptures, cup the ancient pottery. In short, they want to gobble it all up. When children create their own artwork, they ignore boundaries: everything is material, and everything—walls and floors, arms and legs—is a canvas.

Foster your child's love of art through these wonderful titles. The finished piece of art your child is drawn to is just one stage in a long process: oftentimes, the story behind the artist's creation is even more enthralling.

Art Dog by Thacher Hurd (HarperCollins Publishers: 1996) (D)

Read this with your child to go on an art-filled adventure.

Arthur Dog is a guard at the Dogopolis Museum of Art, but when the moon is full he becomes Art Dog and paints beautiful masterpieces without anyone knowing. One night, however, Art Dog witnesses and is framed for the theft of the valuable *Mona Woofa*. Can he catch the real thieves and clear his name?

The Art Lesson by Tomie dePaola (Putnam Juvenile: 1989) (D)

Read when you want to talk about really loving art and art class.

Tommy loves drawing and he really wants to be an artist. His pictures hang all over his house, his dad's barbershop, and his grandparent's grocery store. Tommy was so excited to start school so that he could take art lessons. But when the day finally comes, he is very disappointed—Mrs. Bowers wants Tommy to copy a painting. "Copy? Copy? Tommy knew that *real* artists didn't copy. This was terrible." Will he ever find a solution to his big problem?

Cave Paintings to Picasso: The Inside Scoop on Fifty Art Masterpieces by Henry M. Sayre (Chronicle Books: 2004) (E)

Read to learn about fifty amazing pieces of art from many periods in history.

From cave paintings to surrealism, Sayre surveys fifty pieces of art that represent different cultures and techniques. The book includes large pictures of the art and information on the date, painter, and more about each piece.

Frida by Jonah Winters, illustrated by Ana Juan (Arthur A. Levine Books: 2002) (E→D)

Read to express how exploring talents can help one cope with personal obstacles. If you would like to read more by this author, check out Diego, *about Diego Rivera and his famous murals.*

This story, based on Frida Kahlo's life, describes how painting saved young Frida from her loneliness, and also two near-death experiences. She explores all realms of painting, from copying photographs to painting what she sees under a microscope, and uses her painting to create beautiful works.

I Spy Shapes in Art by Lucy Micklethwait (Greenwillow Books: 2004) (E)

Read to learn about artworks through the classic game I Spy.

Using I Spy, this book allows children to explore the artwork of masters such as Georgia O'Keeffe, Henri Matisse, and Andy Warhol. The book encourages readers to search for ovals, rectangles, and circles in these masterpieces, learning about shapes and the art in which they are found in the process.

Ish by Peter H. Reynolds (Candlewick Press: 2004) (D)

Read to explore when your child feels frustrated because her drawings are not perfect.

Ramon loves drawing. He draws everywhere and all the time. Until one day, his brother Leon laughs at one of his drawings and Ramon realizes that "he kept trying to make his drawings look 'right' but they never did." Will Ramon's sister Marisol be able to help him appreciate his drawings?

Klimt and His Cat by Berenice Capatti and Shannon A. White, illustrated by Octavia Monaco (Eerdmans Books for Young Readers: 2005) (D)

Read to learn about Klimt, a late nineteenth-century painter.

Told from the perspective of his pet cat Katze, this fictionalized biography explores the art of the painter Klimt. The cat takes readers on a journey through the brightly colored and highly imaginative artworks found in Klimt's studio.

The Magic Horse of Han Gan by Chen Jiang Hong, translated by Claudia Zoe Bedrick (Enchanted Lion Books: 2006) (M)

Read for an example of when paintings come alive for you.

Experience the magical ways that paintings can come to life and inspire enormous imagination. Learn about the story of Han Gan, an extraordinarily talented Chinese painter who lived twelve hundred years ago. Legends tell that Han Gan, who grew up too poor to buy paint and paintbrushes, became a Chinese master painter, painting pictures of horses that came to life. "Why do you always draw your horses hitched up?" his friends asked him one day. "Because," Han Gan replied, "my horses are so alive they might leap right off the paper."

Murals: Walls That Sing by George Ancona (Marshall Cavendish Children: 2003) (M)

Read to learn about murals in cities across the United States.

With large color pictures and explanatory text, Ancona explores murals in different communities from Cambridge, Massachusetts, to San Francisco, California. He provides information on the people who create the murals, the materials used, and some of the techniques.

Seen Art? by Jon Scieszka, illustrated by Lane Smith (The Viking Press: 2005) (E)

Read when you want to take a moment to appreciate some of the magical works of art in the MoMA.

The confused young narrator searches for his friend Art on the corner of Fifty-third Street and Fifth Avenue, but ends up discovering all of the amazing artwork in the Museum of Modern Art instead.

Story Painter: The Life of Jacob Lawrence by John Duggleby (Chronicle Books: 1998) (M)

Read to explore the fascinating life of artist Jacob Lawrence.

Working with few materials during the Great Depression, Jacob Lawrence created artworks with a unique and vivid style. Lawrence's story can provide inspiration for readers, who learn that struggles can be overcome, leaving room for beauty to emerge.

Talking with Artists by Pat Cummings (Clarion Books: 1999) (M)

Read to learn about different illustrators and how they create their art.

Children's book illustrators create some of the most beautiful and vibrant artwork. This book contains conversations with thirteen such artists about how they create their work and where their ideas come from. The artists use many different methods and materials, providing a rich spectrum of many different kinds of art.

3-D ABC: A Sculptural Alphabet by Bob Raczka (Millbrook Press: 2007) (D)

Read to learn about different kinds of sculptures.

Actual sculptures from all over the world are photographed on each page of this book. The subject of each sculpture is arranged through the letters of the alphabet, but even more interesting is the author's description of what makes each art form so unique. Each image also includes a caption with the artist's name and where the piece is located.

Talk about It: Use this book to introduce your child to a very important and interesting art form, and to open his mind to different concepts of art. Discuss the similarities and differences between the various sculptures in their location, material, purpose, or the time when they were created.

- Select some of the pieces that you really like. Why do you like them? Are there some sculptures that you do not like? Why?
- Talk about the similarities and differences in the sculptures on facing pages; make comparisons, as the author does sometimes.

Walking the Log: Memories of a Southern Childhood by Bessie Nickens (Rizzoli International Publications: 1994) (M)

Read to learn how visual art can inspire writing. A great way to associate visual images and written memories.

In this book, the collection of memories is inspired by Nickens's beautiful paintings. For each painting that depicts her childhood, Nickens writes about the memories she has of the place, or event.

The Yellow House: Vincent Van Gogh and Paul Gauguin Side by Side by Susan Goldman Rubin (Harry N. Abrams: 2001) (M)

Read to learn about the difficult relationship between two famous artists, Vincent van Gogh and Paul Gauguin.

This book tells the story of two months when Vincent van Gogh and Paul Gauguin, two of the most famous artists of the late nineteenth century, lived and worked together. The author tells the story of each painter's style and methods, as well as the tumultuous personal relationship between the pair.

LOVING HISTORY

History is not just a collection of facts: it is storytelling at its best. It tells how a person or group of people can have an impact on society and on a time period. It is about how we caution ourselves to take care that our leaders do not gain so much power that our community loses its own. If we tell these stories to our children from a very young age, they will come to see history as a living thing, to learn from, to be inspired by. Your child too can be the person who changes the world, who uses power wisely and for good. To understand where great people began their journeys is to see that they were people, boys and girls once, too. To understand great events, we read to find out all the small details that led up to those big moments. Mummies, dinosaurs, ice cream, pyramids, and more: history is capable of riveting even the youngest readers.

Abe Lincoln: The Boy Who Loved Books by Kay Winters and Nancy Carpenter (Aladdin: 2003) (D)

Read when you want to talk about how books can change a person's life.

Abe Lincoln loved words. As he and his family struggled for survival, hunting, building log cabins, and grieving over the death of his mother, Abe longed to attend school so that he could read books. He learned about the power of books and how they can change a person's life: they even helped him to become the sixteenth president of the United States.

Aliens Are Coming!: The True Account of the 1938 War of the Worlds Radio Broadcast by Meghan McCarthy (Knopf Books for Young Readers: 2006) (M)

Read for a great historical story with lessons that remain applicable to this day. This is a fun story to remind your child that not everything he hears is the complete truth.

On October 30, 1938, radio broadcasts throughout the country exclaimed that something had landed in New Jersey; it appeared to be martians! "Is it the end of the world?" Suddenly, people throughout the country were in panic and seeing alien objects everywhere. At the same time, in the radio broadcast studio, actors were in the middle of their rendition of a science-fiction novel in celebration of Halloween.

Talk about It: Use this story as a pilot for talking with your child about the media and entertainment industry, and about being careful in not believing everything that we hear over the airwaves or on the Internet. For a child really interested in history, make sure to read the addendums at the end of the story; discuss the meaning of *War of the Worlds* and why people might be more easily scared during times of war or uncertainty.

- Read the notes and addendum at the end of the story. Discuss *War of the Worlds.* Talk about how the newspapers and other media added to the hysteria. Can you think of anytime in our own lives when people were in panic about something that turned out not to be a real threat?
- Can you think about reasons why we should be careful about trusting everything that we hear, especially through the media?

Behold the Trees by Sue Alexander, illustrated by Leonid Gore (Scholastic: 2001) (D→M)

Read to begin a discussion about the conflicts in Israel and wars fought over political or religious differences.

When Israel was known as Canaan, trees covered the land. As people lived on, fought over, and prayed throughout the land, the trees began to disappear. The land became arid and dry, until new inhabitants replanted the trees and began to bring a new life back to Israel. Through the story of the trees of Israel, learn about the impact the political and religious conflicts have had on the land and the people of Israel.

Freedom River by Doreen Rappaport, illustrated by Bryan Collier (Hyperion Books for Children: 2000) (M)

Read to start a discussion about the Underground Railroad, and the people who helped to create and sustain it. The themes in this book are important, but meant to be discussed with a mature child.

John Parker was once a slave himself, but he escaped by crossing the Ohio River. Yet he returns to the plantation where he once toiled to help free others from the horrors of slavery. Despite the severe danger, John Parker becomes a hero, bringing families to freedom through the Underground Railroad.

Ice Cream Cones for Sale! by Elaine Greenstein (Scholastic: 2003) (D)

Read this book to learn about the controversial debate over who truly invented the ice-cream cone.

Who invented the ice-cream cone? Ernest Hamwi claims he invented the ice-cream cone for the World's Fair in St. Louis, but another person claims he brought the ice-cream cone back from France, while another claims his girlfriend invented the ice-cream cone.

Mr. Williams by Karen Barbour (Henry Holt and Company: 2005) (M)

Read to inspire your child through a biography.

In 1929, a man named Mr. Williams was born in Acadia, Lousiana. He grew up on a farm with his parents, six brothers, five sisters, and many animals. This beautifully illustrated biography tells the story of Mr. Williams's life.

Mummies Made in Egypt by Aliki (HarperCollins Publishers: 1985) (M)

Read when your child wonders about pyramids, mummies, or ancient Egyptians.

Learn about how Egyptians made their mummies, why they made them, and where the mummies were buried. This in-depth book has illustrations and detailed explanations about the history and process of mummification in ancient Egypt.

Independent Dames: What You Never Knew About the Women and Girls of the American Revolution by Laurie Halse Anderson, illustrated by Matt Faulkner (Simon & Schuster Children's Publishing: 2008) (D→M)

Read to teach your child about the vital roles played by women and girls during the American Revolution.

How did women and girls contribute to the American Revolution? Learn all about these Revolutionary heroes in this beautifully illustrated tribute to the brave and inspirational women and girls of the Revolutionary Era. Read the brief snippets about the lives of Margaret Morris and Martha Washington and other special, independent dames.

Passage to Freedom: The Sugihara Story by Ken Mochizuki, illustrated by Dom Lee (Lee & Low Books: 1997) (M)

Read to learn about reaching out to others in difficult times, and about doing the right thing even when it is challenging. It is a historical read, but from a child's perspective and with many relevant themes. Good for an older child.

The narrator's father is a Japanese diplomat living in Lithuania. At the beginning of World War II, he has a chance to help Jewish refugees by issuing them visas to go to Japan. Despite being told by the Japanese government that he should not do so, the narrator's father and family know in their hearts that he must help the refugees be freed; the narrator thinks, "If I were one of those children out there, what would I want someone to do for me?" With his family's support, Hiroki Sugihara's father saved thousands of lives and was a hero to an entire nation during one of the most difficult times in our history.

Talk about It: The many themes in this story run very deep; it's difficult to imagine where to start a conversation. Pick a topic to discuss with your child: World War II, refugees, the struggle between doing what seems right or following the rules, the significance of a Japanese family helping

Jewish refugees. Or, ask your child if something else interests her in the story.

- Let's talk about the meaning of the word "refugee." Why were the Jewish people refugees during this time?
- What do you think about the actions of the narrator's father? Do you think that he did the right thing at the time? Why did he disobey the Japanese government?
- Read the afterword, written by Hiroki Sugihara. How did his family suffer from his father's actions initially, and how were they treated long after the war ended?

Reaching for the Moon by Buzz Aldrin, paintings by Wendell Minor (HarperCollins Publishers: 2005) (D→M)

Read to teach your child about Buzz Aldrin's path to become an astronaut who walked on the moon.

Dreams can be achieved, says Edwin Eugene Aldrin, better known as "Buzz" Aldrin. He explains that determination, hard work, education, and discipline combined made it possible for him to accomplish his dream of walking on the moon. Learn about how in following his dreams, Buzz became an astronaut, a scientist, and an airplane pilot.

Talk about It: Use this book to talk about the importance of having and pursuing dreams. Discuss how Buzz had to study and work very hard to follow his dreams, even when it seemed they might not come true.

- What was Buzz's dream? What did Buzz have to do to accomplish his dream?
- What is your dream? What do you think you will have to do to accomplish your dream?

Sequoyah: The Cherokee Man Who Gave His People Writing by James Rumford, translated by Anna Sixkiller Huckaby (Houghton Mifflin Company: 2004) (D)

Read to learn about the man who brought a written language to the Cherokee.

Sequoyah did not know any written language, but he knew that the Cherokee needed one. Determined to enable the Cherokee to become a nation who could read and write, he created a written language for his people. This is an extraordinary story of determination and how one person can impact a whole community.

Sienna's Scrapbook: Our African-American Heritage Trip by Toni Trent Parker, illustrated by Janell Genovese (Chronicle Books: 2005) (M)

Read to discover the range of ways to enjoy history. This is a great book for an older child with a lot of questions.

Written in the form of a scrapbook or journal, this vibrant, colorful book takes the reader on a journey through both important places and significant historical moments. At first, the narrator is frustrated about her family summer vacation; but, as they drive cross-country exploring the sites that reveal major events, stories, and people in African-American history, she feels a great and beautiful connection to her heritage.

They Called Her Molly Pitcher by Anne Rockwell, illustrated by Cynthia von Buhler (Knopf Books for Young Readers: 2002) (D)

Read to learn about the amazing tactics of Molly Pitcher, a heroine of the Revolutionary War.

Molly Hayes accompanied her husband, a soldier in General Washington's army, to Valley Forge and became a war heroine. On hot days, she provided the soldiers with pitchers of water. When Molly's husband was shot, she quickly tended to him before completing his task of firing the cannon. Read this story about an extraordinary heroine and notice also the accompanying pictures depicting much about life during the Revolutionary War.

LOVING MUSIC

Music is a glorious component in developing literacy. You will see that throughout this book I mention songs and rhymes, music collections that can inform literacy development. Here, let us enjoy a collection of books about music itself. Music is a mirror for culture, and for history, from the spirituals collected by Ashley Bryan to the biography of Bach by Jeanette Winter. When I was teaching deaf students, we went to a concert by a group called Sweet Honey in the Rock. They had a sign language interpreter and a good bass musician. My students stood and sang along, signing as they went, their bodies moving to the steady beat of the bass and their faces alight with the joy of it. The entire audience stood and signed along with them too. Music can be a lifelong joy and a lifelong comfort. Begin early by giving this great gift to your child.

The Deaf Musicians by Pete Seeger and Paul Dubois Jacobs, illustrated by R. Gregory Christie (Putnam Juvenile: 2006) (D)

Read to discover that music is everywhere, and that anyone can appreciate it.

Lee was a great piano man, playing every night at the jazz club with his band. One day, Lee realizes that he can't keep up with the band because he is losing his hearing. Undiscouraged, Lee goes to a school to learn sign language and finds that losing the ability to hear does not mean losing the ability to love or to play beautiful music. Note the brilliant colors and the motion of the bebopping words on each page.

Dizzy by Jonah Winter, illustrated by Sean Qualls (Scholastic: 2006) (D)

Read this book when you want to learn about the history behind the formation of bebop and about a very important musician, Dizzy Gillespie.

Dizzy Gillespie created a new form of music, bebop. In order to turn the music world upside down, Dizzy had to break rules and play the trumpet like no one ever had before. Learn about the incredible story of Dizzy's life and how he came to be a world-famous musician.

Duke Ellington: The Piano Prince and His Orchestra by Andrea Davis Pinkney, illustrated by Brian Pinkney (Hyperion Books for Children: 2007) (D)

Read to learn about Duke Ellington, a famous jazz pianist.

After hearing ragtime music as a child in Washington, D.C., Duke Ellington taught himself piano and became one of jazz's most renowned musicians. Through hard work and talent, Ellington put together an orchestra and wrote more than a thousand compositions during his lifetime.

Ella Fitzgerald: The Tale of a Vocal Virtuosa by Andrea Davis Pinkney and Brian Pinkney (Hyperion Books for Children: 2007) (D)

Read with your child to learn about one of jazz's greatest singers, Ella Fitzgerald.

Told from the perspective of a cat, this book tells the story of Ella Fitzgerald's life. From meager beginnings, performing on street corners, to packed theaters, Fitzgerald's life is a celebration of overcoming obstacles to create beautiful and world-renowned music.

He's Got the Whole World in His Hands by Kadir Nelson (Dial Books for Young Readers: 2005) (E→D)

Read to see a visual interpretation of an old, old song.

The song "He's Got the Whole World in His Hands" began as a spiritual and became a classic tune for children. Kadir Nelson interprets the song as seen from the eyes of a child. Talk about how you could draw your interpretation of a favorite song—and then try.

Jazz by Walter Dean Myers, illustrated by Christopher Myers (Holiday House: 2006) (M)

Read this when you want to explore the styles and rhythm of jazz. The book will take you on a journey from bebop to jazz vocals and much more. A perfect read for music or history lovers.

As you get swept up in the rhythm that Myers creates in *Jazz,* you can also learn about the history and many different styles of jazz.

Jazz ABZ: An A to Z Collection of Jazz Portraits by Wynton Marsalis, illustrated by Paul Rogers, contributions by Paul Schaap (Candlewick Press: 2005) (M)

Read and become mesmerized by some of the world's greatest jazz musicians.

Wynton Marsalis celebrates the vibrant, powerful, and enchanting works of twenty-six jazz musicians. Learn about Sarah Vaughan, Charlie Parker, and Count Basie through these beautiful illustrations and poetic verses.

Lookin' for Bird in the Big City by Robert Burleigh, illustrated by Marek Los (Harcourt: 2001) (D)

Read to learn about the meeting of two jazz greats, Miles Davis and Charlie Parker.

Through word and colorful art, this book tells the story of Miles Davis traveling to New York to meet his idol, Charlie Parker. Seeing New York for the first time, Davis is awed by the sights and sounds of the big city; his feelings are captured in the book's vibrant illustrations. Davis searches New York for, and eventually gets to perform with, Charlie Parker in this evocative introduction to jazz.

Sebastian: A Book about Bach by Jeanette Winter (Harcourt: 1999) (D)

Read to learn about Bach, a famous composer.

From the time he was a child, Bach was surrounded by music. His determination and love for music led him to become a prolific composer, renowned both in his time and today.

The 39 Apartments of Ludwig van Beethoven by Jonah Winter, illustrated by Barry Blitt (Schwartz & Wade: 2006) (D)

Read with your child for a humorous look at Ludwig van Beethoven's life.

Why did Beethoven move so often, living in thirty-nine different apartments in and around Vienna? Winter explores this question in a comical way, using clues from the few facts known about the composer's life. Cartoon-like illustrations show Beethoven changing and becoming more eccentric over time.

Woody Guthrie: Poet of the People by Bonnie Christensen (Dragonfly Books: 2001) (M)

Read to learn about the life of folk musician Woody Guthrie.

Woody Guthrie has become one of the most renowned folk artists of the twentieth century. However, his road to success was not easy—Guthrie grew up poor during the Great Depression. His talent, hope, and perseverance helped him through those times to become the artist beloved today.

Zin! Zin! Zin! A Violin by Lloyd Moss, illustrated by Marjorie Priceman (Aladdin: 1995) (D)

Read to uncover all the instruments you hear in an orchestra. How does each instrument sound? Discover the beauty and magic of listening as so many instruments come together for a special concert.

Learn about all of the unique instruments that make up an orchestra in this delightful rhyming story. Count the many instruments in the orchestra and discover how each instrument makes a special sound, but in harmony: "The strings all soar, the reeds implore, the basses roar with notes galore. It's the music we all adore. It's what we go to concerts for."

LOVING NUMBERS

There are kazillions of great math books for kids. I have chosen the ones I find the most entrancing for all ages. Children love to count, and they love to think about their age. There is nothing as delightful as watching a four-year-old explain how old he is: "I am four and three and a half quarters." They know the value of numbers: first by counting on their fingers and their toes, and then later, by exploring the miracles of disappearing digits. For children who are less than thrilled by math, beloved characters like Miss Spider and Sir Cumference will help ease them along.

Ten Black Dots by Donald Crews (HarperCollins Publishers: 1995) (E)

Read to uncover the diverse places where you might find ten black dots.

This straightforward counting book uses clear graphic illustrations to demonstrate when we might see one dot, two dots, or three dots. First published in 1968, this book has stood the test of time, making it an important counting book for youngsters.

The Best of Times: Math Strategies That Multiply by Greg Tang, illustrated by Harry Briggs (Scholastic: 2002) (M)

Read when learning to crack the multiplication tables.

Every elementary schooler wants to master the multiplication tables and win the math bee; this book will help your child to become comfortable with multiplication in a unique and fun way.

Chicka Chicka 1-2-3 . . . And More Stories About Counting by Bill Martin Jr. and Michael Sampson, illustrated by Lois Ehlert (Simon & Schuster Children's Publishing: 2004) (E)

Read when you want to talk about the order in which we count numbers.

Numbers climb up a tree in orderly twos and threes to gather together. Soon, the swarm of bees that lives in the tree scare the numbers away and they fall out in reverse order.

Counting on Frank by Rod Clement (Houghton Mifflin Company: 1994) (D)

Read this book with an inquisitive child who is interested in learning about the things all around her and thinking about measurement in a new way.

Frank is a dog who becomes a unit of measure for his boy. The boy measures the things all around him according to Frank, learning new facts about numbers, calculation, and the world around him in the process.

G Is for Googol: A Math Alphabet Book by David M. Schwartz, illustrated by Moss Marissa (Tricycle Press: 1998) (M)

Read with a child who wants to learn math terms in a new and humorous way.

Starting with "A is for Abacus," this book goes through the alphabet, finding an unusual math term for each letter of the alphabet. The book offers a funny way to explore new mathematical terms and ideas.

The Grapes of Math by Greg Tang, illustrated by Harry Briggs (Scholastic: 2001) (D)

Read to discover new and creative ways to learn math.

Learn how to solve math problems without even realizing it, using this fun, rhyming book full of math riddles and exciting illustrations. "How many scallops in this bunch; count them quick, it's time for lunch." Or, find out how many mushrooms are on the pizza pie or how many seeds hide in the watermelon.

The Greedy Triangle by Marilyn Burns (Scholastic: 2008) (D→M)

Read this book to learn about different kinds of polygons.

When a triangle becomes bored with having only three sides, he asks a "shape-shifter" to give him a new look. He spends some time as a quadrilateral and a pentagon in his exploration of shapes, an adventure that leaves readers noticing the shapes of the objects around them.

If You Made a Million by David Schwartz, illustrated by Steven Kellogg (HarperCollins Publishers: 1989) (D)

Read this to learn about different types and values of money.

Marvelosissimo the Mathematical Magician and his friends are hired to do some odd jobs, which leads to the discussion of how much they will earn and what their earnings will look like. They learn about money equivalencies—for example, "How much is one hundred dollars in pennies?" The book also has more detailed descriptions of other monetary concepts, such as the bank and income tax, at the end.

Just a Minute: A Trickster Tale and Counting Book by Yuyi Morales (Chronicle Books: 2003) (E→D)

Read this book written in Spanish and English to explore a clever take on counting.

Grandma Beetle is preparing for her birthday party when a skeleton visits her. She says, "Just a minute!" and the skeleton follows her as she does her chores, each one linked to a number from one to ten.

The Librarian Who Measured the Earth by Kathryn Lasky, illustrated by Kevin Hawkes (Little, Brown and Company: 1994) (D→M)

Read to learn about Eratosthenes of Cyrene, a librarian and scientist, and to ask questions about the natural world.

Eratosthenes was a geographer who estimated the circumference of the Earth in around 200 BC. While not much is known about his life, what is certain is that Eratosthenes was fascinated by the world around him—his questions are still relevant and provide important insights on the world around us.

Math Curse by Jon Scieszka and Lane Smith (Viking Books: 1995) (D)

Read to find that everyday problems can often be solved using math.

The day after the narrator's teacher tells him that "you can think of almost everything as a math problem," he starts to realize that daily problems seem to always involve numbers: being late for the bus, picking out clothes, answering questions in social studies class, and disagreeing at the dinner table. Through the story, the reader can help solve the problems of the "math cursed" narrator.

Math Trek: Adventures in the Math Zone by Ivars Peterson and Nancy Henderson (Jossey-Bass: 1999) (M)

Read with an inquisitive child who wants to solve math puzzles.

Each chapter takes readers on an adventure through different parts of an amusement park called "MathZone." Each stop includes puzzles about different mathematical concepts—solutions are provided in the back of the book.

Miss Spider's Tea Party: The Counting Book by David Kirk (Scholastic: 2007) (D)

Read to learn about counting, along with the bigger theme of not judging someone before you know her. Continue following Miss Spider's adventures by reading the other books in the series.

Miss Spider's carefully counted guests run away from her tea party when they learn that spiders are predators. However, when they hear that Miss Spider has been kind to an injured moth, they quickly change their minds and rejoin Miss Spider for tea.

Moja Means One: Swahili Counting Book by Muriel Feelings and Tom Feelings (Puffin: 1992) (D)

Read to learn about counting in Swahili.

Accompanied by drawings of East African life, this book teaches about counting, both in Swahili and English.

Mother Goose: Numbers on the Loose by Leo and Diane Dillon (Harcourt Children's Books: 2007) (E)

Read to learn to count using traditional rhymes.

Using illustrations, animals, and rhymes, the Dillons teach counting to young readers.

Sir Cumference and the Dragon of Pi by Cindy Neuschwander (Charlesbridge Publishing: 2004) (D)

This is one book in a series of Sir Cumference books, including: Sir Cumference and the First Round Table *and* Sir Cumference and the Great Knight of Angleland.

When Sir Cumference drinks a potion that turns him into a dragon, his son must search for the magical, and mathematical, remedy to his father's condition.

We All Went on Safari: A Counting Journey Through Tanzania by Laurie Krebs, illustrated by Julie Cairns (Barefoot Books: 2004) (E)

Read to learn how to count in Swahili and to gather other sorts of information about the Maasai people, and their home in the grasslands of Tanzania.

Learn to count in Swahili. Join this group of Maasai children as they count their way through Tanzania's grasslands. Use the accompanying map and the facts about the Maasai people, animals, and landscape to further unravel the mysteries of Tanzania.

What's Your Angle, Pythagoras? A Math Adventure by Julie Ellis, illustrated by Phyllis Hornung (Charlesbridge Publishing: 2004) (D)

Read to learn how young people can solve great problems that help future generations to understand the world better.

How did a young boy devise the Pythagorean theorem? Learn about the angles and people who inspire Pythagoras, a young Greek boy who loves to solve problems in this fictional story.

LOVING SCIENCE

The essential skill in science is something children do best: close observation. Read these titles to both your boys and girls, so as to encourage the love of science in both. Poring over these books together with your child will bring you both hours of pleasure. Be as much of an inquirer as your child is. Model your own questions and your own wonderings. Don't feel like you have to know everything. My father once told me that the smartest people he knew were the people who asked the most questions. Some of these books are silly, some are serious, but all are about inquiry and investigation, exploration and discovery. And that's what childhood is all about.

Atlantic by G. Brian Karas (Puffin: 2004) (D)

Read when you want to explore the seemingly boundless Atlantic Ocean.

Unravel the mystery of the Atlantic Ocean in this delightful book, which celebrates the amazing forces of nature. Through the story of the Atlantic, learn about how the ocean moves, shifts its shape, and inspires poets.

Bees Live in Hives by Melvin and Gilda Berger (Scholastic: 2003) (D)

Read to learn where bees live.

Have you ever wondered where bees live or what happens in a beehive? Discover the amazing world of the beehive in this book filled with interesting and informative photographs.

Creatures of the Deep by Katharine Kenah (School Specialty Publishing: 2005) (D)

Read to learn about animal life in the ocean. This book is one of the Extreme Readers series.

Discover the exciting creatures who live deep, deep down in the ocean. Learn all about manatees, sea horses, whales, and dolphins.

Diving Dolphin by Karen Wallace, edited by Linda Martin (Dorling Kindersley Publishing: 2001) (E→D)

Read when your child is curious about dolphins. You can read about frogs and tadpoles in Tale of a Tadpole *and about bees in* Busy Buzzy Bee, *also by Karen Wallace.*

Using word repetition and simple sentences, this book allows your child to uncover the extraordinary activities of dolphins. Dodge killer whales and explore the vast expanse of the ocean, as the dolphins share the experience of their daily lives through vibrant images with clear explanations.

Frozen Man by David Getz, illustrated by Peter McCarty (Henry Holt and Company: 1994) (M)

Read to learn about all of the stories told by a very special body, the body of the Iceman.

David Getz tells the captivating story of the discovery and subsequent study of the Iceman found frozen high in the mountains of the Ötztal Alps. The Iceman, who lived more than five thousand years ago, has provided an abundance of information about what ancient people ate, how they lived, and how they died, as detailed in this fascinating book.

Galileo's Treasure Box by Catherine Brighton (Walker Books for Young Readers: 2001) (D)

Read for a unique slant on the life of one of the most famous scientists, who challenged the worldviews of his time.

This book explores the world of Galileo's eldest daughter, Virginia. One day, she wanders into her father's workroom and finds his treasure box, which contains several pieces of glass and a feather. Virginia looks through the different glass shards and sees the world in a different way in each one. She takes the feather to her father, who tells her that this special feather helped him make one of his most important discoveries.

Move! by Robin Page, illustrated by Steve Jenkins (Houghton Mifflin Company: 2006) (E)

Read for an explanation of how an animal moves from place to place.

Rabbits hop and gibbons swing—can you guess how other animals move? This funny book asks readers to guess how animals move and then shows the many unusual ways that animals do so.

The Quest to Digest by Mary K. Corcoran, illustrated by Jef Czekaj (Charlesbridge Publishing: 2006) (D)

Read to discuss how the digestive system works.

Follow an apple as it passes through the digestive system. Watch it journey through the mouth, esophagus, stomach, and intestines and discover how the digestive process causes us to burp, vomit, and pass gas. This is the perfect read for a child who always wants to know where food goes and why we digest food the way we do.

Science Verse by Jon Scieszka and Lane Smith (Penguin: 2004) (M)

Read when you want a fun and creative way to learn exciting scientific facts.

Can you create a science verse? In this book, a little boy finds poetry in everything scientific. Learn about evolution, matter, viruses, and much more in these funny rhyming poems.

Sea Horse: The Shyest Fish in the Sea by Chris Butterworth, illustrated by John Lawrence (Candlewick Press: 2006) (D)

Read to learn about the fantastical sea horse, and to imagine life under the sea.

John Lawrence's beautiful illustrations will captivate your child, and Chris Butterworth's text is simple but factual and very engaging. Descriptions and comparisons will help your child to relate information about the sea horse to things more familiar to her. This is a beautiful introduction to nonfiction and science-related texts.

Surprising Sharks by Nicola Davies, illustrated by James Croft (Candlewick Press: 2005) (D)

Read to learn about the many kinds of sharks in the ocean.

Meet the amazing sharks of the ocean—the swell shark, the lantern shark, and many more. This book is hugely informative and provides detailed information on the physical characteristics of sharks, how they behave, and why sharks should be more afraid of humans than humans of sharks.

The Tiny Seed by Eric Carle (Simon & Schuster Children's Publishing: 2001) (D)

Read to learn about seeds—where they go, how they travel, and how they eventually become plants.

Where do seeds go? Follow the path of these small seeds as they blow off in the autumn wind. The seeds journey far and long, facing danger from birds that eat them, sunshine that burns them, and the ocean that drowns them. The survivors of this amazing migration settle in the ground, where they become plants that send off their seeds the following autumn.

Whose Tracks are These? A Clue Book of Familiar Forest Animals by Jim Nail, illustrated by Hyla Skudder (Rinehart Publishers: 1994) (E→D)

Read when your child wonders who left those prints in the ground.

Can you tell the difference between the tracks of a raccoon or a chipmunk? What prints do foxes leave behind? Learn how to identify the tracks of many different forest animals through the intricate illustrations and descriptions of each paw print. Become a detective and study all of the prints you encounter, big and small.

LOVING SPORTS

Children are often stereotyped into two groups: those who love sports and those who love reading. Children who love sports are sometimes not given the same due considerations as readers (and vice versa). But we can bring these worlds together very easily through literature. Children do not need to feel as if they have to love one or the other. Jumpy, lively, bouncy stories and poems that relate to sports help our children make connections between what they love to do and what they love to read. Read to them as they bounce a basketball or study athletic books together to learn some new techniques. The read-aloud then serves many purposes. And besides, some of the best writing I have ever read in my life is in the sports pages; feel free to read those aloud to your children too.

At Gleason's Gym by Ted Lewin (Henry Holt & Company: 2007) (D)

Read to talk about the training process for world champions and the excitement of a day in Gleason's Gym.

Visit the world-famous boxing gym Gleason's, where world champions Muhammad Ali, Sugar Ray, and Jake LaMotta trained. At Gleason's Gym, "The noise and smell of sweat hit you in the face like a roundhouse right," perseverance reigns, and trainees build courage, confidence, and their skills. Look at the beautifully illustrated images, which depict the hard work and sweat of these world champions and everyday boxers.

Baseball Saved Us by Ken Mochizuki, illustrated by Dom Lee (Lee & Low Books: 1993) (M)

Read with older children to discuss how sports can help to unify groups of people. Use this compelling book to introduce the topic of internment camps or the effects of World War II on Japanese-Americans.

During World War II, Shorty and his family are forced to leave their home and move to an internment camp in the dusty desert. Seeing the demoralizing effect of the camp on the children and adults, Shorty's dad, with the help of the whole community, creates a baseball field, baseball uniforms, and a baseball team. Shorty learns that through playing baseball, he can earn the respect of his friends, family, and even those who once put him down.

Catching the Moon: The Story of a Young Girl's Baseball Dream by Crystal Hubbard, illustrated by Randy DuBurke (Lee & Low Books: 2005) (D)

Read to celebrate the achievements of a girl who won't give up. This is a true story about the childhood of baseball hero Marcenia Lyle.

Marcenia is one of the best baseball players at her school, and she probably loves the game the most. The problem is that Marcenia is a girl; she is the only girl who plays on the team, while the other girls play hopscotch. It is hard enough trying to defend her love of baseball to her parents, but even worse when Mr. Street tells her that girls can't come to his summer baseball camp. But Marcenia is not going to give up. She is going to prove to everyone that she deserves to play ball.

Cross-Country Cat by Mary Calhoun, illustrated by Erick Ingraham (William Morrow: 1979) (D)

Read when you want to discuss the importance of persevering with a sport, even if your first experience is difficult.

Henry is a cat who loves to walk on his hind legs, except when he chases mice, of course. One day, his young owner decides to make Henry a pair of little cross-country skis. At first Henry tries to ski, falls, and gets snow in his whiskers. When his family accidentally leaves him behind, he must once again take to his skis, this time to be reunited with his family.

Short Takes: Fast-break Basketball Poetry by Charles R. Smith Jr., edited by Donna L. Brooks (Penguin Young Readers Group: 2001) (M)

Read when you want to enjoy fast-paced lyrics about a fast-paced game.

These twelve poems explore the gripping excitement, mind-blowing action, and vibrant sounds of the basketball court during a game. Influenced by rap, jazz, and rhymes, these poems, accompanied by snapshots of basketball games, bring the energy and life of a basketball game to the page.

Sixteen Years in Sixteen Seconds: The Sammy Lee Story by Paula Yoo, illustrated by Dom Lee (Lee & Low Books: 2005) (M)

Read to learn about the ultimate perseverance needed to be successful at a sport.

It's the summer of 1932 and Sammy must wait to practice diving in the public pool until Wednesday; on the other days, only white children can swim. Sammy loves diving, is very talented, and dreams about becoming an Olympian. His father, however, believes that Sammy should be a doctor. There are many obstacles in the way of Sammy's dream, but he is prepared to work hard. Will his perseverance pay off?

Talk about It: This is a great book for an older child who enjoys sports. It's also simply an incredible story about overcoming obstacles (discrimination, parental pressure, the loss of a parent, academic struggles) to achieve a dream. The rich topics in this true story could lead to many brilliant conversations with your child.

- ✦ Talk about the unfair treatment that Sammy faced throughout his life; why did he face this discrimination? How did he react? What did his father tell him about dealing with prejudice? Did Sammy take his father's advice?
- ✦ What were some of the obstacles that Sammy faced as he tried to reach his goal? How did he overcome each obstacle? What are some good words for describing Sammy's personality?
- ✦ How was Sammy's father important in his life?

Teammates by Peter Golenbock, illustrated by Paul Bacon (Gulliver Books: 1990) (M)

Read to baseball lovers, who also love heroes, history, and feeling a sense of justice. Good for an older child, who may have heard about the history of segregation in sports in the United States.

Learn about the heroes of the Negro baseball leagues and the challenges these players faced. Learn about the manager who would not accept segregated baseball, and about the fearless Jackie Robinson, who fought racism by agreeing to play with the Brooklyn Dodgers in the major leagues. Learn about the one player who had the courage to stand by his teammate.

Teammates by Tiki and Ronde Barber with Robert Burleigh, illustrated by Barry Root (Simon & Schuster Children's Publishing: 2006) (D)

Read to learn about the bond between the twins and the sport that they love.

This is the true story of NFL superstars and twins, Tiki and Ronde; their relationship as teammates begins as children on the football field. As they grow and practice their sport, they support each other, learn from their coaches, and bond in their struggles and in their successes.

What Athletes Are Made Of by Hanoch Piven (Simon & Schuster: 2006) (D)

Read when you want to talk about what it takes to be an athlete. After reading What Athletes Are Made Of, *try reading* What Presidents Are Made Of, *also by Hanoch Piven.*

What are athletes made of? Find out through the innovative drawings of professional athletes like Martina Navratilova and Kareem Abdul-Jabbar what it takes to be an athlete: hard work, determination, and teamwork, but athletes also need great minds and free spirits.

LOVING WORDS AND LANGUAGE

The alphabet and language itself is funny, tricky, confusing, and thought provoking. The new *Oxford English Dictionary* is all online now, so, as its editor says, the possibilities for collecting words are endless. Words are the building blocks for story and communication. For your children learning a second language, whether it's English or another, a reverence for the language they already know helps them to build off that knowledge and learn something new. Find the silliness in language, in the oddness of English spellings, in the eccentricity of grammar conventions. Enjoy words that are unfamiliar by marveling over them and even collecting them. Best of all, savor these books for the attention they give to the love of language itself and the glorious, marvelous alphabet.

AlphaOops! The Day Z Went First by Alethea Kontis, illustrated by Bob Kolar (Candlewick Press: 2006) (D)

Read to celebrate turning the alphabet upside down, backward, and all around.

What would happen if the letters in the alphabet jumped out of order? Could *Z* go first? The letters let *Z* begin the alphabet, but then *P* decides to find a new spot and suddenly all the letters are finding new places. Can you find all of the letters in the alphabet? Turn the pages and find out which letter will come next.

Chicka Chicka Boom Boom by Bill Martin Jr. and John Archambault, illustrated by Lois Ehlert (Little Simon: 2006) (E)

Read when you want to enjoy a playful alphabet chant.

Race to the top of the coconut tree with all of the letters of the alphabet. "Chicka chicka boom boom! Will there be enough room?" How will all of the letters in the alphabet fit into the coconut tree? Enjoy the rhyming alphabet story and celebrate the exciting letters.

C Is for Curious: An ABC of Feelings by Woodleigh Hubbard (Chronicle Books: 1990) (D)

Read to discover new names for feelings and to learn about the alphabet. You can also read the companion book 2 Is for Dancing: A 1 . . . 2 . . . 3 . . . of Actions.

Find a feeling for any letter in the alphabet. *A* is angry and *Z* is zealous. What other emotions can you find in this alphabet book of feelings?

The Disappearing Alphabet by Richard Wilbur, illustrated by David Diaz (Harcourt Children's Books: 2001) (D)

Read to discover the importance of each letter in the alphabet.

What would happen if the letters in the alphabet disappeared? "What if there were not the letter *O*? You couldn't COME, you couldn't GO." Learn about why words matter in this funny and creative journey through the alphabet.

Gathering the Sun: An Alphabet in Spanish and English by Alma Flor Ada, English translation by Rosa Zubizarreta, illustrations by Simón Silva (HarperCollins Publishers: 2001) (D)

Read to celebrate the beauty of letters, language, and poetry.

Alma Flor Ada captures the beauty and complexity of farms and farmworkers in a series of twenty-eight poems. Using the Spanish alphabet as a guide, her simple poems and the beautiful illustrations tell the story of the farms and the people who live and work on them in loving detail.

Max's Words by Kate Banks, illustrated by Boris Kulikov (Farrar, Straus and Giroux: 2006) (D)

Read if you enjoy hoarding words.

Max's brother Benjamin has a stamp collection and his other brother Karl has a coin collection. Max really wants to have his own collection, so he decides to collect words—he cuts out words from newspapers and magazines. Max's collection grows bigger and bigger, even outgrowing his room. Finally, Max has so many words that he can write a story.

Mom and Dad Are Palindromes: A Dilemma for Words . . . and Backwards by Mark Shulman, illustrations by Adam McCauley (Chronicle Books: 2006) (M)

Read to learn about palindromes and the excitement of words.

Can you find the 101 palindromes hidden in this book? Bob discovers that he is a palindrome and so is his family—Mom, Dad, Nan, and Otto. Enjoy this wonderful book full of wordplays as you learn all about the excitement of palindromes.

Sparkle and Spin: A Book about Words by Ann Rand, illustrated by Paul Rand (Chronicle Books: 1957) (D)

Read to learn about all of the jobs that words can do.

This book does a good job of introducing the many functions of words. Words can help express emotion or tell someone what you are thinking. Sometimes people shout out words, and other times a word is "something to whisper softly as the little breeze that says 'hush hush.'" Let this book help your child start thinking about different kinds of words, and how they can create different meanings in our heads or feelings in our hearts.

The War Between the Vowels and the Consonants by Priscilla Turner, illustrated by Whitney Turner (Sunburst Books: 1999) (D)

Read when you want a funny way to learn about the differences between vowels and consonants.

The Consonants and the Vowels composed two separate groups. From a young age, the Vowels learned never to stray into the Consonant Quarter and the Consonants learned never to trust a Vowel. War breaks out between the Vowels and Consonants—will the two sides ever find a common ground?

Wild about Books by Judy Sierra, illustrated by Marc Brown (Random House Books for Young Readers: 2004) (D)

Read to appreciate a love of books.

Molly McGrew, Springfield's librarian, accidentally drives her bookmobile into the zoo. As Molly sets up her shop in the zoo, the animals quickly plunge into the joy of reading. Through these rhyming lyrics, discover why the animals of the zoo learn to love reading so much that Molly has to find waterproof books for the otters and tiny books for the crickets.

Wonderful Words: Poems about Reading, Writing, Speaking, and Listening selected by Lee Bennett Hopkins, illustrated by Karen Barbour (Simon & Schuster Children's Publishing: 2004) (M)

Read to celebrate reading, writing, speaking, or listening.

Read "Listen" by Lee Bennett Hopkins when you want to appreciate the importance of just listening to the sounds around you. Or, read "How to Learn to Say a Long, Hard Word" by David McCord or "Words Free as Confetti" by Pat Mora when you want to embrace the magic of words. Whichever poem you choose to read, take a moment to think and talk about why we should celebrate reading, writing, speaking, and listening.

Word Wizard by Cathryn Falwell (Clarion Books: 1998) (D)

Read to learn all about anagrams.

Anna discovers that the letters in her bowl of cereal form more than one word. With the excitement of this discovery, Anna and her friend Zack embark on a magical adventure with anagrams. After reading this book, try collecting words of your own. Search through magazines, books, or even bowls of cereal for favorite letters or words.

MAKING A MISTAKE

Making a mistake can sometimes be a little bit funny, but also painful. And sometimes our biggest mistakes lead to our greatest learnings. The great thing about children's literature is that often it is animals who make the silliest mistakes. Somehow, telling our story through animals makes our own stumbles a little less wounding. We can laugh at the funny little animal while feeling reassured that we have done the same things ourselves, and all was well in the end. Another reason to read books and talk about how everyone makes mistakes is to reinforce for your child that at the end of the day, you will love him not only in spite of his stumbles, but even because of them.

Beverly Billingsly Borrows a Book by Alexander Stadler (Voyager Books: 2002) (D)

Read when your child is worried about the consequences of making a mistake.

Beverly Billingsly is so excited to get her first library card. She immediately borrows a book and reads it everywhere; she can't put it down, until she realizes that she is a day late in returning it. Her friends tell her horror stories about people who do not return their library books. Will Beverly have the guts to face the librarian with an overdue book?

Edwurd Fudwupper Fibbed Big by Berkeley Breathed (Little, Brown and Company: 2003) (D)

Read to discuss when a seemingly small fib becomes a giant out-of-control lie.

Edward is always telling fibs. One day Edward tells a very, very big fib that gets lots and lots of people involved—the army, the air force, the dogcatcher, and more. Edward cannot find a way out of his huge lie, until his little sister finds a way to save him from his fibs.

It Wasn't My Fault by Helen Lester, illustrated by Lynn M. Munsinger (Houghton Mifflin Company: 1985) (D)

Read when you want a funny story about the pitfalls of making mistakes and blaming others.

Murdley Gurdson makes a lot of mistakes. His kite gets stuck in a tree. He falls into a wastebasket. His toothpaste oozes all over the bathroom. Murdley knows that most of these mistakes are his fault, but when someone lays an egg on his head, Murdley really wants to find out whom to blame.

Library Lion by Michelle Knudsen, illustrated by Kevin Hawkes (Candlewick Press: 2006) (D)

Read this book when your child has broken a rule and feels very sad about it, or when he has to make the choice between breaking a rule and helping a friend.

One morning, a lion starts visiting the library. After roaring too loudly, the lion learns that in a library one must be quiet. He quickly learns the librarian Miss Merriweather's other rules. The lion soon makes friends with all the children in the library and returns to visit his friends every day. When Miss Merriweather finds herself in trouble, the lion is torn between helping his friend and obeying a rule.

Talk about It: Use this book to explore rules and making mistakes. It is a story about how sometimes you have to break the rules in order to help a friend. Also, use it to talk about what to do when you get in trouble for breaking a rule.

- The library lion found himself in a situation where he had to break a rule in order to help a friend; do you think he did the right thing?

- Sometimes it is hard to learn how to follow rules. But the library lion tried very hard. Have you ever had a hard time obeying a rule?

Mama, Coming and Going by Judith Caseley (Greenwillow Books: 1994) (D)

Read to talk about how sometimes even parents can make mistakes. Also read for the special relationship between a single mother and her firstborn daughter.

After Jenna's little brother Mickey is born, her mom starts to make some funny mistakes: she forgets to defrost the chicken, turn off the water faucet, close the car trunk when the groceries are inside. Jenna is a big help to her mom, in many small and sweet ways.

Martha Speaks by Susan Meddaugh (Houghton Mifflin Company: 1992) (D)

Read to talk about when a small mistake leads to a big problem. Continue following the adventures of Martha by reading the other books in the series.

The trouble begins when Helen feeds the rest of her alphabet soup to her dog Martha. Helen and her family quickly learn how problematic a talking dog can be—especially one who spills family secrets.

Strega Nona by Tomie dePaola (Simon & Schuster Children's Publishing: 1975) (D)

Read to learn about magic, and talk about being tempted to do something that you have been told not to do. This is the first in a series of Strega Nona stories.

Strega Nona, or "Grandma Witch," leaves Big Anthony alone with her magic pasta pot and a warning not to touch it. Big Anthony is tempted by the magic, and determined to prove himself to the town by eliciting the magic pasta.

Talk about It: This book offers a wonderful way to have a conversation about temptation. A child could be tempted to touch or use any number of things, which they have been told not to. Discuss why people feel tempted and what could happen when you disregard a warning and give in to your temptation.

- Magic is very mysterious. Why did Big Anthony want to use the magic pot? Do you think that if you were Big Anthony, you would have been tempted to use the magic pot?
- What was Anthony's punishment? Strega Nona says the punishment must fit the crime. What do we think that means? Does his punishment fit the crime?

Two of Everything: A Chinese Folktale by Lily Toy Hong (Albert Whitman & Company: 1993) (D)

Read this delightful Chinese folktale to talk about how being greedy can be a big mistake.

Mr. Haktak discovers a mysterious pot in his backyard, a magical pot that multiplies everything he or his wife, Mrs. Haktak, put in it. When Mrs. Haktak accidentally drops two hairpins into the pot, she finds out that the pot has produced two more hairpins. When Mr. Haktak puts his coin purse in the pot, he finds out that it has miraculously produced a second coin purse. Mr. and Mrs. Haktak, who are very poor, realize that with the magic pot, they can become rich. All of a sudden, Mrs. Haktak falls into the pot, and the magic pot becomes much more problematic.

Where the Wild Things Are by Maurice Sendak (HarperCollins Publishers: 1967) (E)

Read when your child is feeling mischievous or adventurous.

After yelling at his mother, Max is sent up to his room without any dinner. But soon his room turns into a jungle and he takes a journey across the world, where he meets and tames the wild things, becomes their king, and enjoys a crazy rumpus. Eventually, Max feels lonely and wants to be home, where someone loves him, so he begins his journey back to his own room and his nice, warm dinner.

Talk about It: Even a tough guy like Max misses his mom when he is away on his journey. Use this book to explain that even when a child misbehaves, and receives punishment, his parent still loves him unconditionally. Meanwhile, it is okay to be adventurous but to miss your parents at the same time.

- What did you think of Max? Do you ever feel like making mischief like Max?

- What do you think about Max's journey? Would you like to take a journey to where the wild things are?
- Why does Max return to his room? What do you think about his reasons? Do you think that his mother will be happy to see him?

MAKING FRIENDS/FRIENDSHIP

I first met my friend Elizabeth in the park when our daughters were toddlers. She and I could not get over how similar we were: in everything. Even our husbands looked alike! Or maybe not . . . but when you are instant friends, you look for all kinds of connections. Friendship is a journey too. From a young age, your children experience the emotions, passions, and layers of friendship very deeply. Use these books to explore all the different ways friendships impact our lives. Talk about your own friendships, old and new. Your children will love to hear those stories. My father has a friend from grade school. He calls his friend White Owl, who even knows why anymore? Yet when they are together, I can just picture them as children. And for me, my father becomes all the more complete. I see how hard he has worked at his friendships and I admire him for that and so much more. His dedication to his friends is a form of loving work: it takes discipline, openness, kindness, and a joie de vivre to keep those threads going. There are some classic friendships in great children's literature: Frog and Toad, Ernest and Celestine, Harry Potter and Hermione. Friendships are tender, fierce, bumpy, joyous, loving, and sometimes really, really challenging. They are all about how we practice both giving and receiving love. If you begin talking about the nature of friendship with your child early on through the read-aloud, the conversation will be lifelong, endlessly fascinating, always rewarding.

Alexander and the Wind-Up Mouse by Leo Lionni (Dragonfly Books: 1969) (D)

Read for a beautifully illustrated book about adventure, friendship, and differences.

Alexander befriends Willie, the wind-up mouse. They quickly discover how important friends are.

Alien & Possum: Friends No Matter What by Tony Johnston, illustrated by Tony DiTerlizzi (Aladdin: 2002) (D)

Read to talk about making friends with people who might look or be a little different than you. Continue reading about the adventures of Alien and Possum by reading the other books in the series.

Possum, who loves staying up late, is looking at the stars one night when he sees a spaceship land. When Possum meets Alien, he wonders if they can ever be friends, because they are so different. In fact, Alien and Possum have a lot in common and quickly become best friends.

Cat and Mouse by Tomek Bogacki (Farrar, Straus and Giroux: 1996) (D)

Read this book to your children to teach them about making friends, especially with people who may look or act differently.

On the day Mother Mouse and Mother Cat taught their children about the world, one mouse and one kitten were not paying attention. When those children met in a meadow, they found that despite their physical differences they could be great friends. Eventually all the mice children and all the cat children realized that they could all be friends.

Clara and Asha by Eric Rohmann (Roaring Brook Press: 2005) (D)

Read right before bed, or when you want to talk about having special friends.

As Clara gets ready for bed, her special friend Asha comes by for a visit. Together Clara and Asha have so many adventures: they play in the snow, fly through the sky, and splash in the bath. It is so hard to get ready to fall asleep when you have such a fun friend.

Talk about It: The warmth of friendship can come from many unexpected places. Having friends can be so exciting, as is using your imagination.

- Have you ever had a friend who made you feel very special? Why is that friendship so wonderful?
- Using her imagination, where did Clara visit? What did she do? When you use your imagination, what do you like to do?
- What do you think about when you are going to sleep?

Cowgirl Kate and Cocoa by Erica Silverman, illustrated by Betsy Lewin (Harcourt Children's Books: 2006) (D)

Read when you want to discuss how even though friends may get into arguments, their friendship is still strong.

Cowgirl Kate wants her trusty horse Cocoa to help her herd cattle and ride around on the range, but Cocoa has other plans. Kate wants to count the cows, but Cocoa's independent streak and enormous appetite create small arguments between the two best friends. Readers know that although they fight, these two pals truly care about each other.

Fox by Margaret Wild, illustrated by Rob Brooks (Kane/Miller Book Publishers: 2006) (M)

Read this book to discuss friendships. You can also use the book to discuss the very complex issues of social justice and what it means to be human.

Dog and Magpie became friends after a devastating fire, which blinded Dog and burned the wings of Magpie so she could no longer fly. Dog and Magpie travel through the forest together, Dog carrying Magpie and Magpie guiding Dog. When a lonely Fox sees this friendship between Magpie and Dog, he becomes jealous. In order to destroy their friendship and show them what it means to be lonely, Fox tricks Magpie into leaving Dog and traveling with him.

Talk about It: Use this book to talk about loneliness, jealousy, and deception. Discuss the reasons why Fox was angered by the relationship between Dog and Magpie and how he dealt with his feelings. Also, talk about the important relationship between Dog and Magpie—how they cared deeply for each other and helped each other out during difficult times.

- Talk about the type of friendship that existed between Magpie and Dog. How did they help each other? Have you ever had a friend who you helped and who helped you when you needed it?
- Discuss the motivations behind Fox's actions. Why did Fox behave the way he did? How could he have acted instead? Has anyone you know hurt someone because he was jealous? How did you feel when you saw it happening?
- How did Fox trick Magpie into leaving Dog? How do you think he should have handled the situation?

The Friendly Four by Eloise Greenfield, illustrated by Jan Spivey Gilchrist (Amistad: 2006) (D)

Read this wonderful book about friendship, family, community, and adoption. Use it to talk about the importance of building relationships and the power of friendships.

Drum, who is lonely, finds a new friend when Doreen moves onto his block. Louis, settling with his new mom, joins the group soon after. Finally, when Rae comes to the block while her mother recovers from an illness, the Friendly Four is complete. Drum, Dorene, Louis, and Rae become fast friends who play, break rules, and build a town together. The Friendly Four develop a special friendship during their exciting summer adventure.

Frog and Toad Are Friends by Arnold Lobel (HarperCollins Publishers: 1979) (D)

Read when you want to talk about an enduring friendship.

Frog and Toad share a very special friendship. They care deeply for each other and embark on wonderful adventures. At the first sign of spring, Frog races to Toad's house to find him. They search for buttons and read aloud together. As you read these five stories, bask in their warm friendship.

Girls Together by Sherley Anne Williams, illustrated by Synthia Saint James (Harcourt: 1999) (D)

Read this wonderful celebration of friendship and adventure when you want to talk about the way friends have fun.

Five friends wake up one Saturday morning and want to get away from their mommas who hear everything, their little brothers, and their projects. Follow their adventures through the town and neighborhood.

Hi! Fly Guy by Tedd Arnold (Scholastic: 2005) (E)

Read to introduce the concept of the chapter book to young readers.

Buzz finds a pet fly, Fly Guy, and causes havoc when he brings his new pet to the cafeteria. Everyone's favorite lunch lady likes Fly Guy, but when she gets fired, the replacement hates Fly Guy. Find out how Buzz and Fly Guy get rid of the replacement, much to everyone's delight.

How to Be a Friend by Laurie Krasny Brown, illustrated by Marc Bown (Little, Brown and Company: 1998) (D)

Read when you want to provide an overview of the various types of friends, and also when you want to discuss the ways to reconcile problems in friendships.

Friends can affect our lives in so many different and fantastic ways. This book outlines the many ways you can make a friend or be a friend, and the various kinds of people who can be friends. It also details the ways *not* to be a friend, how to deal with bosses and bullies, and how to resolve an argument.

Leonardo the Terrible Monster by Mo Willems (Hyperion Books for Children: 2005) (E)

Read for a silly story about friends and monsters.

Leonardo really, really wants to be a scary monster like Tony, Eleanor, and Hector, but he cannot seem to scare the tuna fish out of anyone. Will he ever learn to be truly frightening?

Madlenka by Peter Sís (Farrar, Straus and Giroux: 2000) (D)

Read when you want to talk about how friends can be found everywhere; in a store, on a corner, or next to you on a bus.

When Madlenka finds out her tooth is loose, she wants to tell all of her friends: the French baker, the Indian newsstand owner, the Latin American greengrocer, and more. In seeing all of her friends around the block, Madlenka takes a trip around the world. Join Madlenka in her journey; as you do, have fun peeking into the next page through the cutout windows.

Mr. Putter and Tabby Pour the Tea by Cynthia Rylant, illustrated by Arthur Howard (Harcourt Children's Books: 1994) (D)

Read when you want to talk about the importance of friendship and brainstorm some fun activities friends can do together. It is part of the Mr. Putter and the Tabby *series.*

Mr. Putter lives all by himself in his very lonely house. Tabby is also very lonely. When Mr. Putter and Tabby find each other, an unshakable bond is born.

My Best Friend by Pat Hutchins (HarperCollins Publishers: 1993) (D)

Read to celebrate the fun of having a best friend.

Best friends are so much fun. This young girl's best friend can run fast, paint pictures, and even read. When the two best friends have a sleepover, the young girl realizes that she too can help her best friend, who becomes frightened during the night.

My Friends/Mis Amigos by Taro Gomi (Chronicle Books: 2006) (E)

Read this bilingual book to talk about how friends big and small can teach you important lessons.

From her bird friends, this little girl learned to sing. From her friends at school, she learned to play. From her friend the owl she learned to study the night sky. Discover all of the little girl's friends and what important lesson they taught her. Which friend taught you to walk, to study or to smell flowers?

Yo! Yes? by Chris Raschka (Orchard Books: 1993) (E)

Read when you want to discuss the importance of reaching out to make new friends, and how even the simplest gesture can carry a world of meaning to someone else.

When one young boy greets another with a simple "Yo!" the other responds with a "Yes?" The two boys discover that they can learn a lot about each other, even with this short exchange, and once their conversation ends, they have gained a lasting friendship.

A NEW BABY

Families are organic entities: they change and change and change. The arrival of a sibling is startling for a young child. And for an older child whose patterns may be far more set, it is a lot more stressful than we might imagine. The blessing of a great book is that it honors the confusion of all that, while setting a tone of inclusion and the possibility for transcendence and the beginning of a brand new-relationship.

Each book has its own perspective and its own story about the impact of new babies on a family. There is no one right way to feel. Your young children are often very intrigued by how *you* felt when they came into your life. These books offer you the opportunity to tell the story again of their coming, and even the funniness of it all, as you learned to become a parent.

Younger children learning how to be a sibling are also navigating new waters. They may be too young to talk about what a new baby would feel like to the family, and so much of what they are experiencing is barely articulated. A great book will articulate some of their feelings for them, even if it's just looking at pictures of babies in books and realizing that the newness of what they have, other people have too.

I have a photo of Charlotte in her baby crib at the hospital, and if I look really closely I can see the tips of Katie's painted two-year-old toes peeking through the slats of the bassinet. That picture makes me cry every time. It is all about the first moments, all about the entry of a new baby into someone's life and what that can mean.

Babies Can't Eat Kimchee! by Susan Roth and Nancy Patz (Bloomsbury: 2006) (D)

Read to a new older sibling.

Aren't little sisters supposed to be fun? This new baby can't do anything, doesn't know about anything, and spends all day screaming and crying or sleeping. Her older sibling wonders if the new baby in the house will ever be old enough to be fun.

Baby, Come Out! Fran Manushkin, illustrated by Ronald Himler (Star Bright Books: 2001) (E)

Read to an impatient child who is expecting a new sibling. This book can start a conversation with a child about her brother or sister on the way.

Everyone in the family is waiting expectantly for the baby to come. They decide that she needs a little encouragement to realize how comfy and cozy it can also be outside of her mother's womb. The illustrations in this book are deliciously charming, especially the expressions on Baby's face as she listens to the voices of her family, and *especially* when she hears her daddy kissing everyone in the house and wishes for that herself.

The Baby on the Way by Karen English, illustrated by Sean Qualls (Farrar, Straus and Giroux: 2005) (D)

Read for an all-around great book about babies, but also for family bonds connecting the past, present, and future. It's great for a child brimming with questions.

When Jamal asks his grandma if she was ever a baby, he learns that not only was she a baby, she was also a baby on the way. He then has the chance to hear his grandmother tell the story of her birth.

Talk about It: This is a great way of introducing the tradition of passing down stories within a family. Use this book as an introduction to tell stories about your child's birth or entry into the family, as well as your own. You can also use this book to introduce the concept of heritage.

- Did you know that everyone, even grandparents and parents, was once a baby, just like Jamal's grandmother? Let me tell you the story about when I was born . . .
- With an older child, you may want to talk about Jamal's grandmother's *specific* history, as it draws on tradition passed down from times of slavery. Talk about family history, but also cultural history and heritage, whether by birth or adoption.

A Baby Sister for Frances by Russell Hoban, illustrated by Lillian Hoban (HarperCollins Children's Books: 1964) (E)

Read this innovative book that uses rhymes and songs to explore the difficulty of adjusting to a new baby in the house.

After Gloria is born, Frances feels ignored. But then Frances runs away under the dining room table, and even though her journey is not far, she learns a great deal. The Hobans are deeply sensitive to the integrity of a child and the importance of the spirit of a child. Although the child has to accommodate the new situation, it is also our responsibility as parents not to break that spirit and to honor its core.

Bad Baby by Ross MacDonald (Roaring Brook Press: September 2005) (D)

Read this off-the-wall book with an older sibling who is finding the new baby not to be what he or she expected.

Jack is hoping that his new baby sister will be the play companion for whom he has been hoping. Instead, she starts growing out of control (until she could squash Jack with her palm) and her mischievousness begins taking over. Why don't Jack's parents seem to notice?

Jack may be familiar: he is also the hero of MacDonald's book *Another Perfect Day.*

More, More, More, Said the Baby by Vera B. Williams (Greenwillow Books: 1997) (E)

Read to show your baby just how much you love him and to show the love in different families.

Little Guy, Little Pumpkin, and Little Bird are loved so much by the grown-ups in their lives. Follow all of the little babies, as they cannot escape the love of their father, grandmother, or mother. This book's illustrations are beautiful too, especially for how gloriously ethnically diverse the babies are.

Talk about It: Use this book to talk about how much you love your own child. Tell a story about how you remember your parents showing you that they loved you.

- Think about the ways that Little Guy's father, Little Pumpkin's grandmother, and Little Bird's mother showed that they loved their babies. How do I show you that I love you?
- How do you show your parents, grandparents, brothers, or sisters that you love them?

My New Baby illustrated by Annie Kubler (Child's Play International: 2000) (E)

Read this when you want to talk about what it is like to be a new person in the world.

Follow this new baby as she encounters the world in this wordless book. As the baby meets her family, plays, and takes a bath for the first time, you and your child can discuss your own babyhoods and create your own story based on Kubler's charming illustrations.

She Comes Bringing Me That Little Baby Girl by Eloise Greenfield, illustrated by John Steptoe (L. P. Lippincott Co.: 1974) (M)

Read for a great, realistic portrayal of the emotions felt by a new older sibling.

Kevin wishes for his mom to bring home a little brother, but all he gets is a little baby girl who seems to take up everyone's time and attention. It makes Kevin sick . . . until his mama "comes bringing [him] that baby girl" and tells him that now he gets to be an older brother, just as his uncle was to her when she was a little girl.

A Teeny Tiny Baby by Amy Schwartz (Orchard Books: 1994) (E)

Read this when you want to look at the world through the eyes of a teeny, tiny baby.

Have you ever wondered how babies manage to get everything they want? See the world for the first time through the eyes of this baby. Your child will ask you questions about herself as a baby when reading this pleasurable book. Even when the dad stands in the window looking exhausted, you can feel the love and warmth of the new family exuded by the pages.

OVERCOMING ADVERSITY

Everyone from Shy Charles to Martin Luther King Jr. experiences adversity and overcomes it in the following books. Little adversities and big, we as humans learn very early the patterns we set in motion in terms of how we deal with obstacles, with conflict, and with challenges. Literature helps us to talk with our children about practicing resilience. We are always growing. We are not finished with being tested, or learning how to be stronger. I have been honored to come to know many children over the years. The ones who stick with me the most are those who have faced tremendous adversity and persevered. There is Moses, who was a deaf child from Ethiopia who learned to sign and became a lawyer. There is Cynobia, who saw her relative killed in front of her by a stray bullet. There is Edgar, who wished so much he could walk, but did not let his wheelchair stop him from competing in the Special Olympics. The following books are about characters, like the children I've known, speaking up for themselves in sweet and feisty ways. We can all learn something from Brave Irene. With her kind of spunk, we could all change the world.

Armando and the Blue Tarp School by Edith Hope Fine and Judith Pinkerton Josephson, illustrated by Hernán Sosa (Lee & Low Books: 2007) (D)

Read when you want to talk about how people can overcome adversity by uniting as a community; just one person can help to change the lives of others.

Armando grew up in a *colonia* next to the city's dump, spending each day helping his father sort through the trash. When Señor David sets up a school near Armando's home on a blue tarp, Armando longs to attend. Finally, Armando's parents allow him to attend the school. When an unimaginable tragedy occurs, will Armando be able to continue at school? Will the community find a way to overcome their hardships?

Brave Irene by William Steig (Farrar, Straus and Giroux: 1988) (D)

Read to talk about how it can take a lot of courage to overcome obstacles.

When Mrs. Bobbin finally finishes making a beautiful gown for the Duchess, she is too tired and too sick to deliver the dress during the huge, cold, blustery snowstorm that is brewing outside. Brave Irene, Mrs. Bobbin's daughter, is determined to find the courage to go outside and get the dress to the palace in time, but she must overcome several scary obstacles along the way.

Catching the Moon by Myla Goldberg, illustrated by Chris Sheban (Arthur A. Levine Books: 2007) (D)

Read this when your child is becoming discouraged in a long-term goal; it teaches about perseverance and asking for help.

An old fisherwoman is becoming discouraged by spending long nights awake fishing for something she cannot seem to catch. However, one night, she opens her home to a mysterious stranger and finds not only a new friend, but also help in her task from this unexpected source.

The Legend of the Bluebonnet by Tomie dePaola (Putnam Juvenile: 1983) (D)

Read when you want to talk about giving up something special for the greater good.

This book retells a Native American folktale about a girl who is one of the few surviving members of a tribe that has been wiped out by a drought. Her parents are dead and she has one remaining item to connect her to them, a doll that her parents made for her. The tribe's shaman consults with the Great Spirits to ask how to end the drought, and returns stating that the Spirits said the people had become selfish and thus must offer their most valued possessions. While everyone is asleep, the girl goes out and sacrifices her doll. The rains then come and bluebonnet flowers bloom, to remind all of her great sacrifice.

Talk about It: This book demonstrates real courage and sacrifice. The girl gives up her most prized possession for the good of the greater community. This book, since it relates to the death of a child's parents, may upset some children and raise questions for you to address.

- Where do you think the girl found the conviction to burn her favorite possession?
- What would you have done if you were her?
- Was there a time when you felt good about something courageous you did?

Mercedes and the Chocolate Pilot by Margot Theis Raven, illustrated by Gijsbert van Frankenbuyzen (Sleeping Bear Press: 2002) (D)

Read to introduce the topic of war or to talk about the Berlin airlift. A fantastic example of historical fiction, this special picture book illuminates the horrors of war and the importance of giving through the story of a young girl.

Mercedes, a young girl living in Berlin during the Berlin airlift, finds hope through the generosity of the "Chocolate Pilot," Gail Halvorsen. Based on a true story, this beautifully illustrated book tells about how an American pilot's generosity brought hope to a group of children in a war-torn city.

Nothing Scares Us by Freida Wishinsky, illustrated by Neal Layton (Learner Publishing Group: 2000) (D)

Read to talk with your child about expressing his fear of spiders, monsters, or even the dark.

Best friends Lenny and Lucy do everything together, even watch television. One day, when Lenny and Lucy are watching a television show about a monster, Lucy is very, very scared. But Lucy is also afraid to tell Lenny that she is scared of the monster, which she imagines is everywhere. She worries that he will make fun of her. Will Lucy learn to admit to her fears?

Shy Charles by Rosemary Wells (Dial Books for Young Readers: 1988) (D)

Read when your child is feeling very shy and needs the courage to speak to others.

Charles is a very shy mouse who loves playing by himself. Charles hates saying hello and good-bye, or picking up the telephone; that is until an emergency turns him into a hero.

THE POWER OF GRANDPARENTS

In *Sitti's Secrets*, the little girl remembers brushing her grandma's hair. In *Abuela*, a grandchild travels the city with her grandma. When my father had a heart attack and was in the hospital, our little daughters went as soon as they could. When they sat beside him on the bed they carefully patted his hair (what little he has!) to help him feel better. The grandparent relationships in these books speak to love and tenderness. Some of these stories are about loss; some are about discovery. Some, like *Watch Out For the Chicken Feet in Your*

Soup, are about discovering culture and humor through the eyes of someone of another generation. There is exquisite joy in the love between generations shown in these titles, even if your children do not have grandparents of their own. Literature can capture that inestimable care for the older generation and convey it to all children so they reach out for their elders with humility and tenderness.

Abuela by Arthur Dorros, illustrated by Elisa Kleven (Penguin Young Readers Group: 1997) (D)

Read to take an imaginary journey together. A must-read for grandmothers and their grandchildren.

Rosalba loves "going places" with her *abuela*, her grandmother. Together, Rosalba and her *abuela* go to the park and ride on the bus. One afternoon, Rosalba wonders, "What if I could fly?" Suddenly, Rosalba and her *abuela* soar into the sky and fly high above Manhattan. Join them on this fantastic journey that reminds children of why it is so much fun to spend time with their grandmother.

Dear Juno by Soyung Park, illustrated by Susan Kathleen Hartung (Puffin: 2001) (D)

Read when your child needs to find a special way to communicate with someone he loves, and to celebrate the power of writing letters in this age of electronic communication.

Juno loves when his grandmother writes letters to him. Even though Juno's grandmother writes only in Korean and Juno writes only through pictures, they share a very special bond. Juno's grandmother sends Juno a special package to let him know she is on the way.

Grandfather's Journey by Allen Say (Scholastic: 1993) (M)

Read when you want to talk about the impact of war, immigration, change, and courage, or one's family history.

A grandfather and his grandson share a love for two countries as they travel between Japan and California.

Talk about It: This is a beautifully written and illustrated book about the journey of a family from Japan to California and back to Japan again, a journey which begins with a grandfather. It discusses both the impact of war and the sadness of loss.

- Where did Grandfather's journey take him? How did his story influence his grandson?
- Have you ever felt homesick? What did you do when you felt homesick? What did the grandfather do when he felt homesick?

The Hello, Goodbye Window by Norton Juster, illustrated by Chris Raschka (Hyperion Books for Children: 2006) (D)

Read when you want to talk about the excitement of visiting a grandparent and the fun that you can have together. Note that this book is written by the author of the beloved The Phantom Toll Booth.

A little girl loves to visit her Nanny and Poppy, who have a special window that lets her see the weather, the garden, and anyone or anything coming or going. "That's the Hello, Goodbye Window. It looks like a regular window, but it's not." Through this window, the young narrator discovers the magic of observation and the powerful bond that exists between grandparents and grandchildren.

The Hickory Chair by Lisa Rowe Fraustino, illustrated by Benny Andrews (Arthur A. Levine Books: 2001) (D)

Read when you want to talk about the value of memories made with grandparents and the lessons they can teach.

Louis, who was born blind, lives in a world that he can "see" through smells. His Gran, who smells of lilacs and a bit of bleach, teaches Louis this "blind sight" as a new way to experience his surroundings. When she passes away, Louis and his family gather and each finds a personal note left to them by Gran, except for Louis. Louis feels forgotten, but soon realizes that the best gift Gran left him was the memories of their time together, and the new way that he can see without sight.

I Go with My Family to Grandma's by Riki Levinson, illustrated by Diane Goode (Dutton Children's Books: 1986) (E)

Read this book to talk about how families can come together across all differences.

Carrie, Beatie, Stella, Bella, and Millie each live in different places. But, no matter the distance, these children travel with their families to join their cousins, aunts, and uncles at their grandparents' home.

I Love Saturdays y Domingos by Alma Flor Ada, illustrated by Elivia Savadier (Simon & Schuster Children's Publishing: 2002) (D)

Read when you want to celebrate the fun and loving activities you share with your grandparents.

This young girl loves Saturdays *y domingos*, or Sundays. She spends Saturdays with her grandma and grandpa eating scrambled eggs and pancakes. *Los domingos* the girl spends time with her *abuelito y abuelta,* where she drinks papaya juice and eats *huevos rancheros*. With each set of grandparents, this young girl finds love and a wonderfully happy day or *un día maravilloso.*

Lucky Pennies and Hot Chocolate by Carol Diggory Shields, illustrated by Hiroe Nakata (Dutton Children's Books: 2000) (D)

Read when you want to discuss all the fun things you can do with a grandparent and the value of that special relationship.

This endearing book, told from the perspective of a grandfather, relates the adventures he has with his "favorite person," his grandson. They find lucky pennies, tell knock-knock jokes, and put as many marshmallows as they can fit into one cup of hot chocolate. Describing a weekend visit between a grandfather and grandson, this book details the power of a relationship between two people whose love for one another grows with each visit.

Mama Provi and the Pot of Rice by Sylvia Rosa-Casanova, illustrated by Robert Roth (Atheneum Books for Young Readers: 1997) (D)

Read this with a grandparent or to learn about food from different cultures.

Lucy lives on the eighth floor of an apartment building and her grandmother, Mama Provi, lives on the first floor. On her way up to visit her sick granddaughter, Mama Provi, carrying a pot of arroz con pollo, stops on each floor to gather a multicultural feast.

Midnight Eaters by Amy Hest (Aladdin: 1994) (D)

Read to explore the power of a relationship between grandparents and a grandchild.

Samantha and her grandmother are sharing a room as her grandmother recovers from an illness. One night, they sneak down to the kitchen and share a magical night bonding, sharing their secrets over ice cream and other treats.

Sitti's Secrets by Naomi Shihab Nye (Four Winds Press: 1994) (M)

Read this when you and your child are visiting grandparents, or to introduce the topic of war and conflict.

Mona goes to visit her grandmother, Sitti, who lives far, far away in Palestine. Even though Mona and her Grandmother Sitti do not speak the same language, on this unforgettable trip, Mona learns all about her grandmother and her wonderful secrets.

Tales our Abuelitas Told: A Hispanic Folktale Collection by Alma Flor Ada and F. Isabel Campoy, illustrated by Felipe Davalos, Viví Escrivá, Susan Guevara, and Leyla Torres (Simon & Schuster: 2006) (M)

Read when you want to celebrate the power of folktales.

Alma Flor Ada collected twelve folktales passed down through the generations, stories which capture the many ancient traditions of Hispanic culture. Read "Dear Deer! Said the Turtle" or "The Castle of Chuchurumbe" and notice the similarities between each of them and other cultural folktales.

Watch Out for the Chicken Feet in Your Soup by Tomie dePaola (Aladdin: 1974) (D)

Read to introduce the topic of appreciating people from different generations.

"Joey, mi bambino! How nice you come to see Grandma." How happy Joey's grandma is to see him and his friend. But Joey is suddenly embarrassed by his old-fashioned grandma. Will Joey be able to learn how to appreciate his grandma?

What! Cried Granny: An Almost Bedtime Story by Kate Lum, illustrated by Adrian Johnson (Penguin Young Readers Group: 2002) (E)

Read to talk about all the fun things you can do at your granny's house before bedtime.

Patrick is all ready for his first sleepover at Granny's house. Until bedtime, that is. Granny does not have a bed for Patrick, so she goes out and chops wood to make one. Then Patrick discovers that Granny does not have a pillow for him, so she goes out to the henhouse and makes one. What else is Patrick going to discover that Granny does not have for him? Will Patrick and his granny ever fall asleep?

When I Am Old with You by Angela A. Johnson, illustrated by David Soman (Orchard Books: 1990) (D)

Read this with a grandparent.

A little boy imagines all of the fun activities that he and his grandpa will do when the little boy is old with his granddaddy. The grandson promises his granddaddy that they will fish, play cards, and much more when he is "old with you."

Talk about It: Spending time with a grandparent can be very special. Imagining growing older can also be fun. Celebrate how excited this boy is to spend time with his granddaddy and to begin to grow older.

- What activities do you like to do when you spend time with your grandpa?
- Who do you like to spend time with? Why is your relationship with that person important to you?

PONDERING THE WORLD

Every great innovator, scientist, poet, educator, historian asked one question that led to a thousand others: why? It is the most important, most essential question we can ask and any education of our children must begin with it. These books represent a genuine modeling of asking this key question, by people who are paying close attention to the world in which they live. All of the books are quirky, as every person who asks why finds a different chain of answers. We want our children be in a questioning stance for the rest of their lives, because this openness and receptivity to new information is going to help them to create new ideas and to be actively engaged with the world and the people in it. Use these books to practice asking: why?

Actual Size by Steven Jenkins (Houghton Mifflin Company: 2004) (D)

Read this book to answer an inquisitive child's questions about the sizes of animals.

Through illustrations, as well as narrative and numbers, this book shows the relative sizes of all types of animals, from an atlas moth to a great white shark. This book is an interactive and dynamic way to teach your child about a variety of animals and show her wonders of the animal world that numbers alone cannot convey. The illustrations even allow a child to compare animal sizes to her own body.

Benito's Dream Bottle by Naomi Shihab Nye, illustrated by Yu Cha Pak (Simon & Schuster Children's Publishing: 1995) (D)

Read this book to ponder the mysterious nature of dreams.

After Benito finds out that his grandmother hasn't had a dream in years, he is very concerned and asks everyone he knows, "Where do dreams come from?" Despite the interesting answers, Benito already knows that dreams come from the dream bottle, nestled between the stomach and chest. Throughout the story, he works to fill his grandmother's dream bottle and, in the meantime, fills his own dream bottle with new questions.

Confucius: The Golden Rule by Russell Freedman, illustrated by Frédéric Clément (Arthur A. Levine Books: 2002) (M)

Read to teach your child about the ancient teacher Confucius and his long life as an intellectual.

This book tells the tale of Confucius, called Kongfuzi by his students. It contrasts the legends about this famous teacher and politician with the reality of proven facts. Young Confucius had his heart set on learning, and later shared this passion for knowledge with his students. Following Confucius throughout his life, we learn about his unending thirst for new experiences and books as well as his powerful and radical thoughts on the role of government, including the Golden Rule.

A Drop of Water: A Book of Science and Wonder by Walter Wick (Scholastic: 1997) (M)

Read to a child who wonders about water.

Through brilliantly executed photographs, this book uncovers where water comes from, what it looks like in every state, and how it is used.

Encyclopedia Prehistorica Dinosaurs by Robert Sabuda, illustrated by Matthew Reinhart (Candlewick Press: 2005) (D)

Read to learn about prehistoric dinosaurs through beautifully designed pop-up images and well-crafted descriptions.

Learn about prehistoric dinosaurs in this exciting pop-up encyclopedia. Each page features a different dinosaur, which pops up for you to see. Let your younger children delight in the images, while your older ones can soak up the information in the accompanying paragraphs.

How Come? by Kathy Wollard, illustrated by Debra Solomon (Workman Publishing Company: 1993) (M)

Read to a child who always asks: How come? Find a question you want to answer and read just that section, or read the book from cover to cover and answer all sorts of scientific questions.

How can X-rays take pictures of your bones? Why does Jupiter have a red spot? Why does rain fall in drops? Has your child ever wondered about the rain or planets or the zoo or colors or tricks of light? If so, you must read this book, which will answer all of her wonderings and begin to unravel the mysteries that surround us.

The New Way Things Work: From Levers to Lasers, Windmills to Web Sites: A Visual Guide to the World of Machines by David Macaulay (Houghton Mifflin Company: 1998) (M)

Read to your child who always wonders how things work.

What do zippers and pyramids have in common? How do locks work? How do computers actually compute? Learn the answers to all of these questions and many more in this delightfully informative book that unlocks the mystery of machines, explores the history of inventions, and explains the scientific principal behind each device.

If You Decide to Go to the Moon by Faith McNulty, illustrated by Steven Kellogg (Scholastic: 2005) (D)

Read to your child who dreams of being an astronaut.

What would you take if you were going to the moon? What would you see along the way? How would you get home again? Imagine what it would be like to travel to the moon. Follow this boy as he prepares for takeoff, explores the surface of the moon, and of course, comes back home again. Use your imagination to take a trip to Mars or Saturn.

On the Same Day in March: A Tour of the World's Weather by Marilyn Singer, illustrated by Frané Lessac (HarperCollins Publishers: 2000) (M)

Read when your child wonders about the weather outside your home or around the world.

What is the weather like outside your window? Have you ever wondered what it is like in Beijing or the Arctic or Paris? Travel around the world and discover how "polar bears ride on floes of ice" and "people in French cafés turn up their faces to the sun" all on the same day in March.

Quest for the Tree Kangaroo: An Expedition to the Cloud Forest of New Guinea by Sy Montgomery, photographs by Nic Bishop (Houghton Mifflin Company: 2006) (M)

Read to discover the amazing feats of conservationist scientists and the beauty and mystery of the Matschie's tree kangaroo, found deep in the cloud forest of Papua New Guinea.

Scientist Lisa Dabek, author Sy Montgomery, and photographer Nic Bishop take you on an astounding journey though the cloud forest in Papua New Guinea in search of the rare Matschie's tree kangaroo. Along the way, they document the beauty of the wildlife in the depths of the cloud forest.

Rocks & Minerals: Discover the Story of the Earth's Rocks and Minerals—Their Creation, Variety, and Uses by Dr. R. F. Symes (Eyewitness Books: 2008) (M)

Read to unravel the mystery of rocks and minerals with your child.

Does your child love rocks and minerals? Use this book to answer questions your child might have about the variety of rocks, where they come from, and how long they have been around. Study the beautiful photographs of gems, coal, and limestone caves. You can read this book in its entirety or focus on a topic your child is particularly interested in. Read the descriptions of stalagmites, glacier deposits, and amphiboles. Begin a lively discussion about the world around us.

There Is a Flower at the Tip of My Nose Smelling Me by Alice Walker, illustrated by Stefano Vitale (HarperCollins Publishers: 2006) (D)

Read this book with your child to talk about how there is more than one way to view a situation.

Through poetry and vibrant illustrations, Walker challenges readers to see the world through new eyes and from a different perspective. This book will change the way we see the world every day.

Wait Till the Moon Is Full by Margaret Wise Brown, illustrated by Garth Williams (Harper: 1948) (E)

Read when your child is wondering about something, and to teach her how to be patient when learning something new.

A very anxious young raccoon asks his mom when he can go outside to see the night. What does it look like, what is the moon like, he wonders. But his wise mother says, "Wait till the moon is full," and she sings to him about the night when the moon is full. When finally the moon *is* full, off the little raccoon goes.

What Do You Do with a Tail Like This? by Steve Jenkins and Robin Page (Houghton Mifflin Company: 2003) (E)

Read when your child wonders about what animals do with their ears, eyes, noses, and, yes, tails.

Have you ever wondered what animals do with their tails or their ears? Discover the answers in this exciting and interactive book, covered with invigorating illustrations of the animals themselves. A must-read for those who love learning about animals.

Where Do Balloons Go? An Uplifting Mystery by Jamie Lee Curtis, illustrated by Laura Cornell (HarperCollins Publishers: 2000) (E)

Read when your child wonders about the journeys balloons take when people accidentally let them go.

Has it ever happened to you? Have you ever accidentally let a balloon go? This little boy wonders where balloons go when they are set free. He wonders, "Do they tango with airplanes? Or cha-cha with birds?" What do you think happens to balloons as they fly into the sky?

Wildfire by Taylor Morrison (Houghton Mifflin Company: 2006) (M)

Read to talk about wildfires, both the danger they pose to humans and nature and also their necessity for the survival of the forests. Also, discuss the bravery and determination of the firefighters who tackle wildfires all summer long.

What causes wildfires? Can any good come from wildfires? Discover the causes and the devastating effects of wildfires. Learn about the strategies and methods courageous firefighters use to eradicate wildfires.

SAVORING FOOD

Food is the life source. Hunger is something far too many children experience, all across the world, for us to take eating lightly. Food represents family and culture and companionship too. When my daughter was in Ghana a few years ago, her host mother cooked her a stack of toast each morning as she had read somewhere that Americans like toast. I was so deeply touched that so far away, a wonderfully kind person was taking that kind of care with food for my child. It made me think a great deal about the significance of food, both as a way to bring people together and also as a way to define culture. Several summers later, when I sat with my friends in Kenya and ate their delicious *chopati* bread dipped into stew, I could see in their smiling faces how proud they were to share a taste of their family lives with me. I hope food can be this way for everyone: sustenance both for body and spirit. The books we read to our children can reflect this respect for food and a delight in all its varieties. Let us raise our children with a respect for what comes to their tables and for how precious it all really is.

Bread, Bread, Bread by Ann Morris, photographs by Ken Heyman (Lothrop, Lee & Shepard Books: 1989) (E)

Read to discover a simple, beloved food that connects people all over the world.

There are so many kinds of bread, with different shapes, textures, and flavors. Simple text and photographs from around the world show the baking of bread, bread for sale, and the beauty of sharing bread together. Make sure to look in the back at the notes to the photos to see where they are from.

Dim Sum for Everyone! by Grace Lin (Dragonfly Books: 2003) (D)

Read to learn about dining out and sharing a meal with your familiy.

A family with three daughters goes out to a restaurant together to enjoy a meal. They share unique and delicious dishes and end the meal full and sleepily satisfied.

Dumpling Soup by Jama Kim Rattigan, illustrated by Lillian Hsu-Flanders (Little, Brown and Company: 1993) (D)

Read to see how special food traditions can unite a family.

Every New Year's, Marisa's family comes from all over Hawaii to celebrate together. One of the most important traditions is the food, especially the dumpling soup. Marisa loves to help her grandmother and aunties make the dumplings, but is worried that hers don't look as perfect as the rest. But as the family gathers together to eat all the great foods, she realizes that the most important thing is that the whole family eats together.

Good Enough to Eat: A Kid's Guide to Food and Nutrition by Lizzy Rockwell (HarperCollins Publishers: 1999) (D)

Read to learn about the importance of food for nourishing our bodies.

Food doesn't just quell our hunger: it literally keeps us alive, and protects and energizes our bodies so that we can do fun activities. This book is a simple and colorful explanation of the many different nutrients, vitamins, and minerals found in food, how they help our bodies, and which foods are good sources of each one.

Talk about It: This book is a great conversation starter for talking with your child about nutrition. It contains a lot of good information, making it a great learning tool for parents as well. Talk about the different kinds of food your family eats and what kinds of nutrients they contain. Think about the way you feel when you eat certain foods with different kinds of nutrients.

- What kinds of foods are your favorites to eat? What are the nutrients found in those foods?
- Look at the food pyramid and talk in depth about how to use it. Take a day to plan out and make meals with your child (maybe make a special trip to the grocery store) according to the food guide pyramid. Or make one of the recipes written in the back of the book.
- Discuss reasons why people might not get all of the nutrients that they need or may get too much of certain nutrients that should be consumed in moderation.

I Will Never Not Ever Eat a Tomato by Lauren Child (Candlewick Press: 2000) (E)

Read to a picky eater. It's a very funny book and might just sway your child to try new foods.

Charlie has to feed his sister Lola dinner, but the problem is, Lola will not eat carrots or potatoes or peas or spaghetti or any of a whole array of other foods. But Charlie convinces Lola to use her culinary imagination.

Little Pea by Amy Krouse Rosenthal, illustrated by Jen Corace (Chronicle Books: 2005) (E)

Read with your child to enjoy a humorous look at a common mealtime struggle.

Little Pea is happy, except for one thing. Every night he is forced to eat five pieces of candy for dinner before his parents will let him eat spinach, his favorite dessert. His mother tells him, "If you don't eat your candy, you can't have your dessert!" The struggle is one any child or parent can relate to and laugh about.

Yum! ¡MmMm! ¡Que Rico! America's Sproutings by Pat Mora, illustrated by Rafael Lopez (Lee & Low Books: 2007) (D)

Read for a delectable favorite! It will inspire both you and your child to want to try all of "America's sproutings."

On each spread of this vibrantly colored book, Pat Mora uses a haiku poem to celebrate a different food that comes from somewhere in the Americas. Her descriptions of fire hot chilies, fudgy chocolate, yellow corn, syrupy pineapples, and creamy vanilla take the reader on a journey from Mexico to Brazil to the Caribbean to midwestern states of the United States. Along with the haiku poems and beautiful illustrations, the author includes short descriptions about the origins of each food.

Talk about It: Use this book as a lesson in history on where foods came from, a lesson in geography, in poetry, or simply as an enticing celebration of the wonderful colors and tastes we can experience through food.

- Talk about the poetry and illustrations. How do they work together to make the food enticing to you?
- Read the descriptions about where each food comes from. Look for

the country on a map. Discuss whether you have ever tried the food, if you would like to, and the different ways that one can enjoy each food.

SPIRITUALITY

There is a Buddhist saying that life is short, so move slowly. When I watch children, I am always struck by how spiritual they are by nature: reflective, observant, meditative, slow. It is only when we bring them into the adult world that we speed them up, and make them move faster. We are always hurrying them along. What if we made a commitment to slowing down each day, meditatively, together? What if we practiced breathing deeply, together? What if we used the read-aloud time to linger between pages, to let silence fill our hearts, and to hear the sound of each other's hearts beating, together? Let silence, the words of the text, and the sound of our children's voices guide us to our own internal sense of peace and acceptance.

In Every Tiny Grain of Sand collected by Reeve Lindbergh (Walker Books: 2001) (D)

Read to experience poems from a variety of religions and regions that praise the things we love.

This book is a collection of prayers and praises for everything from God and nature, to homes and families. Spanning world religions, and divided into sections such as "For the Day" and "For the Home," this collection provides poetry that can celebrate the wonder of the average day.

Let It Shine by Ashley Bryan (Simon & Schuster Children's Publishing: 2007) (E)

Read for a beautiful way to introduce three traditional spirituals. It's a great book to sing or to read.

Three well-known spirituals, "This Little Light of Mine," "Oh, When the Saints Go Marching In," and "He's Got the Whole World in His Hands" come to life in Ashley Bryan's beautiful, vibrant, colorful book.

The Three Questions written and illustrated by Jon J. Muth, based on a story by Leo Tolstoy (Scholastic: 2002) (D)

Read when you discuss the importance of asking big questions.

This retelling of Leo Tolstoy's classic story follows a young boy's quest to be a good person. Longing to find the path to goodness, Nikoli seeks the answer to three powerful questions: When is the best time to do things? Who is the most important one? What is the right thing to do? Nikoli turns to his friend, Leo, the wise turtle, to answer his questions, but Nikoli discovers that it is not until he meets new friends, a wounded panda and her cub, that he discovers the answer to his query.

The Way to Start a Day by Byrd Baylor, illustrated by Peter Parnall (Aladdin: 1986) (D)

Read to introduce the topic of how people from around the world began their days and honored the world they woke to.

How do you start your days? Learn how the cavemen, Aztecs, Egyptians, and others started their days.

Zen Shorts by Jon J. Muth (Scholastic Press: 2005) (D)

Read when you want to introduce the topics of generosity, luck, or leaving burdens behind through Zen teachings.

One morning, Stillwater, a giant panda, arrives in Addy, Michael, and Karl's backyard. Over three days, Stillwater teaches the trio three essential lessons through the telling of Zen shorts, or classic Zen stories that contain a moral lesson.

Talk about It: This is a beautifully illustrated book. Look through the pictures and talk about them. Ask your child what Stillwater teaches the three children. Take some time to make sure your child understands the lessons that each of these Zen stories teaches.

- What lesson did Stillwater teach Addy? How did the poor man react to the robber? Why do you think he acted in this manner?
- What lesson did Stillwater teach Michael? What does this classic Zen story teach you about luck?
- What lesson did Stillwater teach Karl? How did Stillwater's tale help Karl?

SEPARATIONS

Recently, a friend called to ask for a poem. A child in her daughter's school had tragically died in an accident and they were looking for words that would help sustain them during this time of grief. I sent them "Poem" by Langston Hughes, one of the simplest, most direct poems in the English language: "I loved my friend/he went away." A few of the books in this list are about losing a toy (*Knuffle Bunny*) and others are a bit silly (*Caps for Sale*). The silly books are a salve: they offer a reprieve from the sadness of a separation. Some separations seem silly to an adult but may not be silly to a child (a beloved blanket, for example), and sometimes it is actually a good idea to laugh at a funny separation so as to learn the flow of life will involve some of these. A few of the books are about temporary separations (*The Moon Was the Best*), but at the heart of it, many separations are hard, no matter what form they take. Throughout our lives with children, we too experience separations: when our child goes to school, when our child grows into new kinds of independence. We all struggle with and transcend our worries at times, as we each let the other go. We learn about ourselves when we get separated from what we love most; we find comfort when we seek to salve our vulnerable moments with words and memory that sustain us and give us hope. From the smallest blanket to the dearest friend, we hope we become reunited, but if not, we hope we become stronger.

Adèle & Simon by Barbara McClintock (Farrar, Straus and Giroux: 2006) (D)

Read about losing your belongings.

Simon is always losing things. So when his older sister, Adèle, walks him home from school, she implores him to try not to lose any of his possessions. However, as Adèle and Simon walk home through the streets of Paris, watching the jugglers in front of Notre-Dame, wandering through the Louvre, and enjoying a puppet show in the Jardin de Luxembourg, Simon loses item after item. He loses his drawing of a cat at the grocer's, and his books in a tree, until he is without his hat, gloves, scarf, sweater, drawing, and knapsack. Will Simon be able to retrieve all of his lost belongings?

Caps for Sale by Esphyr Slobodkina (HarperCollins Childrens Books: renewed 1988) (E)

Read to discuss new ways for finding lost objects.

Follow a cap seller who displays his colorful wares piled on top of his head. One day he falls asleep under a tree and wakes with no more hats on his head; he looks up to find a tree full of monkeys, each adorned with a different color cap. What is he to do?

Emily's Balloon by Komako Sakai (Chronicle Books: 2006) (E)

Read to teach your child about the beauty of friendship, the sorrow of separation, and the excitement of reunion.

Emily receives a yellow balloon, a balloon that becomes her friend by the end of the afternoon. Emily delights in the way the balloon reaches the ceiling, joins her for a tea party, and walks beside her. What will Emily do when her balloon is swept from her hand?

Half a World Away by Libby Gleeson, illustrated by Freya Blackwood (Arthur A. Levine Books: 2007) (D)

Read when a friend moves away.

"Amy and Louie built towers as high as the sky. They dug holes deep enough to bury bears, and they saw magical creatures in the clouds." They were best friends. When separated, Louie or Amy called out "coo-eee" across the room or the playground or the fence and the other always came. One day, Amy's family moves very far way. How will Amy and Louie handle this separation?

Hug by Jez Alborough (Candlewick Press: 2002) (E)

Read Bobo's beautiful story about love and, of course, hugs. Its simple, comforting message is told through illustrations with only three words in the whole book.

Bobo, a baby monkey, walks through the jungle, and sees the elephants, giraffes, and lions hugging. But Bobo wants a hug. Will he find a special person who loves to hug him?

If You Listen by Charlotte Zolotow, illustrated by Stefano Vitale (Running Press: 2002) (D)

Read when you want to address the ways that we can carry the love of those who might be separated from us.

When a little girl's father is away for a long time, she asks her mother how she knows that her father still loves her. The mother tells the young girl all the ways that she can experience things through her senses, even though they might be far away, such as the sounds of bells from a distant church steeple. Her mother tells her you must "listen inside yourself" to feel the love of someone far away.

In My Heart by Molly Bang (Little, Brown and Company: 2006) (E)

Read when you want to offer reassurance and comfort in the daily separations your child experiences.

A mother looks deep into her heart and sees her love for her child even when they are separated during the day by work or school.

Knuffle Bunny: A Cautionary Tale by Mo Willems (Hyperion Books for Children: 2004) (E)

Read to discuss the difficulty of leaving things behind and the excitement of reunion after a short separation.

Trixie, her daddy, and Knuffle Bunny, Trixie's very favorite bunny, take an excursion to the Laundromat. When they leave the Laundromat, Trixie's daddy leaves behind Knuffle Bunny. Will Trixie ever find her beloved friend?

Mama: A True Story in Which a Baby Hippo Loses His Mama During the Tsunami, but Finds a New Home, and a New Mama by Jeanette Winter (Harcourt Children's Books: 2006) (E)

Read this book for an extraordinarily simple tale about separation. There are only two words in this beautifully illustrated book: "Mama" and "Baby."

This is a moving tale about a baby hippo who loses his mother during the tsunami but manages to find a new home and mama. As the tsunami sweeps this baby hippo from the shores of Kenya, he calls out "Mama," and his mother calls out "Baby." Separated from his mother, the baby hippo finds solace and comfort from an unusual companion.

The Moon Was the Best by Charlotte Zolotow, photographs by Tana Hoban (Greenwillow Books: 1993) (E)

Read when you are about to be separated from your child, perhaps on the first day of school, before work, or before a trip.

As her parents prepare to leave for Paris, a little girl reminds her mother and father to "remember the special things to tell me." And they do. They remember the parks, the dogs under the chairs at the outdoor cafés, and the fountains.

Talk about It: Times of separation can be very hard for children of all ages. Younger readers of this book will enjoy the beautiful illustrations and the descriptions of Paris (it takes you on a visual and descriptive journey through the city), while older readers will be able to use the book to discuss ways of getting through difficult periods of separation.

- Can you think of a time you felt good about saying good-bye to someone whom you knew you would miss? How did you handle the situation?
- What would you have done if you were the little girl saying good-bye to her parents?

Owen by Kevin Henkes (HarperCollins Publishers: 1993) (E)

Read when your child has to learn to leave behind her very favorite blanket or stuffed animal.

Owen loves Fuzzy, his fuzzy yellow blanket. Fuzzy goes everywhere that Owen goes, to picnics, the sandbox, and playdates. But when Owen wants to bring Fuzzy to school with him, his parents and neighbor, Mrs. Tweezers, say that Owen is too old for Fuzzy. Will Mrs. Tweezers and Owen's parents be able to find a solution?

The Polar Bear Son: An Inuit Tale retold by Lyda Dobcovich (Houghton Mifflin Company: 1999) (D)

Read this powerful tale about friendship, adoption, and how people make sacrifices for those they love.

Lyda Dobcovich retells an ancient Inuit tale about an old Inuit woman who has no family or sons to help her hunt and find food. The woman depends on her neighbors to help her, until she finds and adopts a baby polar bear. The polar bear grows up helping his adoptive mother, providing her with the food and company she seeks. A rich friendship develops between the woman and her polar bear son. Jealous of her friendship, the men in the village threaten the life of the polar bear. Through he must leave to seek safety from these men, the bear continues to provide for his adoptive mother.

Sylvester and the Magic Pebble by William Steig (Aladdin: 1969) (D)

Read to understand how separations can sometimes reveal what is most important in our lives.

Sylvester loves collecting pebbles. One day, he finds a magic pebble that grants his wish for the rain to go away; he begins to imagine all of the wishes that he and his parents could make come true. When he is suddenly face-to-face with a lion, he panics and wishes he were a rock. Not being able to change himself back, he becomes separated from his family, friends, and normal life. His parents feel the same anxieties as they struggle, thinking they have lost their only son.

Talk about It: This is a good book to start a conversation about how we realize what is important when we lose that thing or person. Although the book may feel depressing, as Sylvester goes through the seasons as a rock on Strawberry Hill, there is an excellent surprise ending that celebrates the reunion of Sylvester and his parents. Talk with your child about the difficulty of separations, but how they can help us learn to appreciate our lives, and the people who love us.

- Sylvester thinks that he is very lucky to have found a magic pebble, but it actually leads to a horrible experience that separates him from his parents. Have you ever had an experience that started out well but went sour? What happened? How did you deal with it? Why does Sylvester the rock start to spend more and more time sleeping?
- What happens at the end of the story? Why do Sylvester and his parents put the magic pebble in an iron safe? Do you think that was a good idea?

Wish You Were Here by Moritz Petz, illustrated by Quentin Gréban (North-South Books: 2005) (D)

Read right before a separation. Learn how even when you miss someone, you can think about them all the time in fun and exciting ways.

When Hedgehog has to go away, Mouse and Hedgehog know they will miss each other dearly. Mouse thinks about Hedgehog and Hedgehog thinks about Mouse as they count down the days until their reunion. Finally the day has arrived, but when they get to the station, they cannot find each other. What has happened? Will they ever meet again?

SLEEPOVERS

Sleepovers are weighted with import. They are a way for our children to practice being away from us, albeit briefly. The image of Edward's round and shocked eyes in *Edward's Overwhelming Overnight* remind us of just how big these journeys can be.

And they are not always successful. Sometimes our children come home in the middle of the night. Sometimes they come home in the morning grumpy and out of sorts. These hints tell us our children might not be so ready for such big journeys. But the read-aloud can also help us do something more by preparing our children for the small and big journeys of their lives, the funny aspects of them as well as the more serious ones.

My grandmother Betty Button was sleeping over at my uncle's house one time. Her sister Frieda was also visiting. In the middle of the night, my uncle got up and heard giggling from the bedroom. He peeked in to see two seventy-five-year-old women cuddled up in one bed together. Frieda had crawled in beside her beloved sister in the middle of the night. "I missed her so," she said to my uncle the next morning. You are never too old to love the cuddle potential that a sleepover with someone you adore can bring.

Corduroy's Sleepover by B. G. Hennessy (Penguin: 2007) (E)

Read in preparation for a sleepover.

Corduroy sets out for his first sleepover. After an evening of fun, one of his friends cannot fall asleep. Can Corduroy help him?

Edward's Overwhelming Overnight by Rosemary Wells (Dial Books for Young Readers: 1995) (D)

Read when your child needs reassurance that it is okay to not be ready for a sleepover.

When Edward learns that he is going to have to sleep over at Anthony's house because of a big snowstorm, he becomes very overwhelmed. Anthony's parents dig out their car and help Edward find his way home.

Froggy's Sleepover by Jonathan London, illustrated by Frank Remkiewicz (Puffin: 2007) (D)

Read to give your child a laugh before a big sleepover.

One afternoon, a magical hat arrives in town. As the hat finds its way onto the heads of the townspeople, they become giant, playful animals. Will the wizard who arrives in town be able to solve the problem?

Moon Plane by Peter McCarty (Henry Holt Books for Young Readers: 2006) (D)

Read to take your child on an imaginary adventure.

Have you ever wondered what you would see if you took a plane to the moon? After this young boy hears a plane overhead, he imagines just that journey. Join him on his imaginary trip to and from the moon.

My Chair by Betsy James, illustrated by Mary Newell DePalma (Arthur A. Levine Books: 2004) (E)

Read to encourage your child to use his imagination and make the ordinary extraordinary.

What is your favorite chair? Is it a swing or a tree house or a squeaky folding chair? Follow these neighborhood children as they show off their favorite seats.

The Night Eater by Ana Juan (Arthur A. Levine Books: 2004) (D)

Read to help your child taste the night sky and drink in the clouds.

Every night, the Night Eater follows after his friend, the moon, eating up the night sky. As he nibbles on the nights, cloudy, clear, or dark, he makes way for the sun to bring warmth and light. What will happen when the Night Eater stops eating? Will there ever be daytime again?

No Mirrors in My Nana's House by Ysaye M. Barnwell, illustrated by Synthia Saint James (Harcourt: 1998) (D)

Read this book to explore the hidden power of everyday objects.

A young girl sees the beauty of everything around her as reflected in her Nana's eyes. Without mirrors, she uses her imagination to taste "joy in the dust that would fall" and to hear "the noise in the hallway" as music. This is a beautiful book to explore a new perspective on everyday things.

The Other Side by Istvan Banyai (Chronicle Books: 2005) (M)

Read this book to take a journey into different perspectives.

A book without words, this piece of art is designed to stretch the imagination and pique curiosity. It switches perspectives and alternates points of view. Although the pages do not consecutively create a cohesive story, they connect through reoccurring characters and themes, always presented in new ways. On one page, we see a sign that reads, "The grass is greener on the other side," but does the book agree with this statement?

Talk about It: There are endless opportunities for conversation within this book. Take your child's lead; find out what he thinks is interesting, strange, scary, or what he notices particularly. Talk about point of view and perspective. This is a good book for an older child, and has a bit of a graphic novel feel.

- What do you notice about the style of the illustrations, how they are drawn and the colors that are used? How do they make you feel? Do you like the author's choices?
- Follow some recurring characters throughout the book. Find the pages where that character is looking at a scene, and then the pages where the same character becomes the subject of another person's viewpoint.
- Pick two facing, or consecutive, pages in the book. Spend a long time noticing the details in the illustrations and discussing how perspectives change. Talk about how the characters' situations change or remain constant.

Pirates Don't Change Diapers by Melinda Long, illustrated by David Shannon (Harcourt: 2007) (D)

Read to explore how make-believe can turn an ordinary task into something extraordinary.

Jeremy Jacob's mom asks him to watch baby Bonney Anne while she runs some errands. Things get interesting when a whole crew of pirates show up at the door looking for treasure and end up helping Jeremy Jacob with the baby. Hilarity ensues as the pirates change diapers, feed the baby, and dance to help get the baby back to sleep.

Sector 7 by David Wiesner (Houghton Mifflin Company: 1999) (M)

Read this wordless picture book to help your child practice using context cues and storytelling through pictures.

A school trip to the Empire State Building becomes a great journey for a boy as he is brought by a cloud to visit Sector 7 in this wordless picture book.

Snowmen at Night by Caralyn Buehner, pictures by Mark Buehner (Dial Books for Young Readers: 2002) (E)

Read this on a cold day and imagine a world of playing snowmen.

What happens to snowmen at night? In this witty rhyming story, all of the snowmen in the neighborhood wait for dark to begin the fun and games.

Some Dogs Do by Jez Alborough (Candlewick Press: 2003) (E)

Read to give your child the encouragement to dream big and love his or her imagination.

Sid the dog learns that dogs *do* fly after he flies to school one morning. "Dogs don't fly," say his friends. "Dogs don't fly," says his teacher. Will anyone believe Sid that some dogs do fly?

Superhero by Marc Tauss (Scholastic: 2005) (D)

Read to help your child feel like a superhero.

Maleek is a scientist and a superhero who saves the day. Maleek and Marvyn, his robot, take it upon themselves to figure out why all the parks are disappearing from the city. Will they be able to solve the problem before it's too late?

The Three Witches collected by Zora Neale Hurston, adapted by Joyce Carol Thomas, illustrated by Faith Ringgold (HarperCollins Publishers: 2006) (M)

Read when you want to share the mystery of folktales. If you have a child who is frightened easily, the subject matter may disturb, so be cautious, but for others this is a lively, exciting retelling of a famous folktale.

Joyce Carol Thomas retells the folktale of three long-toothed witches who try to outsmart two children, their grandma, three dogs, and a slithery snake. Can the children and their grandmother find the courage to survive these scary witches?

Traction Man Is Here by Mini Grey (Random House Books for Young Readers: 2005) (D)

Read before bath time or while washing dishes when your child needs an imaginary friend to help him through those trying chores.

A young boy sets out on a series of adventures. He defeats the mysterious toes in the bathtub who are stealing his pet, Scrubbing Brush, all with the help of his friend, Traction Man, the boxed toy superhero who comes to life through this young boy's imagination.

What Elephant? by Geneviève Côté (Kids Can Press: 2006) (E→D)

Read when you want to discuss the difference between dreams, imagination, and reality.

Can George really see an elephant sitting in his living room, or is he going crazy? His friends say he is going crazy, that is, until they too see the elephant wreaking havoc on George's house, flower garden, and life. But no one knows quite what to believe in this funny story about a large elephant crashing into George's life.

Zuni Folk Tales by Frank H. Cushing (Kissinger Publishing Company: 2006) (D)

Read when you want to talk about the power of storytelling, oral history, and folklore.

Read "How the Coyote Ate the Beetle" or "How the Summer Birds Came" or one of the many other folktales Cushing collected to discover the rich history of the Zuni tribe.

YOUR BODY

Later in life, many of us reject our bodies in all kinds of ways, big and small. We don't like the way we look; we criticize ourselves; we think we are too fat or too skinny. But children really don't start out that way. They start out loving the way they look and the way their bodies make them feel. They do not differentiate what is beautiful by someone's physical size or blemishes. Somewhere along the way, American culture tells them to doubt the beauty of their bodies and to doubt beauty in others. These books are designed to restore that love and reverence for the human body. The following titles are fun and playful and respectful, the way our interactions with the human body should always be. Read them aloud with an eye toward what you are trying to build in your child: a self-concept that is healthy and affirmed, exuberant and confident, strong and sound.

Everyone Poops by Taro Gomi, illustrated by Amanda Mayer Stinchecum (Kane/Miller Book Publishers: 1993) (E)

Read with your child to learn about what happens after eating.

Vivid illustrations and singsong text show children that all creatures, from a mouse to a horse to a human child, poop after eating.

Five for a Little One by Chris Raschka (Simon & Schuster Children's Publishing: 2006) (E)

Read to explore the excitement of the five senses: touching, feeling, tasting, smelling, and hearing.

Join this bunny as he rejoices in using his five senses. Can you use your five senses? What do you taste? What do you smell? What do you hear?

Hair Dance! by Dinah Johnson, photographs by Kelly Johnson (Henry Holt and Company: 2007) (D)

Read to celebrate the many different hairstyles for many different kinds of hair.

Photographer Kelly Johnson says, "Hair is our crowning glory, and every day we should appreciate its grace, color, and texture." The brilliant photos of the beautiful girls in this book, and the short bits of text, show how different styles of hair contribute to the vibrancy of the girls' lives.

Talk about It:

- ✦ Talk about the photographs in this book. How do photos of real girls contribute to the greatness of the book?
- ✦ Talk about the different kinds of hair textures and styles of people you know. What is something that you like about your own hair?
- ✦ Talk about how our heritage/history influences the way we look and how we choose to create the look we have.

More Parts by Tedd Arnold (Penguin Young Readers Group: 2003) (D)

Read with your child for a funny lesson on common sayings about the body.

The young protagonist of this brightly illustrated sequel to *Parts* is horrified when he hears expressions such as "hold your tongue" and "lend me a hand." Children will love to learn about their body and common sayings through this wildly fun medium.

My First Body Board Book by DK Publishing Staff (Dorling Kindersley Publishing: 2004) (E)

Read with your child to begin learning to identify parts of the body.

Pictures of babies and toddlers illustrate the parts of the body in this colorful book. Children will learn not only to identify ears, toes, hair, and other body parts, but also what those parts do.

On Your Mark, Get Set, Grow! A "What's Happening to My Body?" Book for Younger Boys by Lynda Madaras (Newmarket Press: 2008) (M)

Read with your son to talk about puberty and changing bodies.

With just enough information for a preteen, Madaras discusses puberty, with ample reassurance about the changes that are taking place.

Parts by Tedd Arnold (Penguin Young Readers Group: 2000) (E)

Read with your child for a funny lesson about the body.

A young boy is upset to see some of his hair in the bathtub, his skin peeling, and lint from his belly button—he thinks he is falling apart. His parents reassure him, however, telling him that these things are natural; hair, skin, and the like will grow back.

Toes, Ears, & Nose! by Marion Dane Bauer and Karen Katz (Simon & Schuster Children's Publishing: 2002) (E)

Read with your child to learn about body parts.

Lifting flaps reveals toes behind shoes and hands behind mittens in this colorful introduction to parts of the body.

The "What's Happening to My Body" Book for Girls by Lynda Madaras with Area Madaras (Newmarket Press: 2007) (M)

Read with your daughter to discuss puberty and her changing body.

Incorporating anecdotes, scientific facts, and illustrations, Lynda Madaras and her daughter Area discuss the changes a girl undergoes when she hits puberty. From information on bodily and emotional changes to eating disorders, and everything in between, this book is a must-read for any preteen girl.

Whose Knees Are These? by Jabari Asim, illustrated by LeUyen Pham (Little, Brown and Company: 2006) (E)

Read when your child wonders about knees, or toes, or noses, and feels a little silly.

Follow a trail of knees and try to figure out to whom the knees belong.

YOUR OWN CATEGORY

This is the fiftieth, and last category. It's my favorite one, really. I had a wonderful time developing the forty-nine others, but there are of course countless more we can imagine. So this one, number fifty, is for you and for your child. Is there a category I did not include that you think is really important? Add it here, along with your favorite books that would fit inside the category. And then visit whattoreadwhen.com and let me know what you came up with! I would love to hear your suggestions and share them on our Web site. You and your child may very well invent the one category or recommend the one book that will inspire another adult/child partnership for lifelong literacy.

Please join me on the next and final pages for a closing meditation on the joys of literature, and, through literature, the joys of connectedness with children.

Conclusion: Blueberries, Silvery Moons, and a Purple Plastic Purse

Harry Potter has a scar on his forehead and invisible wounds in his heart. By going to Hogwarts, Harry is not only able to find courage and become proud of his scars, he is able to do so through a return to childhood. Hogwarts is all about learning to do magic. We spend so much time helping our children to grow in the land of the ordinary when in truth, as J. K. Rowling understood better than anyone, childhood is where the extraordinary can happen. Picasso said he spent his whole life trying to learn to paint like a child. So much of the greatest children's literature is about children finding ways to be extraordinary *without adults*. Little Sal walking along with her blueberry bucket is walking in the face of danger, next to a big brown bear, but she is calm and unafraid, and she is alone. The funny thing about the best of children's literature is this interesting fact: most great books are about children coping and transcending their struggles completely on their own. And isn't it true that this is what we want for all our children? So they can go out there in the world without us and not only be fine, but be great. The world can and will bruise our children. This is nearly unbearable to think of, but it is true. I sometimes think that by reading aloud to my children and to the children I meet in my travels, I am fortifying them with words. I think, if I can fill them with stories and words, these can be their talismans in a vast and unpredictable world. And if, in a dark time, they remember my voice, or the voice of someone else they love reading to them, they will never be truly alone.

Tonight, as I reach the final pages of this book, is the eve of my daughter's graduation from high school. I hope for her and for all children everywhere that the words contained in the pages of the books we read to them not only protect them but also liberate them. Show them the potential of who they are and who they can be. But because the read-aloud is a shared experience, these lessons are for us too.

One of my all-time favorite characters in fiction, Lilly, is just a child, with her purple plastic purse, but I want to be just like her in my own life. She is fearless, funny, proud, and keeps her chin up. Sal is just a child, but I want to be just like her too, living in the moment, plucking the berries, *kerplink, kerplank, kerplunk*. A peaceful, peaceful sound. Her mother is not right there, but she is nearby. Her presence, her presence is felt. In *Kitten's First Full Moon*, the kitten is just a kitten, but he can look up to the darkened sky and witness the illumination of the first full moon he has ever seen. He might think it is a saucer of milk, not because he knows nothing but because he knows so much. He knows that it is entirely possible to dream a world where moons are saucers and the night sky is full of possibility. I want to be like that too.

Here's to the journey that is full of hope, courage, imagination, and possibility. This is all we can ask for. This is all we can do: sit down and read to our children and give them the stories that might teach them all of those things. So that when they step up for their diploma, or have their hearts broken for the first time, or reach a hand to someone who needs help, or struggle through hard times, they will never be alone.

And neither will you.

Good travels, friends.

Index

Abe Lincoln (Winters and Carpenter), 237
Abuela (Dorros; Kleven, ill.), 275
access (physical), 22–23, 24–25, 59, 65
access (reading levels), 23–25, 30, 36, 56, 118
Actual Size (Jenkins), 279–80
Adèle & Simon (McClintock), 289
adoption, 120–23
adversity
  bad days, 130–33
  obstacles and challenges, 272–74
age-appropriate selections. *See* Reader's Ladder
Aggie and Ben (Ries; Dormer, ill.), 163
Alexander and the Terrible, Horrible, No Good, Very Bad Day (Viorst; Cruz, ill.), 130–31
Alexander and the Wind-Up Mouse (Lionni), 263
Alexie, Sherman, 38
Alfie Gets in First (Hughes), 175
Alien & Possum (Johnston; DiTerlizzi, ill.), 263–64
Aliens Are Coming! (McCarthy), 237
alphabet books
  AlphaOops!, 256
  Chicka Chicka Boom Boom, 256
  C Is for Curious, 256–57
  Disappearing Alphabet, 257
  Gathering the Sun, 257
  G Is for Googol, 246
  Gone Wild, 126
  I Stink!, 154–55
  3-D ABC, 235–36
AlphaOops! (Kontis; Kolar, ill.), 256
Amazing Grace (Hoffman; Binch, ill.), 186
Amber on the Mountain (Johnston; Duncan, ill.), 181
Amber Was Brave, Essie Was Smart (Williams), 167
Anansi stories, 102–3
And Tango Makes Three (Richardson and Parnell; Cole, ill.), 149–50
Andy and the Lion (Daugherty), 54–55
Annie and the Old One (Miles; Parnell, ill.), 194
Armando and the Blue Tarp School (Fine and Josephson; Sosa, ill.), 272
Arrival (Tan), 222
art appreciation and artists, 232–36
Art Dog (Hurd), 232
Art Lesson (dePaola), 232–33
arts and literature magazines, 83, 94, 111
At Gleason's Gym (Lewin), 253
Atlantic (Karas), 249

Babies Can't Eat Kimchee! (Roth and Patz), 269
Baby, Come Out! (Manushkin; Himler, ill.), 269
baby face books, 60–61
baby in family, new, 268–72
Baby on the Way (English; Qualls, ill.), 269–70
Baby Sister for Frances (Hoban; Hoban, ill.), 270
Bad Baby (MacDonald), 270
Bad Day at Riverbend (Van Allsburg), 131
bad days, 130–33
Badger's Parting Gifts (Varley), 194
Bark, George (Feiffer), 138
Barney Is Big (Weiss), 211
Baseball Saved Us (Mochizuki; Lee, ill.), 253
bath time, 64, 133–35
Bathtime for Biscuit (Capucilli; Schories, ill.), 133
Becoming Butterflies (Rockwell; Halsey, ill.), 227
bedtime
  books about, 201–6
  ritual, 58–59
Bedtime for Frances (Hoban; Williams, ill.), 201
Beegu (Deacon), 230

Bees Live in Hives (Berger and Berger), 250
Beetle Bop (Fleming), 125
Behold the Bold Umbrellaphant and Other Poems (Prelutsky; Berger, ill.), 214
Behold the Trees (Alexander; Gore, ill.), 237–38
Benito's Dream Bottle (Nye; Pak, ill.), 280
Best Friends for Frances (Hoban; Hoban, ill.), 230
Best of Times (Tang; Briggs, ill.), 245
Best Pet of All (LaRochelle; Wakiyama, ill.), 214
Beyond the Ridge (Goble), 195
Big Alfie and Annie Rose Storybook (Hughes), 167
Big Sister and Little Sister (Zolotow; Alexander, ill.), 167–68
bilingual books
 Calabash Cat and His Amazing Journey, 222–23
 Doña Flor, 177
 Gathering the Sun, 257
 Hairs/Pelitos, 151
 Just a Minute, 247
 Moja Means One, 248
 My Friends/Mis Amigos, 268
 My Name is Gabito/Me Llamo Gabito, 221
 Poems to Dream Together, 204
 for seven-year-olds, 95
Bintou's Braids (Diouf; Evans, ill.), 138–39
Birthday Box (Patricelli), 145
Birthday For Frances (Hoban; Hoban, ill.), 145
Birthday Presents (Rylant; Stevenson, ill.), 145
birthdays, 144–48
birth to age two, 57–64
Biscuit (Capucilli; Schories, ill.), 201
Black, White, Just Right! (Davol; Trivas, ill.), 139
black-and-white books, 58
Black Is Brown Is Tan (Adoff; McCully, ill.), 150
Blueberries for Sal (McCloskey), 1, 150
board books, 61–63, 135, 302
body, human, 300–303
Books for Boys initiative, 5, 14, 28
Bookshop Dog (Rylant), 181
boys' reading preferences, 28–29, 106
Boy Who Loved Words (Schotter; Potter, ill.), 136
Brave Charlotte (Stohner; Wilson, ill.; Cole, trans.), 176
Brave Irene (Steig), 272–73
bravery, 175–81, 272–73
Bread, Bread, Bread (Morris; Heyman, photos), 284
Bread and Jam for Frances (Hoban; Hoban ill.), 45
Brother Eagle, Sister Sky (Seattle; Jeffers, ill.), 217
Brothers in Hope (Williams; Christie, ill.), 158
Brown, Margaret Wise, 2, 40–41, 77
Brown, Stuart, 71
Building an Igloo (Steltzer), 187–88
bullies, 159–63
Bully (Caseley), 160
Butter Battle Book (Seuss), 158

C Is for Curious (Hubbard), 256–57
Calabash Cat and His Amazing Journey (Rumford), 222–23
Caps for Sale (Slobodkina), 289–90
Captain Raptor and the Space Pirates (O'Malley and O'Brien), 223
caring, 163–66, 172–74
Cars and Trucks and Things That Go (Scarry), 154
Cat and Mouse (Bogacki), 264
Catching the Moon (Goldberg; Sheban, ill.), 273
Catching the Moon (Hubbard; DuBurke, ill.), 253–54
Cat in the Hat (Seuss), 42
Cave Paintings to Picasso (Sayre), 233
Chair for My Mother (Williams), 182
Charlotte's Web (White; Williams, ill.), 41–42
Cherry Tree (Bond; Eitzen, ill.), 145–46
Chicka Chicka 1-2-3 . . . And More Stories About Counting (Martin and Sampson; Ehlert, ill.), 245
Chicka Chicka Boom Boom (Martin and Archambault; Ehlert, ill.), 256
Chicken Sunday (Polacco), 206
chronological reading journey. *See* Reader's Ladder
Chrysanthemum (Henkes), 176
Clara and Asha (Rohmann), 264
classic books. *See* Landmark books
classic stories. *See* folktales and classic stories
Collins, Billy, 4, 113
Come on, Rain! (Hesse; Muth, ill.), 182
Come with Me (Nye), 223
comfort
 cozy books, 58–60, 86
 through read-aloud, 13–14
communication through literature, 25–27
community, 181–85, 265–66, 272
complex thinking, 105–6
comprehension
 barriers to, 32
 building, 12
 reading levels, 23–25, 30, 36, 56, 118
computer use, 22, 25, 37
concept books, 64
Confucius (Freedman; Clément, ill.), 280
controlled text, 74
cookbooks, 73, 97
Corduroy's Sleepover (Hennessy), 294
counting, 68–69, 245–49
Counting on Frank (Clement), 246

courage, 175–81, 274
Cousins (Caseley), 150
Cow Who Clucked (Fleming), 139
Cowgirl Kate and Cocoa (Silverman; Lewin, ill.), 264–65
Crazy Horse's Vision (Bruchac; Nelson, ill.), 217–18
creation stories, 103
creativity and imagination
  books, 76–77, 86–87, 111, 187–90, 295–300
  role of play, 70–71, 295
Creatures of the Deep (Kenah), 250
critical thinking skills, 15
Cross-Country Cat (Calhoun; Ingraham, ill.), 254
Crow Boy (Yashima), 230
culture magazines, 83, 95, 112
curiosity, 74–75, 81, 99, 279–84
Curious George (Rey and Rey), 40
Cyrus the Unsinkable Sea Serpent (Peet), 176–77

Dad, Jackie, and Me (Uhlberg; Bootman, ill.), 218
Daddy's Roommate (Willhoite), 150–51
Deaf Musicians (Seeger and Jacobs; Christie, ill.), 242
Dear Juno (Park; Hartung, ill.), 275
death, 194–98
dialogue with child, 25–27, 52–55
Diary of a Wombat (French; Whatley, ill.), 227–28
Dim Sum for Everyone! (Lin), 284
Dinosaurs Divorce (Brown and Brown), 199
Dino Wars (Johnson and Benton), 228
Disappearing Alphabet (Wilbur; Diaz, ill.), 257
Diving Dolphin (Wallace; Martin, ed.), 250
divorce, 198–200
Dizzy (Winter; Qualls, ill.), 242
Dog Heaven (Rylant), 195
Do Like Kyla (Johnson; Ransome, ill.), 168
Doña Flor (Mora; Colón, ill.), 177
Don't Let the Pigeon Drive the Bus! (Willems), 214
Do Pirates Take Baths? (Tucker; Westcott, ill.), 133–34
Do You Know What I'll Do? (Zolotow; Steptoe, ill.), 168
Dream Carver (Cohn; Córdova), 295–96
Drop of Water (Wick), 280
Duck and Goose (Hills), 163
Duke Ellington (Pinkney; Pinkney, ill.), 242
Dumb Bunnies (Pilkey), 215
Dumpling Soup (Rattigan; Hsu-Flanders, ill.), 285

Each Little Bird That Sings (Wiles), 195
Eats, Shoots & Leaves (Truss; Timmons, ill.), 136
Edward's Overwhelming Overnight (Wells), 294
Edwurd Fudwupper Fibbed Big (Breathed), 260
Egg Is Quiet (Aston; Long, ill.), 124–25
eight-year-olds, 95–101
Eleanor, Ellatony, Ellencake, and Me (Rubin; Fowler, ill.), 139
Eleanor Roosevelt (Freedman), 218
Elizabeti's Doll (Stuve-Bodeen; Hale, ill.), 163–64
Ella Fitzgerald (Pinkney and Pinkney), 242–43
Ella Sarah Gets Dressed (Chodos-Irvine), 139
Ella the Elegant Elephant (D'Amico; D'Amico, ill.), 211
Ellington Was Not a Street (Shange; Nelson, ill.), 218
Elvis the Rooster Almost Goes to Heaven (Cazet), 173
Emily's Balloon (Sakai), 290
Emma's Rug (Say), 188
emotional turning points. *See* themes
emotions
  bad days, 130–33
  grief, 194–98
  loneliness, 229–31, 265
  sadness in response to illness, 172–74
  Yum! Yuck! A Foldout Book of People Sounds, 229
Encyclopedia Prehistorica Dinosaurs (Sabuda; Reinhart, ill.), 280–81
Enemy Pie (Munson; King, ill.), 160–61
environment for reading, 21–23, 31, 70
Epossumondas Saves the Day (Salley; Stevens, ill.), 146
Estelle Takes a Bath (Esbaum; DePalma, ill.), 134
Everyone Poops (Gomi; Stinchecum), 301
exploration. *See* interests
Extreme Animals (Davies; Layton, ill.), 125–26
Eyes of a Gray Wolf (London; Van Zyle, ill.), 126

Fairyopolis (Barker), 296
fairy tales. *See* folktales and classic stories
Families, 151
family relationships
  adoption, 120–23
  building through read-aloud ritual, 20
  concept of, 149–54
  divorce, 198–200
  grandparents, 274–79
  new baby, 268–72
  siblings, 166–70
Fancy Nancy (O'Connor; Glasser, ill.), 140
fears and worries, 90, 175–81, 274
fiction, 12–13, 101–2
Fine, Fine School (Creech; Bliss, ill.), 211
Five for a Little One (Raschka), 301
five-year-olds, 78–83
Floating Home (Getz; Rex, ill.), 228

Fly Away Home (Bunting; Himler, ill.), 207
folktales and classic stories
  Anansi stories, 102–3
  creation stories, 103
  Doña Flor, 177
  for four-year-olds, 72–73
  Polar Bear Son, 292
  retellings, 102, 110
  Tales our Abuelitas Told, 278
  Three Witches, 299
  Two of Everything, 262
  Zuni Folk Tales, 300
food and cooking, 73, 97, 284–87
Forbidden Schoolhouse (Jurmain), 207
Forest (Nivola), 177–78
For You Are a Kenyan Child (Cunnane; Juan, ill.), 182–83
four-year-olds, 70–78
Fox (Wild; Brooks, ill.), 265
Frankenstein Makes a Sandwich (Rex), 215
Freedom River (Rappaport; Collier, ill.), 238
Freedom Train (Sterling), 42
Freedom Walkers (Freedman), 219
Free to Be You and Me (Thomas and Friends), 186
Freight Train (Crews), 154
Frida (Winters; Juan, ill.), 233
Friendly Four (Greenfield; Gilchrist, ill.), 265–66
friendship
  Jitterbug Jam, 168
  making and keeping friends, 97, 263–68
  Name Jar, 230–31
  Other Side, 209
  Stevie, 169–70
Frog and Toad Are Friends (Lobel), 266
Froggy's Sleepover (London; Remkiewicz, ill.), 294–95
Frozen Man (Getz; McCarty, ill.), 250
funny/silly books, 76, 81–82, 100–101, 214–17

G is for Googol (Schwartz; Marissa, ill.), 246
Galileo's Treasure Box (Brighton), 250–51
Gathering the Sun (Ada; Silva, ill.; Zubizarreta, trans.), 257
Geisel, Theodore (Dr. Seuss), 42–43, 76, 147
genres, exposure to, 12–13, 24–25, 29, 79
Gimme Cracked Corn & I Will Share (O'Malley), 215
girls' reading preferences, 28, 106
Girls Together (Williams; Saint James, ill.), 266
global view, development of, 15–16
Gone Wild (McLimans), 126
Good-Bye, Daddy! (Weninger; Marks, ill.), 199
Good Enough to Eat (Rockwell), 285
Good Masters! Sweet Ladies! Voices from a Medieval Village (Schlitz; Byrd, ill.), 186
Good Night, Good Knight (Thomas; Plecas, ill.), 201–2
Goodnight Moon (Brown; Hurd, ill.), 40–41, 202
Gorilla (Browne and Enfield), 296
Gorilla Doctors (Turner), 126–27
Grandfather's Journey (Say), 275–76
Grand Old Tree (DePalma), 195–96
grandparents, 274–79
Grapes of Math (Tang; Briggs, ill.), 246
Grass Sandals (Spivak; Demi, ill.), 136–37
Great Blue House (Banks; Hallensleben, ill.), 191
Great Fuzz Frenzy (Stevens and Crummel), 215
Great Kapok Tree (Cherry), 127
Greedy Triangle (Burns), 246
grief and sadness, 172–74, 194–98
growing up, 144–48
Guess How Much I Love You (McBratney; Jeram, ill.), 164

Hair Dance! (Johnson; Johnson, photos), 301
Hairs/Pelitos (Cisneros; Ybáñez, ill.), 151
Half a World Away (Gleeson; Blackwood, ill.), 290
Halibut Jackson (Lucas), 178
Happy Birthday, Moon (Asch), 146–47
Happy Birthday, Sam (Hutchins), 147
Happy Birthday to You! (Seuss), 147
happy endings, 66
hard days, 130–33
Haring, Keith, 43
Harlem (Myers; Myers, ill.), 191
Harold and the Purple Crayon (Johnson), 296
Harry Potter series (Rowling), 46–47, 305
Harry the Dirty Dog (Zion), 134
Hello, Biscuit (Capucilli; Schories, ill.), 164
Hello, Goodbye Window (Juster; Raschka, ill.), 276
Hello Twins (Voake), 168
Help! A Story of Friendship (Keller), 161
Henry's Freedom Box, 219
"here and now," 77–78
Here Comes the Bus! (Haywood), 211–12
heroes. *See* role models
He's Got the Whole World in His Hands (Nelson), 243
Hickory Chair (Fraustino; Andrews, ill.), 276
Hi! Fly Guy (Arnold), 266
history, 107, 236–41, 274
Hoban, Russell, 45
homosexuality, 150–51
Hooway for Wodney Wat (Lester; Munsinger, ill.), 161
Horton Hears a Who! (Seuss), 43
How Are You Peeling? (Freymann and Elffers), 131
How Come? (Wollard; Solomon, ill.), 281

How I Came to Be a Writer (Naylor), 137
How the Ladies Stopped the Wind (McMillan; Gunnella, ill.), 188
How to Be (Brown), 228
How to Be a Friend (Brown; Brown, ill.), 266–67
How to Eat Like a Child (Ephron; Koren, ill.), 186
How to Lose All Your Friends (Carlson), 161
How We Are Smart (Nikola-Lisa; Qualls, ill.), 140
Hug (Alborough), 290
human body, 300–303
humorous books, 76, 81–82, 100–101, 214–17
Hurricanes (Simon), 127
hurtful people, 159–63
Hush (Ho; Meade, ill.), 202

I Am Absolutely Too Small for School (Child), 212
I Can Make a Difference (Edelman; Moser, ill.), 208
Ice Cream Cones for Sale! (Greenstein), 238
identity as reader, 15, 35
If You Decide to Go to the Moon (McNulty; Kellogg, ill.), 281
If You Listen (Zolotow; Vitale, ill.), 290–91
If You Made a Million (Schwartz; Kellogg, ill.), 246–47
If You're Not Here, Please Raise Your Hand (Dakos; Karas, ill.), 212
I Go with My Family to Grandma's (Levinson; Goode, ill.), 276
I Like to Be Little (Zolotow; Blegvad, ill.), 147
I Live with Daddy (Vigna), 200
illness, 172–74
I Love Saturdays y Domingos (Ada; Savadier, ill.), 277
I Love You Like Crazy Cakes (Lewis; Dyer, ill.), 120–21
imaginary lands, 109
imagination. *See* creativity and imagination
I'm Gonna Like Me (Curtis; Cornell, ill.), 140
I'm in Charge of Celebrations (Baylor; Parnall, ill.), 189
I Miss You (Thomas; Harker, ill.), 196
I'm Not Going Out There! (Bright; Cort, ill.), 178
Imogene's Antlers (Small), 140
In Daddy's Arms, I Am Tall (Steptoe), 151
Independent Dames (Anderson; Faulkner, ill.), 239
individuality, 138–44, 176, 186
In Every Tiny Grain of Sand (Lindbergh, collector), 287
In My Heart (Bang), 291
inspiration. *See* role models
interests
  emergence of talent, 103–4
  interest development books, 65
  learning, 227–29
  mechanical processes, 79, 99, 154–56, 281
  questioning and wondering, 74–75, 81, 279–84
  research books, 82–83
In the Fiddle Is a Song (Bernhard), 141
In the Forest (Ets), 183
Ira Sleeps Over (Waber), 295
Ish (Reynolds), 233–34
I Spy Shapes in Art (Micklethwait), 233
I Stink! (McMullan and McMullan), 154–55
It's Not Your Fault, Koko Bear (Lansky), 200
It Wasn't My Fault (Lester; Munsinger, ill.), 260
I Want to Be (Moss; Pinkney, ill.), 141
I Will Hold You 'Til You Sleep (Zuckerman; Muth, ill.), 202–3
I Will Never Not Ever Eat a Tomato (Child), 286

Jamberry (Degen), 223
Jazz (Myers; Myers, ill.), 243
Jazz ABZ (Marsalis; Rogers, ill.; Schaap, contributor), 243
Jin Woo (Bunting; Soentpiet, ill.), 121
Jitterbug Jam (Hicks; Deacon, ill.), 168
journeys, 222–27
Journey That Saved Curious George (Borden; Drummond, ill.), 223–24
Julio's Magic (Dorros; Grifalconi, ill.), 164
Julius, the Baby of the World (Henkes), 169
Just a Minute (Morales), 247

Kami and the Yaks (Stryer; Dodson, ill.), 224
Keats, Ezra Jack, 44
Kempton, Susan, 70
Kheru Nefer (Beautiful Night) (Maa; Fasolino, ill.), 203
kindergarten books, 79
King Bidgood's in the Bathtub (Wood; Wood, ill.), 134
King & King (de Haan and Nijland), 152
Klimt and His Cat (Capatti and White; Monaco, ill.), 234
Knoxville, Tennessee (Giovanni; Johnson, ill.), 191–92
Knuffle Bunny (Willems), 291

label books, 69, 135
Landmark books
  Bread and Jam for Frances, 45
  Cat in the Hat, 42
  Charlotte's Web, 41–42
  Curious George, 40
  Freedom Train, 42
  Goodnight Moon, 40–41
  Harry Potter series, 46–47
  Horton Hears a Who!, 43
  Madeline, 39, 141

Landmark books *(cont.)*
Make Way for Ducklings, 40
Pat the Bunny, 39–40
Runaway Bunny, 40
Snowy Day, 44
Where the Sidewalk Ends, 45–46
Where the Wild Things Are, 44–45
language
books about, 80, 112, 256–59
early print awareness, 67–68
learning about, 2, 11–12, 13
See also alphabet books
writing, 135–37
learning, 227–29
Legend of the Bluebonnet (dePaola), 273
Leonardo the Terrible Monster (Willems), 267
Leo the Late Bloomer (Kraus; Aruego, ill.), 141
Let It Shine (Bryan), 287
Let's Be Enemies (Udry; Sendak, ill.), 162
Let's Talk About Race (Lester; Barbour, ill.), 140–41
Let the Celebrations Begin! (Wild; Vivas, ill.), 208
levels of reading, 23–25, 30, 36, 56, 118
Librarian of Basra (Winter), 219–20
Librarian Who Measured the Earth (Lasky; Hawkes, ill.), 247
Library Lion (Knudsen; Hawkes, ill.), 260
Lifetimes (Mellonie), 196
Lightship (Floca), 155
Lilly's Big Day (Henkes), 171
Lilly's Purple Plastic Purse (Henkes), 131–32
Lion, the Witch and the Wardrobe (Lewis), 3–4
literary magazines, 83, 94, 111
Literate Kindergarten (Kempton), 70
LitLife organization, 5
Little Green Goose (Sansone; Marks, ill.), 121–22
Little Night (Morales), 203
Little Peace (Kerley), 157–58
Little Pea (Rosenthal; Corace, ill.), 286
LitWorld initiative, 5
loneliness, 229–31, 265
Lookin' for Bird in the Big City (Burleigh; Los, ill.), 243–44
Look Out, Kindergarten (Carlson), 212
Look to the North (George; Washburn, ill.), 127
loss. *See* separation
Lou Gehrig (Adler; Widener, ill.), 220
Luckiest Kid on the Planet (Ernst), 152
Lucky Pennies and Hot Chocolate (Shields; Nakata, ill.), 277
Lullaby Raft (Nye; Flesher, ill.), 203

Macaulay, David, 99
Madeline (Bemelmans), 39, 141
Madlenka (Sís), 267
magazines
selections, 83, 94–95, 110–12
value of, 33
magical worlds, 89–90, 92, 101–2
Magic Hat (Fox; Tusa, ill.), 296–97
Magic Horse of Han Gan (Hong), 234
Make Way for Ducklings (McCloskey), 40, 224
Mama, Coming and Going (Caseley), 261
Mama, Do You Love Me? (Joosse; Lavallee, ill.), 164–65
Mama, I'll Give You the World (Schotter; Gallagher, ill.), 171
Mama Provi and the Pot of Rice (Rosa-Casanova; Roth, ill.), 277
Mama (Winter), 291
Man Who Walked Between the Towers (Gerstein), 178–79
Man Who Went to the Far Side of the Moon (Schyffert), 220
Martha Speaks (Meddaugh), 261
Martin's Big Words (Rappaport; Collier, ill.), 208
math and numbers, 68–69, 245–49
Math Curse (Scieszka and Smith), 247
Math Trek (Peterson and Henderson), 247–48
Max's Words (Banks; Kulikov, ill.), 257
mechanical processes, 79, 99, 154–56, 281
Mei-Mei Loves the Morning (Tsubakiyama; Van Wright and Hu, ill.), 192
Mercedes and the Chocolate Pilot (Raven; van Frankenbuyzen, ill.), 274
Mercy Watson Fights Crime (DiCamillo; Van Dusen, ill.), 179
Meteor! (Polacco), 192
Michael Rosen's Sad Book (Rosen; Blake, ill.), 196
Midnight Eaters (Hest), 277
Mighty Jackie (Moss), 220
Mike Mulligan and His Steam Shovel (Burton), 189
Minnie and Moo, the Case of the Missing Jelly Donut (Cazet), 216
Mirette on the High Wire (McNully), 179
Miss Rumphius (Cooney), 183
Miss Spider's Tea Party (Kirk), 248
mistakes, 87, 259–63
Mitten (Brett), 224–25
Miz Berlin Walks (Yolen; Cooper, ill.), 173
Moja Means One (Feelings and Feelings), 248
Mom and Dad Are Palindromes (Shulman; McCauley, ill.), 257–58
Mommy, Carry Me Please! (Cabrera), 165
Moon Plane (McCarty), 297
Moon Was the Best (Zolotow; Hoban, photos), 291–92
More, More, More, Said the Baby (Williams), 270–71
More Parts (Arnold), 301–2
Mother for Choco (Kasza), 122

Mother Goose (Dillon and Dillon), 248
Mother's Journey (Markle; Marks, ill.), 128
Mountains of Tibet (Gerstein), 196–97
Move! (Page; Jenkins, ill.), 251
Mr. Gumpy's Outing (Burningham), 183
Mr. Putter and Tabby Pour the Tea (Rylant; Howard, ill.), 267
Mr. Rabbit and the Lovely Present (Zolotow; Sendak, ill.), 3, 147
Mr. Williams (Barbour), 238
Mrs. Biddlebox (Smith; Frazee, ill.), 132
Mummies Made in Egypt (Aliki), 238–39
Murals (Ancona), 234
music. *See* songs and music
My Best Friend (Hutchins), 267
My Best Friend (Rodman; Lewis, ill.), 230
My Chair (James; DePalma, ill.), 297
Myers, Walter Dean, 60
My Family Is Forever (Carlson), 122–23
My Father's Hands (Ryder; Graham, ill.), 165
My First Body Board Book (DK Publishing), 302
My First Word Bath Book (DK Publishing), 135
My Friends/Mis Amigos (Gomi), 268
My Grandson Lew (Zolotow; du Bois, ill.), 197
My Kindergarten (Wells), 212
My Little Island (Lessac), 192
My Name is Gabito/Me Llamo Gabito (Brown; Colón, ill.), 221
My Name is Yoon (Recorvits; Swiatkowska, ill.), 142
My New Baby (Kubler, ill.), 271
My Secret Bully (Ludwig; Marble, ill.), 162
mystery books, 108
My Wobbly Tooth Must Not Ever Never Fall Out (Child), 148

Name Jar (Choi), 230–31
Nana Upstairs & Nana Downstairs (dePaola), 197
Napping House (Wood; Wood, ill.), 203–4
nature, 96–97, 124–30, 252
Neeny Coming, Neeny Going (English; Saint James, ill.), 152
new baby in family, 268–72
newborns to age two, 57–64
newspapers, exposure to, 24
New Way Things Work (Macaulay), 281
Night Driving (Coy; McCarty, ill.), 225
Night Eater (Juan), 297
Nina Bonita (Machado), 142
nine-year-olds, 101–8
Nobody Knew What to Do (McCain; Leonardo, ill.), 162
Nobody Particular (Bang), 221
Nocturne (Yolen; Hunter, ill.), 204
Noisy Way to Bed (Whybrow; Beeke, ill.), 204
No Mirrors in My Nana's House (Barnwell; Saint James, ill.), 297
nonfiction
  book selections, 96
  as genre, 12–13
nonverbal dialogue, 27
Not a Box (Portis), 189
Nothing Ever Happens on 90th Street (Schotter; Brooker, ill.), 137
Nothing Scares Us (Wishinsky; Layton, ill.), 274
Now One Foot, Now the Other (dePaola), 173
numbers, 68–69, 245–49

obstacles, overcoming, 272–74
Odd Boy Out (Brown), 221
Oh No, Ono! (de Beer; Martens, trans.), 142
Old Woman Who Named Things (Rylant; Brown, ill.), 231
Olivia (Falconer), 142
Once Upon a Time, The End (Asleep in 60 Seconds) (Kloske; Blitt, ill.), 204
One City, Two Brothers (Smith; Fronty, ill.), 158
One in the Middle Is the Green Kangaroo (Blume; Trivas, ill.), 169
one-year-olds. *See* birth to age two
online reading, 22, 37
On the Night You Were Born (Tillman), 148
On the Same Day in March (Singer; Lessac, ill.), 281–82
On Your Mark, Get Set, Grow! (Madaras), 302
Other Side (Banyai), 297–98
Other Side (Woodson; Lewis, ill.), 209
Out of the Ballpark (Rodriguez; Morrison, ill.), 221
Out of the Egg (Matthews), 184
overnights, 294–95
Over the Moon (Katz), 123
Owen (Henkes), 292
Owl Moon (Yolen; Schoenherr, ill.), 165

Pablo's Tree (Mora; Lang, ill.), 123
Pancakes for Supper (Isaacs; Teague, ill.), 180
Papá and Me (Dorros; Gutierrez, ill.), 152–53
Parts (Arnold), 302
Passage to Freedom (Mochizuki; Lee, ill.), 239–40
Pat the Bunny (Kunhardt), 39–40
peace and conflict, 156–59
Penelope Nuthatch and the Big Surprise (Gavril), 132
Perfectly Orderly House (McKenzie; Lloyd, ill.), 216
picture books, sophisticated, 108–9, 110
Pie in the Sky, 189–90
Pierre in Love (Pennypacker; Mathers, ill.), 165–66
Pigeon Finds a Hot Dog! (Willems), 171
Pinky and Rex (Howe; Sweet, ill.), 172

Pirates Don't Change Diapers (Long; Shannon, ill.), 298
Pitching in for Eubie (Nolen; Lewis, ill.), 153
place and time, 77–78, 191–93
Place My Words Are Looking for (Janeczko), 137
play, value of, 70–71, 295
plays and performance pieces, 104, 185–87
poems and rhymes, annotated list of
- *Amber Was Brave, Essie Was Smart,* 167
- *Baby Sister for Frances,* 270
- *Beetle Bop,* 125
- *Behold the Bold Umbrellaphant and Other Poems,* 214
- *Come with Me,* 223
- *In Daddy's Arms, I Am Tall,* 151
- *In Every Tiny Grain of Sand,* 287
- *Fathers, Mothers, Sisters, Brothers,* 151
- *Free to Be You and Me,* 186
- *Gathering the Sun,* 257
- *Goodnight Moon,* 40–41, 202
- *Grapes of Math,* 246
- *Happy Birthday to You!,* 147
- *Harlem,* 191
- *If You're Not Here, Please Raise Your Hand,* 212
- *Knoxville, Tennessee,* 191–92
- *Place My Words Are Looking for,* 137
- *Poems to Dream Together,* 204
- *Science Verse,* 251
- *Short Takes,* 254
- *Snowmen at Night,* 299
- *Soul Looks Back in Wonder,* 190
- *Stopping by Woods on a Snowy Evening,* 128
- *Sun Is So Quiet,* 128–29
- *There Is a Flower at the Tip of My Nose Smelling Me,* 282–83
- *Today I Feel Silly and Other Moods That Make My Day,* 216–17
- *Welcome to the Ice House,* 124, 129
- *Where the Sidewalk Ends,* 45–46
- *Wild About Books,* 258
- *Winter Eyes,* 129
- *Wonderful Words,* 258–59
- *Yum! ¡MmMm! ¡Que Rico! American Sproutings,* 286–87
- *Zin! Zin! Zin! A Violin,* 244–45
- *See also* poetry and song

Poems to Dream Together (Alarcon; Barragan, ill.), 204
poetry and song
- birth to age two, 63
- two- to three-year-olds, 68
- four-year-olds, 75–76
- five-year-olds, 80–81
- six-year-olds, 87–88
- seven-year-olds, 92–93
- eight-year-olds, 99–100
- nine-year-olds, 104–5
- ten-year-olds, 112–13

poetry as genre, 12–13
Polar Bear Son (Dobcovich), 292
pop-up books, 69, 156, 280–81
Pot That Juan Built (Andrews-Goebel; Diaz, ill.), 190
potty-training books, 69–70
print awareness, 67–68
Priscilla Twice (Casely), 200
Problem with Chickens (McMillan; Gunnella, ill.), 184

Quest for the Tree Kangaroo (Montgomery; Bishop, photos), 282
questioning and wondering, 74–75, 81, 99, 279–84
Quest to Digest (Corcoran; Czekaj, ill.), 251

Rainbow Fish (Pfister), 184
Rain Came Down (Shannon), 184
Rainy Day! (Lakin; Nash, ill.), 132
Rattlesnake Mesa (Weber), 197–98
Reaching for the Moon (Aldrin; Minor, ill.), 240
Reader's Ladder
- birth to age two, 57–64
- two- to three-year-olds, 65–70
- four-year-olds, 70–78
- five-year-olds, 78–83
- six-year-olds, 84–90
- seven-year-olds, 90–95
- eight-year-olds, 95–101
- nine-year-olds, 101–8
- ten-year-olds, 108–13

readiness for reading, 31–32, 73–74
reading aloud
- beyond start of independent reading, 5, 29–31, 37
- connection and bonding, 1–2, 5
- dialogue, 25–27
- environment for, 21–23, 31, 70
- fostering of literacy, 5–6
- guidelines for, 52–55
- parent's dislike of reading, 35–36
- physical access to books, 22–23, 24–25, 59, 65
- reading levels, 23–25, 30, 36, 56, 118
- reasons for, 11–16
- as ritual, 20–21

reading identity, 15, 35
reading levels, 23–25, 30, 36, 56, 118
Really Rosie (Sendak), 186–87
Recess Queen (O'Neill; Huliska-Beith, ill.), 162–63
recipe books, 73, 97
reflection and introspection, 100–101
relationships. *See* family relationships; friendship
Relatives Came (Rylant; Gammell, ill.), 153
Remember, Grandma? (Langston), 173–74

Remembering Grandpa (Krishnaswami; Johnson, ill.), 174
rereading of books, 33–35, 93
Rescue Vehicles (Gould and Epstein), 155
research books, 82–83
rewards for reading, 31
Rey, Margret and Hans A., 40, 223–24
rhymes. *See* poems and rhymes, annotated list of
rhythm of language, 2, 57–58, 75
ritual
  bedtime reading, 58–59
  bookmarking, 53
  books about, 98
  to build, 59–60
  to foster lifelong reading, 20–21
  reading aloud beyond start of independent reading, 29–30
Robots Everywhere (Hebson; Hoffman, ill.), 155
Rocks & Minerals (Symes), 282
role models
  Forbidden Schoolhouse, 207
  heroes and great people, 109, 217–21
  How I Came to Be a Writer, 137
  Man Who Walked Between the Towers, 178–79
  parents as, 16–17, 52
  Snowflake Bentley, 128
routines, 67
Rowling, J. K., 46–47, 305
Rudi's Pond (Bunting; Himler, ill.), 198
Runaway Bunny (Brown; Hurd, ill.), 40

sadness and grief, 172–74, 194–98
Sammy the Seal (Hoff), 212–13
Sayonara, Mrs. Kackleman (Kalman), 169
school, 79, 85, 210–13
science
  exploration and discovery, 92, 249–52
  magazines on, 94, 111
  nature, 96–97, 124–30, 252
Science Verse (Scieszka and Smith), 251
scrapes, 87
Sea Horse (Butterworth; Lawrence, ill.), 251–52
Seashore Book (Zolotow; Minor, ill.), 192–93
Sebastian (Winter), 244
Second Is a Hiccup (Hutchins; Denton, ill.), 228–29
Sector 7 (Wiesner), 298–99
Seen Art? (Scieszka; Smith, ill.), 234–35
Selznick, Brian, 4
Sendak, Maurice, 2, 44–45, 56
sensory experiences
  children's relationship with books, 56–57
  pop-up books, 69, 156, 280–81
  tactile books, 39–40, 61–63, 69, 135
separation
  death, 194–98
  loss and parting, 289–93
  overnights, 294–95
  school, 79, 85, 210–13
Sequoyah (Rumford; Huckaby, trans.), 240–41
series books, 89, 98–99
Seuss, Dr. (Theodore Geisel), 42–43, 76, 147
seven-year-olds, 90–95
sharing, 170–72
She Comes Bringing Me That Little Baby Girl (Greenfield; Steptoe, ill.), 271
Sheila Rae, the Brave (Henkes), 169
Shortcut (Crews), 225
Short Takes (Smith; Brooks, ed.), 254
Shy Charles (Wells), 274
shyness, 178
siblings, 166–70, 268–72
sickness, 172–74
Sienna's Scrapbook (Parker; Genovese, ill.), 241
Silent Music (Rumford), 159
Silly Billy (Browne), 180
silly/funny books, 76, 81–82, 100–101, 214–17
Silverstein, Shel, 45–46
Sir Cumference and the Dragon of Pi (Neuschwander), 248
Sitti's Secrets (Nye), 16, 278
Sixteen Years in Sixteen Seconds (Yoo; Lee, ill.), 254–55
six-year-olds, 84–90
Sky Boys (Hopkinson; Ransome, ill.), 155
sleep
  bedtime ritual, 58–59
  books about, 201–6
Sleeping Ugly (Yolen; Stanley, ill.), 143
sleepovers, 294–95
Sleepy Boy (Konevsky; Anderson, ill.), 204–5
Small Knight and George (Armitage; Robins, ill.), 180
Small Tall Tale from the Far Far North (Sís), 225
Smash! Crash! (Scieszka; Keytoon, Inc., ill.), 156
Snowflake Bentley (Martin), 128
Snow in Jerusalem (da Costa; Van Wright and Hu, ill.), 159
Snowmen at Night (Buehner; Buehner, ill.), 299
Snowy Day (Keats), 44
social justice, 206–10
Some Dogs Do (Alborough), 299
songs and music
  Baby Sister for Frances, A, 270
  for birth to age two, 63
  for four-year-olds, 75–76
  Free to Be You and Me, 186
  Kheru Nefer (Beautiful Night), 203
  Let It Shine, 287
  Lullaby Raft, 203
  musicians and music appreciation, 241–45
  Really Rosie, 186–87

songs and music *(cont.)*
Take Me Out of the Bathtub and Other Silly Dilly Songs, 135
for two- to three-year-olds, 68
So Sleepy Story (Shulevitz), 205
Soul Looks Back in Wonder (Feelings, compiler), 190
Sparkle and Spin (Rand; Rand, ill.), 258
Special Kids in School (Taking Diabetes to School, and more) (Gosselin; Freedman, ill.), 174
speed of reading, improvement in, 34
spirituality, 287–88
Splish-Splash (Harper), 135
sports
books, 252–56
magazines, 83, 94, 111
Sterling, Dorothy, 42
Stevie (Steptoe), 169–70
Stone Soup (Muth), 185
Stopping by Woods on a Snowy Evening (Frost and Jeffers), 128
Story of Ruby Bridges (Coles; Ford, ill.), 209
Story Painter (Duggleby), 235
Strega Nona (dePaola), 261
Stringbean's Trip to the Shining Sea (Williams and Williams), 225–26
Sumi's First Day of School (Kim and Pak), 213
Sun Is So Quiet (Giovanni; Bryan, ill.), 128–29
Superhero (Tauss), 299
Surprising Sharks (Davies; Croft, ill.), 252
Sylvester and the Magic Pebble (Steig), 293
Sylvia Jean, Drama Queen (Ernst), 143

Tacky the Penguin (Lester; Munsinger, ill.), 143
tactile books, 39–40, 61–63, 69, 135
Take Me Out of the Bathtub and Other Silly Dilly Songs (Katz; Catrow, ill.), 135
Tale of Pale Male (Winter), 129
Tales our Abuelitas Told (Ada and Campoy; Davalos, Escrivá, Guevara, Torres, ill.), 278
Talking with Artists (Cummings), 235
Tar Beach (Ringgold), 226
Teammates (Barber, Barber, and Burleigh; Root, ill.), 255
Teammates (Golenbock; Bacon, ill.), 255
Teeny Tiny Baby (Schwartz), 271–72
television, 21–22
Tell Me Again About the Night I Was Born (Curtis; Cornell, ill.), 123
Ten Black Dots (Crews), 245
Tenth Good Thing About Barney (Viorst; Blegvad, ill.), 198
ten-year-olds, 108–13
themes
adoption, 120–23
adversity, 272–74
art appreciation and artists, 232–36
babies, 268–72
bad days, 130–33
bath time, 133–35
bedtime, 201–6
birthdays, 144–48
body, human, 300–303
bullying, 159–63
caring, 163–66
community, 181–85
courage, 175–81
creativity, 187–90
death, 194–98
divorce, 198–200
food, 284–87
friendship, 263–68
grandparents, 274–79
heroes, 217–21
history, 236–41
illness and sadness, 172–74
imagination, 295–300
individuality, 138–44
journeys, 222–27
language, 256–59
learning, 227–29
loneliness, 229–31
mechanical processes, 154–56
mistakes, 259–63
music appreciation and musicians, 241–45
nature, 124–30
numbers, 245–49
plays and performance, 185–87
questioning and wondering, 279–84
school, 210–13
science, 249–52
separation, 289–93
sharing, 170–72
siblings, 166–70
silliness, 214–17
sleep, 201–6
sleepovers, 294–95
social justice, 206–10
spirituality, 287–88
sports, 252–56
time and place, 191–93
world events, 156–59
writing, 135–37
See also individual topics
themes, strong or intense, 110
There Is a Flower at the Tip of My Nose Smelling Me (Walker; Vitale, ill.), 282–83
There's a Nightmare in My Closet (Mayer), 205
They Called Her Molly Pitcher (Rockwell; von Buhler, ill.), 241
Things I Learned in Second Grade (Schwartz), 213
Thirteen O'Clock (Stimson), 216

39 Apartments of Ludwig van Beethoven (Winter; Blitt, ill.), 244
This Is the House That Jack Built (Taback), 215–16
3-D ABC (Raczka), 235–36
Three Questions (Muth), 287–88
Three Witches (Hurston, collector; Thomas, adapter; Ringgold, ill.), 299
three-year-olds. *See* two- to three-year-olds
Thunder Cake (Polacco), 181
Tibet Through the Red Box (Sís), 226
time and place, 77–78, 191–93
Time of Wonder (McCloskey), 193
Timothy Goes to School (Wells), 213
Tiny Seed (Carle), 252
Today I Feel Silly and Other Moods That Make My Day (Curtis; Cornell, ill.), 216–17
Toes, Ears, & Nose! (Bauer and Katz), 302
toilet-training, 69–70
tooth milestones, 84–85, 148
Touch and Feel Bathtime (DK Publishing), 135
touch-and-feel books, 39–40, 61–63, 69, 135
Traction Man Is Here (Grey), 300
Trains (Crowther), 156
travel and transition, 222–27
Traveling Man (Rumford), 226–27
Tupelo Rides the Rails (Sweet), 231
Two Is for Twins (Lewison; Nakata, ill.), 170
Two of Everything (Hong), 262
Two of Them (Aliki), 198
two- to three-year-olds, 65–70

uniqueness and individuality, 138–44, 176, 186

Very Lonely Firefly (Carle), 231
Voices in the Park (Browne), 229

Wait Till the Moon Is Full (Brown; Williams, ill.), 283
Walking the Log (Nickens), 236
war and conflict, 156–59, 274
War Between the Vowels and the Consonants (Turner; Turner, ill.), 258
Was It the Chocolate Pudding? (Levins; Langdo, ill.), 200
Watch Out for the Chicken Feet in Your Soup (dePaola), 278
Way to Start a Day (Baylor; Parnall, ill.), 288
We All Went on Safari (Krebs; Cairns, ill.), 249
Wednesday Surprise (Bunting; Carrick, ill.), 209
Welcome to the Ice House (Yolen; Regan, ill.), 124, 129
Welty, Eudora, 67
What Athletes Are Made Of (Piven), 255–56
What! Cried Granny (Lum; Johnson, ill.), 278
What Do You Do with a Tail Like This? (Jenkins and Page), 283
What Elephant? (Côté), 300
"What's Happening to My Body" Book for Girls (Madaras and Madaras), 302–3
What's Your Angle, Pythagoras? (Ellis; Hornung, ill.), 249
What You Know First (MacLachlan), 193
When I Am Old with You (Johnson; Soman, ill.), 279
When I Was Five (Howard), 148
When I Was Little (Curtis), 148
When I Was Young in the Mountains (Rylant; Goode, ill.), 193
When Sheep Sleep (Numeroff; McPhail, ill.), 205
When Sophie Gets Angry—Really, Really Angry (Bang), 132–33
When the Wind Stops (Zolotow; Vitale, ill.), 205–6
When We Married Gary (Hines), 153–54
Where Do Balloons Go? (Curtis; Cornell, ill.), 283
Where's the Baby? (Hutchins), 170
Where the Sidewalk Ends (Silverstein), 45–46
Where the Wild Things Are (Sendak), 44–45, 262–63
Whingdingdilly (Peet), 143
Whistle for Willie (Keats), 229
White, E. B., 41
Whose Knees Are These? (Asim; Pham, ill.), 303
Whose Tracks are These? A Clue Book of Familiar Forest Animals (Nail; Skudder, ill.), 252
Why the Banana Split (Walton; Holder, ill.), 217
Wild About Books (Sierra; Brown, ill.), 258
Wildfire (Morrison), 283–84
Wild Lives (Zoehfeld), 185
Wilfrid Gordon McDonald Partridge (Fox; Vivas, ill.), 174
Willems, Mo, 4
Will I Have a Friend? (Cohen; Hoban, ill.), 213
Winter Eyes (Florian), 129
Wish You Were Here (Petz; Gréban, ill.), 293
Wolves (Gravett), 129–30
Wonderful Words (Hopkins; Barbour, ill.), 258–59
wondering and questioning, 74–75, 81, 99, 279–84
Won't You Be My Kissaroo? (Ryder; Sweet, ill.), 166
Woody Guthrie (Christensen), 244
Woolbur (Helakoski; Harper, ill.), 143–44
words. *See* language
Word Wizard (Falwell), 259
world events, 156–59

worldview, 15–16, 39
worries and fears, 90, 175–81, 274
writing, 135–37

Yellow House (Rubin), 236
Yo! Yes? (Raschka), 268
Yum! ¡MmMm! ¡Que Rico! American Sproutings (Mora; Lopez, ill.), 286–87
Yum! Yuck! A Foldout Book of People Sounds (Park, Durango, and Rama), 229

Zelda and Ivy (Kvasnosky), 170
Zen Shorts (Muth), 288
Zin! Zin! Zin! A Violin (Moss; Priceman, ill.), 244–45
Zuni Folk Tales (Cushing), 300